THE CHANGING POLITICS OF SCHOOL FINANCE

THE CHANGING POLITICS OF SCHOOL FINANCE

Edited by

NELDA H. CAMBRON-McCABE
Miami University, Oxford, Ohio

and

ALLAN ODDEN
Education Commission of the States
Denver, Colorado

Third Annual Yearbook of the
American Education Finance Association
1982

BALLINGER PUBLISHING COMPANY
Cambridge, Massachusetts
A Subsidiary of Harper & Row, Publishers, Inc.

International Standard Book Number: 0-88410-896-1

Library of Congress Catalog Card Number: 82-13849

Printed in the United States of America

Library of Congress Cataloging in Publication Data

Main entry under title:

The Changing politics of school finance.

Includes bibliographies and index.
1. Education—United States—Finance—Addresses, essays, lectures.
I. Cambron-McCabe, Nelda H. II. Odden, Allan.
LB2825.C43 1983   379.1'21'0973   82-13849
ISBN 0-88410-896-1

TRIBUTE TO
JOEL S. BERKE
January 7, 1936 — December 8, 1981

Joel Berke: teacher, scholar, advocate, leader. In all of these roles Joel has made a major and lasting contribution. Joel's interest was in substantive issues, issues that mattered, issues that always had a public policy relevance. Joel's world was the public policy world, but not because of any great interest in politics. In fact, the game interested him very little. It was to accomplish substantive goals that Joel practiced advocacy and exercised leadership. Using his research and policy analysis as a resource base, Joel invaded courts, legislatures, executive branch agencies, and official and unofficial commissions, forcing—by the soundness of his analysis—the policymakers to listen and, frequently, to act.

Joel's chosen field was the financing of education, but more important than the field was his philosophy. The heart of that philosophy inspiring Joel's study and advocacy was equity: a belief that resources should flow in accord with need rather than follow the channels of political power and influence. Joel believed that genuine equality of educational opportunity was the right policy. For him this required, in the financing of education, that resources be distributed in a way that contributed to accomplishing that equity. Because of Joel's work, students disadvantaged by discrimination, by geographic or jurisdictional location, or by handicapped conditions are more likely to have a fair amount of resources devoted to their education. That, in my judgment, was Joel's major contribution. Could there be a more magnificent legacy? I don't think so.

Alan K. Campbell
Executive Vice President
ARA Services, Inc.

Joel S. Berke, one of the foremost leaders in the politics of school finance, was a senior research scientist with the Educational Testing Service. His extensive experience included serving as deputy assistant secretary of education for policy development in the Department of Education, professor at Syracuse University and University of Vermont, and finance consultant to several federal agencies. Dr. Berke was the author of *Answers to Inequity: An Analysis of the New School Finance Laws* and the coauthor of *Politicians, Judges and City Schools—Reforming School Finance in New York*, and *Federal Aid to Education—Who Benefits? Who Governs?*

CONTENTS

LIST OF TABLES

PREFACE

School finance has embarked upon a new era. The expanding resources of the 1960s and the reform consciousness of the 1970s have given way to retrenchment as the 1980s begin. This third yearbook of the American Education Finance Association (AEFA) addresses the changing political context of education finance decisions. Dynamic economic, demographic, and societal conditions have substantially impacted the political process by which financial resources are distributed. It is in this context that the editors have developed the 1982 yearbook. It is hoped that significant political issues have been raised to encourage further discussion, debate, and research on the politics of school finance.

Over the past several decades, educators have acknowledged that education is intertwined with the broader political processes of local, state, and federal governments. No longer can education be viewed as either autonomous or insulated from politics. A range of issues highlights the nexus—accountability demands, racial segregation, tax and expenditure limitation movements, demographic trends, and public aid to nonpublic schools. As governmental policy in general evolves from the interaction of social, economic, and environmental factors, so does educational policy.

In the politics of education, one of the primary agenda items is the financing of public education. Educational finance has been the

recent focus of attention because of rising costs, declining enrollments, and voter resistance to tax increases. These problems occur at
a time when governmental financial responsibility is shifting. Educational finance is in a state of transition; national priorities have
changed. As some analysts have proclaimed, 1980 may indeed be a
watershed year in national fiscal policy. The emphasis on "federalism" portends a significant realignment in federal, state, and local
relations.

With the "new federalism" and the constrained revenue-generating
ability at the local level, attention has been focused on the state
level. The expectation is that states will assume greater fiscal responsibility. This occurs at a time when states are faced with severe fiscal
problems. The condition is further exacerbated by retrenchment in
public and legislative support.

Concomitant with federal withdrawal and the greater reliance on
the states, other factors affecting the political context for school
finance in the 1980s include demographic shifts, economic uncertainties, and attitude changes toward a smaller public sector. These
conditions indicate that fewer funds will be available for most public services. Education will be placed in a more competitive position
with other governmental services, and it will become imperative for
educators to form more cohesive and unified coalitions to compete
effectively.

The yearbook is designed to present an overview of the arenas,
actors, and issues involved in the changing politics of school finance.
The central theme is that conditions have changed: Policies are now
directed toward retrenchment, consolidation, and cutbacks; roles are
being redefined. Each author has attempted to identify the major
shifts which have occurred in the designated arenas or issues, and to
discuss the implications for educational finance policy decisions.

OVERVIEW

The national political context for the yearbook is established in
Chapter 1 by Laurence Iannaccone, professor of education, University of California, Santa Barbara, who is one of the foremost scholars
in the politics of education. He speculates that the American political
system is undergoing a fundamental turning point in its history. Using
research on turning-point election periods (TPEPs) in local school

districts, Iannaccone traces the themes or phases of realignment election periods at the national level—ascension of voter discontent, a triggering election, a realignment election, articulation of a new policy mandate, and a final test election. A TPEP is critical at the national level; it signals a challenge to established idealogical assumptions, a fundamental shift in values. The impact of the present TPEP on educational policymaking will be significant. The new policy mandates of the Reagan administration following the 1980 realignment election have shown a new government philosophy toward education—one that shifts educational decisions to the states. According to Iannaccone, a Republican victory in 1984 will signal a final test election. This will indicate that the new federal policies reflect the voters' philosophical predispositions. The consequence will be a further decline of education as a national priority.

In Chapters 2 and 3, the authors focus on the politics of the changing federal and state roles. Jack Jennings, associate general counsel, Committee on Education and Labor, House of Representatives, addresses the influence of the social, economic, and political environment on leadership options. Although he notes the essential role of leadership in national policymaking, he emphasizes that the environment must be supportive for policies to succeed. Jennings discusses the changed conditions and a de-emphasis in the federal role. He concludes by stressing that educators must act if the present trend in federal withdrawal is to be reversed.

The uncertainty of state level politics is highlighted in Chapter 3 by Susan Fuhrman, research associate, Eagleton Institute of Politics, Rutgers University. Fuhrman, who has conducted extensive research on the politics of state level school finance decisions, reviews the political developments of the seventies and speculates on the trends for the eighties. She notes that the recent fiscal and political trends have resulted in a retreat of legislators and governors from the support of education. Similarly, conditions have significantly impacted interest groups and could result in the formation of new coalitions. All in all, new conditions may mean a renewed and stronger role for educators.

Although courts assumed a new role in education finance policy in the seventies, it has been difficult to predict judicial impact regarding policy changes. Tyll van Geel, professor in the Graduate School of Education, University of Rochester, advances a theoretical model to account for the influence of the judiciary in the political process in Chapter 4. He probes two basic questions: (1) Is there any reason to expect that a judicial decree in a given state is a *necessary condition* for reform and (2) is the issuance of a judicial decree ordering reform a *sufficient condition* for bringing about real reform or only symbolic reform?

In Chapter 5, the impact of school finance reform is analyzed by Patricia R. Brown, assistant professor, Department of Political Science, University of California, Berkeley, and Richard F. Elmore, associate professor, Graduate School of Public Affairs, University of Washington. Unlike most analysts of reform, they go beyond simply examining reform in terms of equity—that is, reducing expenditure disparities or the relationship between wealth and expenditures. Instead, Brown and Elmore propose a model of political choice where equity is treated as only one of several objectives and one of several outcomes. This analysis recognizes the political nature of reform where policymakers are faced with multiple objectives, multiple tradeoffs, and varied constraints. The authors posit that reform cannot be declared successful or unsuccessful on the basis of a single goal such as equity; rather, impact must be evaluated in terms of the purposes of an individual state. According to Brown and Elmore, "reform is more a matter of political organization than it is of principle or technical expertise."

One of the most visible threats to the local–state finance structure in the late 1970s was the initiation of tax and expenditure limitation efforts. In Chapter 6, Mary Frase Williams, social scientist with the School Finance Project, Department of Education, examines the politics of tax and expenditure limitations, the impact of these limitations on school finance, and the potential impact of future limitation efforts. She provides an exhaustive review of the research on campaigns and voting behavior in states that faced referenda on limits. The overriding question posed by Williams is, "Was there a national tax revolt?"

Public aid to private schools surfaced again in 1982 as a volatile issue. Chester E. Finn, Jr., professor of education and public policy, Vanderbilt University, examines the politics of this struggle in Chapter 7. He notes that the current debate occurs in a political context that includes a deepening schism within private education, declining support for education, the continuing threat of competition and rivalry between private and public education, and the increasingly healthy financial condition of private institutions. In this context,

Finn delineates several distinct themes in efforts to secure aid for nonpublic schools, explores viable options for aid, and reviews the tax exemption issue. Overall, he concludes that the politics of efforts to secure public aid are changing; future efforts of private educators will be directed more toward curbing government than seeking additional financial support.

In Chapter 8, Joseph M. Cronin, president, Massachusetts Higher Education Assistance Corporation and former state superintendent of education in Illinois, discusses the politics of financial support for urban schools. He emphasizes that three major factors intensified urban school finance problems in the 1970s: race, retrenchment, and receivership. At the beginning of the 1980s, the problem is further complicated because of federal cutbacks and the unlikelihood that nonurban state legislators will rescue the cities. According to Cronin, these demographic changes, court orders, state fiscal controls, and federal cutbacks have placed urban schools in an untenable position.

The retrenchment of the 1980s is exemplified in school closings at the local level. In Chapter 9, William Lowe Boyd, professor of education, Pennsylvania State University, focuses on the politics of declining enrollments and the management of conflict resulting from cutbacks and school closings. His research reveals an interesting phenomenon: The rational problem-solving and consensus-building process often recommended may not be the most efficacious model. The decisionmaking processes in many districts, especially urban, were characterized by political bargaining. One of Boyd's major conclusions is that "school officials need not be deterred by the inability of the rational planning approach to perform as advertised: The politics of school closings really is far more a 'divide and conquer' than a 'plan and agree' process."

ACKNOWLEDGMENTS

The editors wish to express their appreciation to the numerous individuals who contributed to the completion of the 1982 yearbook. A deep gratitude is due to each of the ten authors whose contribution of time and energy made this project possible. Special thanks are extended to Edwin Steinbrecher, 1981–82 AEFA president, for providing needed support and assistance; to the AEFA board of directors for their thoughtful criticism and interest; and to the members of the publication committee for their input and suggestions—Susan Fuhrman of Rutgers University; K. Forbis Jordan of the Congressional Research Service, James Phelps of the Michigan State Department of Education, and Stephen B. Thomas of St. Johns University.

Special appreciation is extended to Peggy Zimmerman, graduate assistant, Miami University, for editorial assistance, and Jan Fulton, office manager, Department of Educational Leadership, Miami University, for typing the final manuscript. Finally, the editors wish to acknowledge their indebtedness to K. Forbis Jordan, 1981 yearbook editor, for his advice and counsel throughout the various stages of this publication.

Oxford, Ohio   Nelda H. Cambron-McCabe
April 1982   Allan Odden

1 TURNING-POINT ELECTION PERIODS IN THE POLITICS OF EDUCATION

Laurence Iannaccone

This chapter discusses the meaning of turning-point election periods (TPEPs), the chief tension-management mechanism of the American political system. TPEPs are preceded by a growing imbalance between political and socioeconomic systems and display the primary processes through which the political system is recurrently brought back into a more balanced relationship with the changing socioeconomic system. The chief mechanism by which a TPEP restores that balance is a realignment election, the clearest signal that the political system is undergoing a fundamental turning point.

TPEPs are also characterized by increased political conflicts resulting from competing philosophies of government and its service mission. The real prize at stake in a critical realignment and its aftermath is the power to define the issues for the public. The general significance of TPEPs for educational policymaking is their impact upon the politicoeconomic assumptions and ideological premises that guide policy long after a TPEP has run its course.

This chapter is also concerned with the implications of TPEPs and the meaning of the 1980 national realignment election and its aftermath. The knowledge of TPEPs gained from local school districts provides a perspective from which to view the present national scene.

*Laurence Iannaccone, Professor, Graduate School of Education, University of California, Santa Barbara.

1

This knowledge supplies a conceptual context that suggests that the 1984 election will probably test a new mandate for government.

THE UNIVERSALITY OF TPEPs

Turning-point election periods (TPEPs) are a recurring phase in the governmental life cycle of American polities. Evidence of their existence has been reported in the research on the politics of the national government, the states, the largest American cities, middle-size municipal reform cities, and all types of local school districts. Each of these polities may display some unique features in their TPEPs, which reflect in large part structural variations in the representative mechanisms embedded in different types of polities. One such difference is that between partisan and nonpartisan election systems.

Another is the method by which the chief executive of American polities is chosen. The common significance of that office lies in the impact on policy of its combined legislative and executive responsibilities. It is the customary initiator of new policies and programs within the legislative process, whether these emerge as federal statutes or board policies. Its executive responsibilities can materially shape policy implementation, especially its power over appointments and administrative regulations. Whether the chief executive of a polity is elected or appointed by elected representatives makes some difference in the specific sequence of events leading to the close of a TPEP. The reorganization of the key policymaking offices is a TPEP's central feature. It leads to the authoritative articulation of new policy assumptions. This argument may be illustrated by noting the common realignment functions but unique mechanisms in the selection of an American president and a local school superintendent.

In a critical national realignment election the party that previously held the presidency loses it. But this is not its essential aspect. In essence, critical realignment elections are intense disruptions of traditional voting patterns. These reflect sharp reorganizations of the coalitions of voter constituencies within and between the two major parties, a redivision of the mass voter bases along different lines from their predominant configuration in the preceding years. Realignment elections may well be concurrent with changes in the presidency—even the defeat of an incumbent president as in 1932, and 1980, the two most recent national realignment elections. It is the shift in basic voter coalitions, however, that has long-term consequences on politics and policymaking.

The local school district shift in voting behavior with long-term consequences is not usually concurrent with the replacement of an incumbent superintendent. Given the appointive nature of that office and the constraining costs of terminating a superintendent's contract, some time passes between the board election resulting in the replacement of a superintendent and that event. Only with a new superintendent in place is the local district's policymaking system a functional equivalent of the national policymaking system produced by a realignment election. Then the policy processes move on to the articulation of new governance assumptions by the new chief executives in both of these polities. Despite differences in specific mechanisms and their particular operations, the political functions of these in the TPEPs of their respective polities are the same.

In all of these American polities, TPEPs are cyclic, patterned over time—not random. This common pattern may be illustrated again by reference to the local school district. Over an extended era of a typical school district, shorter TPEPs of high politicization and expanded political conflicts alternate with longer periods of quiescence and low political conflict. The alternation of political quiescence and the politicization of a TPEP for a shorter period is the common cyclic characteristic of American polities. Their TPEP tension adjustment functions are the same; the major internal sequences of TPEPs also are the same.

This chapter uses the finer grained findings, concepts, and conclusions from the studies on typical local school district TPEPs to enhance the understanding of TPEPs and their implications for educational policymaking. While the research on the politics of TPEPs in local school districts is the primary empirical base used, the universality of TPEPs among American politics deserves discussion. All American polities display their own TPEPs alternating with periods of political quiescence. Research on the tenure of city managers in medium-size municipal reform cities found recurring periods of politicization resulting in the involuntary termination of the city manager (Kammerer et al. 1962, 1963). The other crucial feature that distinguishes these TPEPs from politics as usual is a conflict in policy orientations (Kammerer et al. 1962: 73). In larger urban governments without city managers, periodic eras of reform display the characteristic TPEPs with impact in Chicago and New York of structural changes in the school board (Iannaccone and Wiles 1971; Lowi 1964; Peterson 1976). Reanalyses of the earliest research on the state politics of education reveal the same cyclic pattern (Iannaccone 1966, 1967). Finally, the findings of research on local school district politics during such periods result from a vastly larger number of TPEPs because of the many American local school districts across the country. These provide a conceptual frame of reference for examining the national politics of the last two decades (Chase 1981; Criswell and Mitchell 1980; Danis 1981; Iannaccone 1967; Iannaccone and Lutz 1970; Lutz and Iannaccone 1978).

POLICYMAKING IN TPEPS AND
QUIESCENT PERIODS

Changes in the character of policymaking processes in each type of polity mentioned above display a similar cyclic pattern. The predominant distinguishing feature of the policy process during the longer periods of political quiescence was aptly described by Lindblom (1968) as "incrementalism." Incrementalism rests to a large degree on ideological premises widely shared by the citizens of a polity. As Lindblom (1968: 23) pointed out,

> Any even loosely organized set of interlocking generalizations or principles . . . about politicoeconomic organization—is of enormous help to policy analysis. . . . In effect an ideology takes certain beliefs out of the gunfire criticism. . . . These . . . can thereafter be introduced into policy analysis as though they were settled fact.

Although dependent on these premises, incremental policymaking is increasingly influenced by precedent. The accretion of a body of policy analyses and decisions consistent with its premises forges additional links in the ideological chain affecting policymaking. The political meaning that policy premises once held and the salient issues of previous conflicts are lost in that process, except to historians. Their influence as the ideological bases of policy analyses may be even stronger, though indirect, as the newer links in the policy chains derived from these become the more immediate parameters within which new politics are incrementally produced. The newest of these rather than earlier ones or their foundation principles are the focal issues of current political conflicts.

The policymaking process characteristic of TPEPs stands in contrast to that of political quiescence. It reverses to a degree the developmental progress of the previous period. TPEPs tend first to challenge more recent aspects of policy; later that challenge expands to engulf earlier policies and their more remote premises. As the politicization of TPEPs continues, political conflicts expand in their scope of issues and intensity (Schattschneider 1960). These conflicts affect the character of policymaking, disrupting to a degree its customary incrementalism. Policymaking in the shorter TPEP is more abrupt, less consistent, and sometimes contradictory. It reflects the polarized ideological positions of earlier fragmented political coalitions and newly organized interests. The ideological course followed tends in part to retrace the policy chains forged earlier during quiescence and thus moves back toward their ideological premises. In this way, aspects of beliefs previously held as settled facts are reintroduced into the gunfire of criticism as salient political issues.

The emergence of vouchers as an issue in educational policy analysis is a useful current illustration. It rests on libertarian assumptions about politicoeconomic organization that were held and articulated somewhat differently by John Stuart Mill (1913) in his essay *On Liberty*. Although Mill believed that a democratic society ought to provide for the education of its children through the use of taxation, he argued that the vehicle for this should not be a public school system. Instead, he advocated something akin to the present voucher proposal. This argument and its underlying assumptions were salient issues in political conflicts about education over a century ago. The victory of a competing set of assumptions—those of the common school movement—pushed aside the libertarian ones. The subsequent incremental development of the public school and educational policy has rested to a large extent on the policy premises that won in those previous political conflicts.

Most important in understanding the long-term policy influence of TPEP winning beliefs is the historic fact that the general perception of these as issues for political debate and conflict disappeared for all practical purposes. They became instead the premises of educational policymaking for a century because they were held as settled fact. The emergence through the voucher debate of previously set aside libertarian assumptions challenges the settled nature of the predominant premises. Their reintroduction into the gunfire of political criticism in competition with the previously defeated and largely ignored assumptions of older political conflicts is typical of TPEP policy conflicts. The coexistence as salient political issues of different ideological assumptions jostling side by side without the synthesizing discipline of a shared political paradigm is the characteristic ideological base of policymaking in TPEPs. The incrementalism of quiescence does not cease, nor are its policy premises erased. They must, however, descend from their previous lofty perch of settled fact and compete with other assumptions in the electoral arenas of TPEPs. Their place in the next political paradigm of interlocking assumptions about the politicoeconomic organization of the polity must be won. At best they are likely to be subsumed beneath other elements involved in the ideological conflicts of the TPEP. Incrementalism resumes its sway in policymaking only after the TPEP has produced another amalgam—a different configuration of interlocking principles supported by the voters in a new mandate for the polity.

National TPEPs are significant for educational policymaking because such periods are critical transitional ones in domestic policymaking. Citizens by their voting choices redirect policy premises for the subsequent allocation of values, including fiscal policy. For years thereafter, until the next TPEP, the resolution of issue conflicts about fiscal policy will bear the stamp of the new predominant political paradigm's premises relevant to such issues as fiscal adequacy, equality, stability, and incentives—for these are value ladden issues at best only illuminated by science, technology, and research findings. They are resolved for a time by public policy choices that are guided to a degree by value laden policy premises (Mitchell and Iannaccone 1980).

THE 1980 ELECTION AND EDUCATIONAL POLICY

The third concern of this chapter is understanding the implications of the 1980 election and its political aftermath. The present educational situation in national politics is markedly different from previous realignment elections. National education policies and the education policymaking function of the national government were an important feature of the 1980 campaigns. A change in that function is a salient part of the challenge the Reagan administration makes to the policy premises of the previous quarter century.

> I am convinced that whether the Republicans win in 1984 or not the 1980 realignment election will have durable consequences in the transformation of the general shape of the national policy agenda ahead. The political conflicts of the next era will be organized around that agenda. And I do not believe that education will occupy a salient place on that agenda (Iannaccone 1981:55)

This assertion, written in late 1980, partly reflects two distinct and originally unrelated bodies of research and theory. One is the body of studies on American national realignment elections (Burnham 1970; Key 1955; MacRae and Meldrum 1960; Schattscheider 1960; Sellers 1965). The other is the corpus of research in the politics of education. This education research beginning about 1960, is concerned with the politicization of education during the last thirty years at the state, local school district, and national levels (Iannaccone 1977, 1981; Iannaccone and Cistone 1974). In addition, it rests upon the author's observations and interpretations of the meaning of the 1980 national elections, the relationship between President Reagan's rhetoric and behavior as governor in California, and his subsequent campaigns for the presidency projected to his probable behavior as president of the United States. His administration's first year and the public's opinion of that has strengthened this conviction further. These interpretations, however, also reflect the bias of the author's previous lectures and writing, which since 1966 have predicted a revolution ahead in the politics and governance of education (Iannaccone 1967, 1977). Caveat emptor! Few things bias a scholar's interpretation more than one's previous public predictions, especially those in print.

LESSONS FROM TPEPs IN TYPICAL LOCAL SCHOOL DISTRICTS

The research on which this section rests is a twenty-year line of cumulative studies. Some of the findings are familiar to students in the politics of education. The best known of these is the empirically established sequence of three events: school board member incumbent defeat (ID), followed by involuntary superintendent turnover (ivSTO), followed in turn by outside succession (OS). The attention given these has produced a perception similar to the narrow focus on the TPEP in which these events take place. It is that contextual ground that gives meaning to the more familiar events in the research. Unfortunately, semantic simplicity among politics of education students has, as Mitchell (1978) pointed out, dubbed these studies as addressing incumbent school board member defeat and superintendent turnover, and the author bears no small part of the responsibility for this misperception. The linguistic symbolism contributed by the shorthand symbol ID−ivSTO−OS has largely ignored and obscured the basic and explicit assumptions of the model (i.e., redefinition of the educational mission and resulting policy priorities) (Iannaccone 1967).

One painful consequence of this is the attribution of closedness per se to educational policymaking. Instead, the attribution of closedness *within the context* of the theory and research reported refers to the universal tendency of organizations to develop over time toward a homeostasis of reduced intraorganizational fluctuations, especially in their organizational elites (Iannaccone 1967:15). The central point lost is that the mechanisms of ID−ivSTO−OS are the characteristic pattern found that *reopens the previous relative closedness* of the school district's policy subsystem. This closedness is increasingly seen in the last phases of political quiescence prior to the politicization and realignment of the school district's policymaking subsystem (Iannaccone and Lutz 1970:85−88). Even more misdirecting is the simplistic emphasis on ID−ivSTO−SO as an indicator exclusively of a change in the school district's policymaking elite. Again the ground lends meaning to the figure. The narrow view ignores much of the theoretical argument and empirical evidence. These demonstrate that the chain of ID−ivSTO−OS in policymaking regimes is, instead, the most observable of the basic recurring means by which the citizenry of school districts redirect educational policy. In short, the entire corpus of this line of research does not demonstrate that the politics of education and school district policymaking are closed. Rather it demonstrates that internal tendencies toward closedness are recurringly checked through the powerful intervention of voters in TPEPs, resulting both in much greater openness for a period and in changed policy (Iannaccone 1967:98).

The progressive unfolding of a TPEP in a typical local school district may be seen in the development of a sequence of five themes: (1) the ascension of voter discontent; (2) a triggering election; (3) realignment of its policymaking subsystem; (4) articulation of a new policy mandate; and (5) a final test election of the new mandate.[1] Like the movements of a large musical composition, each of these themes is partly developed under the dominance of its preceding ones. Similarly, as each successive theme rises to become the dominant strain, it subsumes and modulates its precursors without extinguishing them. It reorders the relationship among those that emerged earlier. The duration of each of these themes as the major element in the process underway varies from school district to school district (Burlingame 1978; Eblen 1975; Minar 1966) as well as from one era to another (Criswell and Mitchell 1980; LeDoux and Burlingame 1973). The existence of the first themes in the politicization of a school district does not always guarantee the emergence of each of the others. Politicization may diminish in some cases without the completion of the five-theme process. However, when each of these does appear in a school district's politics—and that is the more common case—the sequence of their emergence is invariate.[2] Characteristically these movements rise to a crescendo of politicization on the eve of the articulation of a new policy mandate. A final test election is followed by the end of the TPEP and a gradual return to political quiescence.

The *ascension* of discontent is most often foreshadowed by changes in the socioeconomic and demographic composition of the school district (Iannaccone and Lutz 1970; Kirkendall 1966; LeDoux and Burlingame 1973), which appeared some years before evidence of discontent appears in voting behavior. The specific indicator in the research is a significant shift from the district's characteristic baseline ratio of assessed valuation to its average daily attendance (between six and ten years prior to statistically significant evidence of increasing voting discontent).

Despite these early socioeconomic and demographic changes, the school district's policymaking continues to follow the directions it has previously taken. It either ignores the adjustment of programs required by changing social composition of its citizens and their children or underestimates the magnitude of these (Gabarina 1978). It operates on the policy premises, precedents, and assumptions that have guided its ideological decisions for years. The gap between the political discontent reflecting demands to meet changing conditions and the policy outputs of the board/superintendent policy system increases further. In this sense the district's policymaking tends to be closed to the new changes underway in its environment. The ascension of voter discontent (DIS) with the established policy system of school board incumbents and the incumbent superintendent is measurable in changes in the customary base line of the district's ratios of votes for and against incumbent board members cast in school board elections (Minar 1966; Thorstead 1974). Absent the two-party system in most typical school districts, these ratios register functional equivalents of changes between party voting outcomes of national and state elections. Increased factionalism in voter constituencies may be seen in the local district research: It appears in increases in the number of challengers running against incumbents as well as the ratios reflected both in Minar's Conflict Index (MCI) and in Thorstead's (TCI). In fact, on the eve of a triggering election, the total votes for challengers may exceed those for incumbents. The latter may be reelected because of the scattering of opposition votes among a number of challengers.

The first election in which one or more incumbent school board members are defeated (ID) after a period of no incumbent defeats for several successive elections may be thought of as *triggering* additional incumbent defeat elections, especially the next immediate election and the one after that (Criswell and Mitchell 1980). Alternately, the decision in the same election year by two incumbent school board members not to run functions the same as an initial incumbent defeat after a period of political quiescence (Burlingame 1978; Mitchell 1978). The first ID also sets into motion the beginning of significant conflict within the school district's policymaking subsystem—the board/superintendent meetings (Iannaccone and Lutz 1970). These conflicts between the new member or members and the established incumbents tend to expand rapidly. Polarization of the district's policymaking unit takes place. Often the incumbent superintendent leads the older board faction in these conflicts. Sometimes some members of the previous board swing over to join the new board members.

The sharpening of this cleavage within the board/superintendent subsystem also functions within the district to surface and sharpen ideological differences related to the governance of the schools. The ideas of the past are challenged as inappropriate to changes in the district or as a worn-out overemphasis of some educational values of a bygone era. The old board members naturally tend to defend the programs they supported earlier. The superintendent is usually defending programs he or she initially proposed to the old board. In the rhetoric of political conflict, the defense of existing programs is easily attacked as rigidity and lack of responsiveness. Often enough, the old board majority led by the superintendent has the votes to carry further the direction of the past even in the teeth of bitter intraboard conflicts. If the newer board member represents more accurately the district's developing educational ideology, then these decisions carry the board's policies further toward or beyond the limits of the zone of tolerance citizens normally accord their governments. The conflict measures (the MCI and TCI) continue high or rise higher. Thus the authority and legitimacy of the board and superintendent come into question. The initial ID election is usually followed by an additional ID election, and often this is followed by yet another (Criswell and Mitchell 1980). A realignment of the school's policy system ensues.

Despite the general pattern, there is some empirical basis for arguing that rather than triggering additional IDs, an ID after a quiescent political era can be followed by a return to political quiescence (Danis 1981). The reported instances of this in the research suggest that the following correlative conditions characterize most of these: (1) neither the socioeconomic changes nor the political ones characteristic of the first TPEP phase, DIS, appear to precede the incumbent defeat; (2) their antecedent campaign rhetoric highlights personal candidate characteristics rather than educational policy issues; and (3) incumbent board members are reelected in the immediately following election, and challengers are defeated. Clearly the policymaking and political significance of most of these instances are different from the more general pattern. A very few other IDs deserve more research attention than they have received to date (Freeborn 1966). These are deviate cases only in their aftermaths.

The superintendent does not become an ivSTO. This case is one in which the school district's policy subunit—board and superintendent—perceive correctly the importance of the ID in their district and work to adjust the policies, policymaking process, and school programs immediately. These in effect cut across the rest of the process shortening the period of political conflicts by adjustments reestablishing the necessary balance between the schools and their publics without further TPEP phases.

The third theme to appear in the TPEP is its policy system *realignment* through the school superintendent. The amount of STO following one or two ID elections is significantly greater than when the

IDs are not present (Freeborn 1966). Moreover, it is involuntary turnover (Walden 1966). When the chain is found, the new superintendent is an outside successor (OS), an alien to the district. In contrast, when succession in the superintendency takes place without the first two TPEP themes, the chances of inside succession are significantly greater (Freeborn 1966). Hence the sequence of DIS-ID-ivSTO-OS is well-established in the local school district research. The research indicates further that the reason for involuntary STO is conflict with the board over policy questions (Walden 1966). The related work by Bradshaw (1974) on community college succession and Schafer (1966) on superintendent appointment in newly unified districts also demonstrates that policy conflicts determine the choice of inside versus outside successors. Carlson's (1962:69-70) research on executive succession distinguishes the conditions and board expectations related to inside versus outside succession:

> School boards elect insiders to the superintendency only when the judgment has been made that the schools are being properly administered. . . . [S]chool boards will be satisfied if the insider keeps things as they are, but they expect and are satisfied with an outsider only when some changes are made.

He also pointed out that boards guide outsiders in the general direction of policy changes they expect. Most recently case studies by Chase (1981) and Danis (1981) confirm the importance of policy redirection in the selection of outsiders during TPEPs. The characteristic sequence of DIS-ID-ivSTO-OS are the salient features of the first three themes of the local school district's TPEP.

The fourth theme in the progression of TPEPs is the *articulation of a new policy mandate* by the changed board and new superintendent. As noted earlier, the first ID need not immediately lead to the replacement of the incumbent superintendent. A series of two or three ID elections may intervene with continued politicization between the triggering election and the ivSTO-OS events. So, too, the third theme of superintendent succession may predominate for a longer period in some TPEPs extending the time before the fourth theme emerges. In fact the initial case (Lutz 1962), which led to most of the links in the chain of studies used here, displayed an extended succession theme of repeated turnover in the superintendency (Iannaccone and Lutz 1970:219-222). One explanation suggested for this was rapidity in socioeconomic and demographic district changes. These may produce new cross currents of clashing interests and ideological orientations making the task of articulating a new policy mandate virtually impossible for a time. The changed board may fail to provide the new superintendent with appropriate guidance or the new superintendent may fail to articulate a new mandate and delay its implementation. All of these factors appear present in a recent study of four repeated ivSTOs (Chase 1981). But sooner or later the sequence of DIS-ID-ivSTO-OS produces the articulation of a new mandate.

The articulation of policy requires a combination of a philosophy of governance, technical understanding appropriate to the enterprise, and choices of pragmatic alternatives for implementation. The public discontent leading to the selection of an outsider and the board's orientation shared with the superintendent supply the basis for the needed governance philosophy. The superintendent's professional training and experience supplies the technical expertise and leadership for the necessary pragmatic and programmatic definition of policy choices. Information and communication are essential to the articulation of interests. The new chief executive does this in many ways, including policy statements, the selection of key personnel, the revision of regulations, and the initiation of school program changes. A clarification of values and a definition of the policy issues in effect place a new mandate before the voters.

The fifth theme that emerges from the articulation of a new policy mandate involves the aggregation of interests in a *final test election.* This requires the mobilization of voters choosing between well-defined alternatives.[3] The exportation in effect of board/superintendent actions defines the issues for their political environment of voters. In the election, voters make a choice of supporting the board and by inference the superintendent, of rejecting them, or of staying home. There is far less research on this phase of TPEPs in local school districts than on any of the preceding four. The direct evidence available is from a few case studies (Chase 1981; Danis 1981; Iannaccone and Lutz 1970). There appears to be a larger than usual turnout of voters in final test elections of a new mandate in local school districts. The victory of the new mandate given the size of that turnout rather than the margin of victory appears in effect to suppress opposition voting later. Criswell and Mitchell (1980) found that by the third election biennium the number of incumbent school board member defeats in districts previously high in incumbent defeats significantly suppressed the probability of further IDs.

Placed in the context of TPEPs, the politicization of the school district visibly beginning with the ascension of voter discontent reaches its apogee in a final election test. After this the new policies, policymakers, and programs become increasingly more secure in their political support. The politics of quiescence reemerges. Incrementalism in policymaking holds sway as it did before the TPEP. The twin forces of incremental policymaking and quiescent politics shape the implementation of rules and programs inferred from the new policy premises until a new ascension of voter discontent emerges to usher in the next TPEP.

THE PRESENT NATIONAL TPEP

The conceptualization of the progressive unfolding of TPEPs in local school districts is employed to examine national politics. The sequence of the same five themes is used to organize the description of the last two decades: (1) the ascension of voter discontent; (2) a triggering election; (3) a realignment election; (4) articulation of a new policy mandate; and (5) a final test election.

National policymaking of the most recent quiescent political era in large part reflected the dominance of New Deal political philosophy. The policy premises that emerged victoriously from their 1936 final test election of that era's TPEP incrementally shaped to a degree politics and policymaking. The socioeconomic conditions after World War II and the impact of the cold war on partisan politics interpreted by that dominant political philosophy helped define the issues for governmental decisions. Together, for example, these led to a national consensus on a bipartisan foreign policy. Despite its many positive aspects, this consensus in turn substantially subordinated other potential political cleavages between and within the two major parties. For instance, in the Democratic party differences appeared among the party's three basic voter constituencies: the solid south, the liberals, and organized labor. These were contained by a coalition of cold war warriors and of liberals concerned with socioeconomic equality. Policies of the latter years of that quiescent era (circa 1954–64) reflected these coalitional interests and extensions of the dominant political paradigm, New Deal governance philosophy.

These same years saw a new politicization of education, unlike any since the TPEP of the municipal reform era at the turn of the century (Callahan 1962, 1967; Tyack 1974). Three events between 1954 and 1964 stimulated this politicization and national governmental policymaking in education. These were the 1954 *Brown* v. *Board of Education* decision, 1957 Sputnik, and the 1960 New York City teachers' strike (Iannaccone 1977). The saliency of education in national politics from 1954 to the creation of the Department of Education in Carter's presidency reflects socioeconomic conditions emerging from World War II (the cold war especially) in the combined interests of the Democratic Party's predominant coalition and New Deal policy premises.

The industrial productivity of the United States was high at the end of the war, and it continued to grow. It was fueled by low-cost energy, and little competition existed internationally given the devastation of Japanese and European industries. Within this benign economic environment, the post-war baby boom increased both the demand for education and the number of parents supporting it at the same time that the schools were subjected to the criticisms following *Brown* and Sputnik. The concerns over the economic inequalities of the educational system and its perceived failure in science and math were translated into national intervention policies through categorical grant programs consistent with the dominant New Deal political philosophy. Washington educational policy initiatives reflected the combined concerns both of cold-war warriors for the international image of the United States due to segregation and the need for trained manpower highlighted by Sputnik and of the liberals for racial and socioeconomic equality.

The politicoeconomic assumptions of the New Deal are fundamentally supportive of centralization and bureaucratization, emphasizing the importance of the hierarchical flow of policy. The educational policies and programs became a national overlay superimposed upon a basically different structure of state and local governments. The incremental extension of this governance ideology reached a new high in the Johnson era by fashioning basic changes in American intergovernmental relations, for example, in education centralizing policymaking in Washington. Resistance to national governmental intervention was overcome by a combination of dependence on an expanding national economy and traditional New Deal fiscal policies.

The use of grants-in-aid made national policy intervention more palatable. So the domestic policies of the national government including education took a carrot rather than whip intervention character throughout the 1960s.

The ascension of discontent, the first theme of the present TPEP, appeared around the mid-1960s. The economic conditions favorable to the Great Society programs began to decrease almost as soon as the passage of the Elementary and Secondary Education Act (ESEA) in 1965: The competitive rise of Japanese and European economies was felt, and the expansion of the war in Viet Nam demanded national monies. By the late 1960s the favorable economic conditions were reversed. There were ideological indicators of the rise of discontent, too. As early as the 1964 national campaign, the Republican party displayed a new polarization. More clearly revealing that a new TPEP's ascension theme had emerged in American national politics was the division within the Democrats in the 1968 nomination campaign. Robert Kennedy, one of the party's most powerful senators and the heir of its previously assassinated president, challenged his own party's incumbent president in primary elections across the nation. The disruption of the party's national convention by ideological clashes taken literally into the streets of Chicago and the violence that ensued there are classic indicators of national TPEPs. So, too, is the rise of third-party votes. Most significant as an indicator of the ascension of discontent in national elections is a generational division around conflicting ideological assumptions. A generation gap was evident in the party divisions between Kennedy and Johnson.

TPEPs are separated in American history by approximately a generation: There are thirty-six years between 1968 and the realignment of 1932 and between 1932 and 1896, the year of the previous realignment. Thirty-six years earlier, the Lincoln election of 1860 produced the necessary balance between political and socioeconomic systems but only through the Civil War. The year 1824 saw the breakup of the Democratic party, which was realigned in 1828 with the establishment of Jacksonian party dominance. Why one generation? Because ideas translated into political philosophies, formulas of governance, and governmental missions rule the world of politics. They shape the agendas of political conflicts.

The triggering election of 1968 was similar to the first ID in local school district research. Increased polarization in both parties after this triggering election is clear and also was expressed through third-party voting in the 1970s and the 1980 election.

Domestic policymaking also reflected these continuing and growing ideological polarities, as can be seen by an examination of educational policymaking in the years between 1968 and 1980. It no longer revealed a complex coalition of interests producing omnibus educational legislation like ESEA in 1965. Instead, the major national educational policies since 1968 have been distinctively differentiated responses to narrow, single-issue, interest groups. These more recent policies include P.L. 94–142, affirmative action (especially in higher education), bilingual education, and the creation of the Department of Education. However worthwhile in themselves, these clearly have been responses to distinguishably different organized education lobbies rather than policy reflecting the crafted compromise of a dominant coalition. Response to polarized strong interests marked much of the rest of federal policies and legislation during the last twelve years. The once vital political paradigm, which held sway from 1932 and guided the Johnson Great Society programs as its last policy restatement, appeared in the 1970s as burnt-out policy ashes.

The interdependency of policy and politics characteristic of the first themes of TPEPs may be illustrated by examining some aspects of the concern for social equality in educational policies. The policy increasingly focused on schools as prime instruments for solving problems much more pervasive than schooling. The socioeconomic conditions that had in part given rise to this viewpoint were substantially reversed by the late 1960s preceding the triggering election of 1968. In brief, the SES context of these policies had changed. Energy became expensive. The trade balance became unfavorable. Productivity in American industry declined. Personal savings from a previous era were depleted. The Viet Nam war bill had to be paid. The economic system became characterized by stagflation—inflation in costs with lowered production. The ideological interpretation of these facts by the Democratic party revealed that their policy premises about central governmental expansion to solve the problems of the society had temporarily played themselves out. Never explicit, it implicitly declared an era of limits or a steady state. This was to be a disastrous interpretation for the Democratic party when held beside its continued efforts to extend their ideological commitments to solving the problems of equality and social justice through national programs.

The argument can be illustrated by briefly noting the peregrination of equality in and through national education policy. Its first emphasis was on its racial character. Beginning with the 1954 *Brown* decision, the first step was the elimination of legal barriers separating segregated schools. Desegregation had relatively wide consensual support except in the southeast, but intense political conflicts were experienced in some areas. The next problem examined was de facto desegregation. Integration, rather than simple desegregation, became the new goal. The public support for integration, however, was weaker than for desegregation, and the specific focus on school busing as the solution—the national government program substitute for coping with the basic causes of de facto segregation—produced a wide but still not dominant political backlash by the time of the 1968 triggering election.

During the 1970s the peregrination of national policies for equality took another form. What had once been an effort to provide relief from legal segregation and fiscal equality had spawned a variety of equity programs. By the late 1970s this policy metempsychosis revealed the internal chaos of the dominant Democratic party's polarities. Its programs became viewed as special-interest give-aways. The policy rhetoric of equity was edging toward quotas based on racial, ethnic, or sexist discriminations. Policy so defined leaves only one question to the political arena—that is, "Whose ox shall be gored?" Worse, the changed economic conditions meant that the era of carrot inducements had given way to a punitive era of regulatory whips. The late stage came on the eve of the 1980 election. It was characterized by a proactive stance of national agency interventions to solve social problems in states, local districts, and higher education campuses. One high point of bureaucratic arrogance was the bilingual regulations proposed even after the 1980 election. They would have to a degree reversed the transitional stance of congressional legislation passed by a Democratic Congress in the Carter administration. The voter perception that the Democrats supported bureaucratic interference and special interests was one consequence of the journey that began in 1954. What these governmental actions of the 1970s also reveal are the characteristic decisions of established policy systems seen in local school districts. They go beyond the zone of tolerance in the years after the triggering election and before its re-alignment.

The 1980 *realignment election* is the third theme of the present TPEP. Its significance is far greater today than it was in 1968. Not only was an incumbent president defeated in 1980, but never in its 180-year history has the Democratic party lost more seats to an opposing party in a single election. Further, as revealed in Congress since January 1981, many of the Democrats elected share Reagan's ideological assumptions. The socioeconomic conditions that made national educational programs salient issues of political conflict and national policy have played themselves out. The public perception of inconsistency between these changed socioeconomic conditions and the previous governmental philosophy was a major factor in the election. These conditions have produced a new set of policy parameters for the next years.

The *articulation of a new policy mandate* is well underway. The ideological assumptions of Reagan's rhetoric beginning as early as 1964 and consistent in their major outlines have begun to appear in programs and policy statements. The most important of these are his recent proposals to transfer many domestic programs to the states. These are consistent with his positions on the national budget and taxation, but they even better express the central ideological issues of the governmental philosophy he represents. Implicit in the political clashes that lie ahead between the present administration and its opponents is the sharpening of issues around a predominant cleavage of values. The administration's political efforts will be aimed at making the central political agenda question of the 1984 election concern for industrial productivity and the transfer of domestic policy and programs to the states and local governments.

The 1984 election will be a test of the Reagan policy articulation. Whether it will be a *final test election* drawing to a close the present TPEP remains to be seen. The election will probably turn on whether the administration or the Democratic party better articulates the voters' ideological predisposition. In a mature national TPEP following a realignment, the administration has three distinct advantages: the opportunities of its new incumbency, the disarray of the previously dominant party, and the lessons of the off-year election, in this case 1982. Despite negative fallouts from Reagan's domestic policies, to date these have produced more public support than opposition. Reagan's foreign and defense policies have, instead, drawn much less support, and the administration has far less clearly articulated its policies in these areas than in its domestic policy. The evidence indicates President Reagan was elected in spite of voter fears about him in these areas. His expanded defense budgets and failures in foreign affairs may unseat the Republicans in 1984.

Instances of continued superintendent overturn between the fourth and fifth movements of school district TPEPs do exist. Explanations of these continued overturns seem plausible. One is rapid socioeconomic and demographic changes cutting *across the previous trends* and thus reopening ideological conflicts. The other is the failure of the new policy system to articulate in action the voters' new politicoeconomic assumptions. The Reagan administration is more in danger from the first of these than from the second. The impact of increased national indebtedness on the economy as a whole is its greatest present danger in the domestic area. Otherwise, President Reagan's rhetorical mastery and sense of voter response makes it most unlikely that he will lose the voters. His domestic programs are not out of tune with the voter masses that supported him in 1980. The other side of the 1984 test is the question of what the Democrats will do. The research on TPEPs suggests that their return to power in 1984 is not probable if they seek to reinstitute the political philosophy and governmental programs of the previous two decades. The interpretations President Reagan and the Democratic party leaders place on the 1982 congressional elections will shape the respective policy articulation and political agenda they place before the voter for the 1984 election. If the 1982 election goes against the Republicans, the Democrats will be misled into reiterating their past in the 1984 election. Ironically, if instead the 1982 election supports the Republicans, President Reagan is likely to interpret that as support for his foreign policy and defense budgets, increasing his risk in his weakest areas of voter fears. In sum, other things being equal, the 1982 losers have a better chance of *seeing the need* to adjust their 1984 agenda. In either case the realities of economics, demographics, and ideology say that education will not be given much attention in these contests. It would appear that the most significant educational politics and policy conflicts ahead will be *within* the states whether the 1984 election provides a final TPEP test and victory for the GOP or not.

THE FUTURE FOR EDUCATIONAL
FISCAL POLICY

Inferences for educational fiscal policy in the long run may be drawn from the foregoing analyses regardless of which party wins in 1984. A Republican victory and retention of the White House would signal a final test election of the national policy mandate articulated by the present Reagan administration. A Republican loss of the presidency in 1984 would, instead, be a functional equivalent of repeated incumbent defeats and executive turnovers in the local school districts. This would indicate a continuation of realignment rather than a final test election in 1984. It would extend the present period of disarray in educational policy premises produced by contradictory elements embedded in national policy prior to the 1980 elections and increased by the actions of the Reagan administration and Congress since January of 1981. It would also signal a need for further clarification of the issues and a sharper articulation of the new policy mandate, leading to a subsequent final test election closing the present TPEP.

The spring of 1981 signaled the end of an era in national fiscal policy for education. The decrease in federal funding, consolidation of fiscal intervention programs, deregulation in many areas within education, and other actions having immediate impact on education had by the fall of 1981 already set into motion the articulation of a new philosophy of government in education—one that significantly shifts to the states the function of educational policymaking. The subsequent budgetary and governance proposals of the administration articulates even more sharply the transfer of responsibility for education to the states. The continued erosion of public support confronting the White House in the winter and spring of 1982 reflects its lack of credibility in its foreign policy coupled in the minds of voters with growing national deficits and high interest rates rather than a rejection of its philosophy of domestic policymaking.

The diminution of the national government's role in domestic policymaking and the decentralization of programs in domestic affairs are the manifestations of the ideological change in American voters. Within a context of increased concern for productivity and fears about declining economic circumstances, that ideological driving force will shape the fiscal policies in education during the years ahead. An additional major constraint on education fiscal policy is the demographic reality: Fewer citizens have children in the schools today than was the case in the previous three decades. Unfavorable demographics, economic decline, hostility toward government spending, and the rejection of federal intervention constitute the politically feasible parameters of fiscal policy in education during the next years.

Education will continue to experience diminished federal aid in the years ahead, with two immediate consequences: (1) There will be greater reliance on state and local sources of funds; and (2) less obvious, but equally certain, there is a need to focus energy on fiscal acquisition at the expense of attention to allocation. Neither are the states nor the localities likely to spend more for education. Competition for these funds will increase among many domestic services. Reducing the probable losses will require enhanced ability to compete. In turn, this demands a sharp reduction of political fragmentation and conflicts among educational interest groups. Stronger coalitions within a more competitive environment require that their previously conflicting members abandon portions of their previous agendas. Specifically, they must give up those elements that have divided them. Their claims to funds to foster their unique concerns must receive lower priority than their fears of losing general funds for the enterprise. Many of the interest groups that emerged in the last fifteen or so years will not be able to make the necessary adjustment. Understandably, they will fight to survive with their unique agendas, special funds, and categorical programs. In the process, such battles will delay the formation of effective coalitions concerned primarily with general funds.

Fiscal policy in education may be viewed as involving a mutual dependency of adequacy, stability, incentive, and equality aspects. A shortage of funds and a major concern for fiscal acquisition rather than allocation issues lead to greater attention to adequacy and stability at the expense of incentive and equality considerations. These concerns would also reduce reliance on categorical aid and increase the importance of general aid in fiscal policy, even without the influence of the ideological shift away from centralized intervention in policymaking. Fiscal policy aimed at the schools to produce directly increased social equality will suffer. The most feasible countercurrent element in the situation is categorical aid as incentive for programs directed toward expanded productivity. Even this is more likely to increase the differences between the educationally advantaged and disadvantaged, at least in the short run, by allocating resources for improved academic and technical achievement. Nevertheless, public concern for economic production offers the only major potential source of new fiscal acquisition in education. That potential can be realized only if the conceptual connection between education and productivity is made for the voter. The articulation of that connection is a task that can be initially undertaken by finance specialists and educators working on public school policy. To be effective, however, it must be ultimately adopted by central political figures at national and state levels. Implicit in that connection is public awareness that human capital and investment in it play an essential part in a significantly stronger system of economic productivity. The present Reagan agenda ignores this need. The agenda of the Democratic congressional opposition does not appear ready to accept the assumptions implicit in the emphasis on productivity. Whether the specialists in educational finance and policymaking are ready to lead the way toward filling this present vacuum remains to be seen. The situation is opportune for articulating and publicizing the connections between productivity, investment in human capital, and education.

NOTES TO CHAPTER 1

1. The author is particularly indebted to Dr. Ruth Danis for her work, "Policy Changes in Local Governance" (1981), and even more to the lengthy discussions of her data on internal phases of TPEPs.
2. Having made that strong assertion I must now repair to the traditional social science refuge of ceteris paribus. For example, the selection of a new superintendent following the death or voluntary turnover of a predecessor *in the midst of rising discontent* might produce conflicts between the superintendent and the board resulting in the defeat of incumbent board members and support for the superintendent's policies. These events would, indeed, reverse the second and third themes and could theoretically at least concurrently fold in the fourth and fifth.
3. The distinction drawn by Almond and Powell (1966) between interest articulation and interest aggregation is followed here.

REFERENCES

Almond, Gabriel A., and G. Bingham Powell, Jr. 1966. *Comparative Politics: A Developmental Approach*. Boston: Little, Brown and Company, Publishers.

Boyd, William L. 1975. "Community Status and Suburban School Conflict." In *The Polity of the School*, edited by Frederick M. Wirt, pp. 103–121. Lexington, Mass.: D. C. Heath and Company.

Bradshaw, R. H. 1974. "Executive Succession in the Community College." Ph. D. dissertation, Claremont Graduate School.

Brown v. Board of Education, 347 U.S. 483 (1954).

Burlingame, Martin. 1978. "Downward Trends in Socioeconomic-Political Indicators and Incumbent Defeat." In *Public Participation in Local School Districts*, edited by Frank W. Lutz and Laurence Iannaccone, pp. 45–53. Lexington, Mass.: D. C. Heath Co.

Burnham, W. D. 1970. *Critical Elections and the Wellsprings of American Politics*. New York: W. W. Norton.

Callahan, Raymond E. 1962. *Education and the Cult of Efficiency*. Chicago: University of Chicago Press.

_____. 1967. *The Superintendent of Schools: An Historical Analysis*. Washington, D.C. U. S. Office of Education.

Carlson, Richard O. 1962. *Executive Succession and Organizational Change*. Chicago, Ill.: Midwest Administration Center, University of Chicago.

Chase, Wynelle M. 1981. "Superintendent Turnover—Antecedent Conditions and Subsequent Organizational Changes." Ph. D. dissertation, University of California, Santa Barbara.

Criswell, Larry W., and Douglas E. Mitchell. 1980. "Episodic Instability in School District Elections." *Urban Education* 15, no. 2 (July): 189–213.

Danis, Ruth. 1981. "Policy Changes in Local Governance: The Dissatisfaction Theory of Democracy." Ph. D. dissertation, University of California, Santa Barbara.

Eblen, D. R. 1975. "School District Conflict and Superintendent Turnover in Transitional Suburban Communities." Ph. D. dissertation, University of Chicago.

Freeborn, Robert M. 1966. "School Board Change and the Succession Pattern of Superintendents." Ph. D. dissertation, Claremont Graduate School.

Gabarina, William L. 1978. "School Board Response and Incumbent Defeat." In *Public Participation in Local School Districts*, edited by Frank W. Lutz and Laurence Iannaccone, pp. 55–71. Lexington, Mass.: D. C. Heath Co.

Iannaccone, Laurence. 1966. "The Future of State Politics of Education." In *Struggle for Power in Education*, edited by Frank W. Lutz and Joseph J. Assarelli, pp. 49–66. New York: Center for Applied Research in Education.

_____. 1967. *Politics in Education*. New York: Center for Applied Research in Education.

_____. 1977. "Three Views of Change in Educational Politics." In *The Politics of Education*, edited by Jay D. Scribner, pp. 255–286. Chicago: University of Chicago Press.

_____. 1981. "The Reagan Presidency." *Journal of Learning Disabilities* 14, no. 2 (February): 55–59.

Iannaccone, Laurence, and Peter J. Cistone. 1974. *The Politics of Education*. Eugene, Ore.: University of Oregon Press.

Iannaccone, Laurence, and Frank W. Lutz. 1970. *Politics, Power and Policy*. Columbus, Ohio: Charles E. Merrill Books.

Iannaccone, Laurence, and David K. Wiles. 1971. "The Changing Politics of Urban Education." *Education and Urban Society* 3, no. 3 (May): 255–64.

Kammerer, G.; C. Farris; J. Degrave; and A. Clubok. 1962. *City Managers in Politics*. Gainesville, Florida: University of Florida Press.

_____. 1963. *The Urban Political Community*. Boston: Houghton Mifflin Co.

Kerchner, C.; D. Mitchell; G. Pryor; and W. Erck. 1981. "The Logic of Citizen Participation in Public School Labor Relations." Paper presented to the Informational Project for Education-Network, San Francisco, January 30.

Key, V.O., Jr. 1955. "A Theory of Critical Elections." *Journal of Politics* 17, no. 1 (February): 3–18.

Kirkendall, Richard S. 1966. "Discriminant Social, Economic, and Political Characteristics of Changing versus Stable Policy-Making Systems in School Districts." Ph.D. dissertation, Claremont Graduate School.

LeDoux, Eugene, and Martin Burlingame. 1973. "The Iannaccone and Lutz Model of School Board Change: A Replication in New Mexico." *Educational Administration Quarterly* 9, no. 3 (Autumn): 48–65.

Lindblom, Charles E. 1968. *The Policy-Making Process*. Englewood Cliffs, N.J.: Prentice-Hall.

Lowi, Theodore J. 1964. *At the Pleasure of the Mayor*. New York: Free Press.

Lutz, Frank W. 1962. "Social Systems and School Districts." Ph.D. dissertation, University of Chicago.

Lutz, Frank W., and Laurence Iannaccone, eds. 1978. *Public Participation in Local School Districts*. Lexington, Mass.: Lexington Books.

MacRae, Duncan, Jr., and James A. Meldrum. 1960. "Critical Elections in Illinois: 1888-1958." *The American Political Science Review* 54, no. 3 (September): 669–83.

Mill, John Stuart. 1913. *On Liberty*. London: Longmans, Green, and Co.

Minar, David W. 1964. "Community Characteristics, Conflict, and Power Structures." In *The Politics of Education in the Local Community*, edited by Robert S. Cahill and Stephen P. Hencley, pp. 125–143. Danville, Ill.: Interstate Printers and Publishers.

_____. 1966. "Commmunity Basis of Conflict in School System Politics." *American Sociological Review* 31, no. 6 (December): 822–35.

Mitchell, Douglas E. 1978. "Measurement and Methodological Issues Related to Research on Incumbent Defeat and Superintendent Turnover." In *Public Participation in Local School Districts*, edited by Frank W. Lutz and Laurence Iannaccone, pp. 73–99. Lexington, Mass.: D. C. Heath and Co.

Mitchell, Douglas, and Laurence Iannaccone. 1980. *The Impact of California's Legislative Policy on Public School Performance.* Berkeley: University of California.

Peterson, Paul E. 1976. *School Politics Chicago Style.* Chicago: The University of Chicago Press.

Schafer, E. 1966. "Unification: A Change of Power Structure Reflected in Board Composition and Superintendent Selection." Ph.D. dissertation, Claremont Graduate School.

Schattschneider, E.E. 1960. *The Semisovereign People.* New York: Holt, Rinehart and Winston.

Sellers, Charles. 1965. "The Equilibrium Cycle in Two-Party Politics." *The Public Opinion Quarterly* 29, no. 1 (Spring): 16–38.

Stelzer, Leigh. 1975. "Institutionalizing Conflict Response: The Case of Schoolboards." In *The Polity of the School*, edited by Frederick M. Wirt, pp. 69–84. Lexington, Mass.: D. C. Heath and Co.

Summerfield, Harry L. 1975. "The Neighborhood-Based Politics of Education." In *The Polity of the School*, edited by Frederick M. Wirt, pp. 165–185. Lexington, Mass.: D. C. Heath and Co.

Thorsted, R.R. 1974. "Predicting School Board Member Defeat: Demographic and Political Variables that Influence School Board Elections." Ph.D. dissertation, University of California, Riverside.

Tyack, David B. 1974. *The One Best System.* Cambridge, Mass.: Harvard University Press.

Walden, John C. 1966. "School Board Changes and Involuntary Superintendent Turnover." Ph.D. dissertation, Claremont Graduate School.

2 POLITICS OF FEDERAL AID

*John F. Jennings**

INTRODUCTION

One needs only to read last week's newspaper to realize the extent to which the events of the day are overstated. Although certain critical junctures do appear, most fundamental shifts occur over a long period of time and have a wide variety of causes.

Leadership is very important, but it requires a propitious moment in order to succeed. President Lyndon Johnson did indeed create many new federal programs of aid to education, and President Ronald Reagan, nearly twenty years later, is doggedly trying to eliminate or sharply curtail not only these programs but also many predating programs. Neither man, however, —regardless of his leadership abil-ity—could have hoped to succeed unless events over time had created the right environment, and neither man could or will achieve ulti-mate success in his desires because pressures in the system inhibit even a forceful leader. Consequently, in order to understand how federal aid to education got to where it is today and where it is go-ing, one must look beyond the moment of decision.

For instance, in 1980 it seemed that federal aid to education was to be a large and growing part of the federal system. In dollar terms,

*John F. Jennings, Associate General Counsel, Committee on Education and Labor, and Counsel and Staff Director, Subcommittee on Elementary, Secondary, and Vocational Education, House of Representatives, United States Congress.

this aid amounted to $14.2 billion overall. The federal government was contributing 8.7 percent of the cost of elementary and secondary education and 14.0 percent of the cost of postsecondary education. In certain areas, this federal contribution was even higher: approximately 70 percent of the funds expended for compensatory education; approximately 48.5 percent of the funds in the school lunch program; and over 74 percent of postsecondary student aid. The number of students benefitting was staggering—forty-six million in elementary and secondary schools and almost twelve million in postsecondary institutions (National Center for Education Statistics 1981: 6).

The magnitude and complexity of the federal involvement was even more obvious in the various federal laws and regulations concerning education. Those laws amounted to 2,400 pages of statutes, and the regulations to carry them out took up almost 1,800 pages of the very small type in the *Federal Register.*

In 1980, the new Department of Education was only a year old, but it was a very aggressive one-year-old. Its first secretary, Shirley Hufstedler, was interviewed by all of the major news magazines and television networks and gave a high visibility to this creation of the Carter administration. The department also vigorously enforced statutes affecting civil rights, sex discrimination, bilingual education, and protection of the handicapped.

Within one year, the scene changed tremendously. In 1981 federal aid to education was cut by $1.8 billion, a 12 percent reduction from 1980's aid level. A block grant was enacted that terminated twenty legislative appropriations and eliminated and repealed forty-four categorical programs. The Department of Education was in long-term jeopardy because of its proposed legislative abolition and in immediate danger because of the termination of hundreds of employees. In addition, enforcement of the various federal anti-discrimination statutes had come to a standstill.

After these successes of his first year in office, President Reagan proposed in 1982 an even more drastic reduction of a strong federal role in education. Under the banner of "new federalism," he submitted a budget calling for severe cuts in education. For example, the basic programs of compensatory education and student aid were targeted for cutbacks of one-third to one-half of their funds.

More broadly, the president was proposing a massive "swap" of forty programs with the states, which would lead to the elimination of federal funding for vocational and adult education, the school lunch program, the new "block grant" (including library assistance and aid to state departments of education), and many other programs. The only major programs left at the federal level would be compensatory education (Title I of the Elementary and Secondary Education Act), handicapped education, Head Start, and postsecondary student assistance, but all of these would be retained at greatly reduced funding levels.

The federal role in education was not created by one man, and it will not be eliminated by one man. The large programs and their vigorous administration in 1980 owed much to Lyndon Johnson, but they were also the creation of far older and deeper forces. The initial successes of Ronald Reagan were likewise due to both larger forces and also his leadership, and these larger forces will help determine how successful he will be in achieving his ultimate objectives.

In the following discussion, a brief description of the evolution of federal aid for education serves as a backdrop for this overview of the politics of federal aid. The next major section focuses on the role of interest groups in building the coalitions that contribute to the enactment of legislation. In the third major section, attention is given to the impact of changing social, political, and economic conditions on federal actions. This section is followed by a series of speculative principles about future federal involvement in education.

What exactly then are the long-term prospects for federal aid? Will the federal government fund only a few major federal programs and leave the rest to be eliminated or carried on locally, or will all federal funds and programs for education be terminated?

BACKDROP

The national government of the United States has always recognized the importance of education. Over the years, the federal government has enacted various statutes to initiate programs and promote the formation of schools.

Early History

Underlying the "new federalism" is an assumption that many of the federal government's domestic assistance programs, including education, came out of the Great Society or at least out of the New Deal. Although there is much truth to that assumption, the antecedents of federal aid in certain areas are of much longer duration.

The national government started to provide aid to education even before the Constitution was adopted. In the Ordinances of 1785 and 1787, when the thirteen original colonies were still being governed under the Articles of Confederation, the weak national government required that in the sale of land within the present midwest, certain sections had to be sold for the purpose of raising funds to support local public schools. Under the new Constitution of 1789, land grants for education were continued in the various statehood acts, beginning with the Ohio Enabling Act of 1802. The federal government eventually granted nearly a hundred million acres to the states for public schools, and our nationwide system of local public education was born.

The federal government played an equally significant role in the establishment of the great state universities. In the very midst of the Civil War, the Congress enacted the Morrill Act of 1862, which again made land grants available to the states, but this time for the express purpose of establishing colleges of agricultural and industrial education. From the Pennsylvania State University to the University of California, the land grant universities trace their growth and development to this national policy.

Subsequent significant federal actions in education included the establishment of a system of vocational schools with the enactment of the Smith-Hughes Act of 1917, the opening of higher education to the common man through the G. I. Bill of Rights, the establishment of near-universal school feeding through the National School Lunch Act of 1946, and advances in mathematics and science due to the passage of the National Defense Education Act of 1958.

Federal aid to education was not new at the time of the New Deal and certainly not by the time of the Great Society. It was an old and well-established part of the federal system of government.

The Last Twenty Years

Nonetheless, it is true that a great spurt of new aid and new programs occurred during the 1960s principally during the Johnson administration. School revenues from federal sources grew from $3.2 billion in

1963–64 to $7.5 billion in 1969–70. Dozens of new federal education programs were enacted during this period.

President Nixon did not agree with these new education programs or with the variety of other Great Society programs. Consequently, in 1971, using almost the same rhetoric as President Reagan was to use a decade later, he tried to sharply cut back on the funding for almost all of these new domestic assistance activities and to turn them over to the states. He proposed consolidating 105 programs into six "special revenue-sharing" block grants (New Concepts 1973: 97). Only two, the Comprehensive Employment and Training Act and the Community Development Block Grant, were enacted and these not until 1973 and 1974, respectively. Educational programs were spared by the Congress from a massive block grant, although several smaller programs were consolidated.

President Nixon's assaults on these education programs caused a strong reaction, so that the Democratic Congresses over the next few years not only fought off his attempts at cutbacks but also actually began to expand and better fund these programs. Over time, Republicans in Congress came to identify themselves with some federal programs of aid to education; Senators Stafford from Vermont and Weicker of Connecticut supported the Education of All Handicapped Children's Act; Congressman Quie from Minnesota was an advocate for vocational education; Congressman Buchanan from Alabama for the Women's Educational Equity Act; and Senator Javits from New York for the Gifted and Talented Children's Act and state student incentive grants.

In retrospect, President Nixon's attacks on these programs may have made them stronger, since political coalitions and interest groups were formed locally and nationally to defend the programs. This defensive support then grew into a force to expand the programs.

President Carter came into office with Vice-President Walter Mondale, whose record in Congress was as a strong and vigorous advocate of federal education programs. Moreover, by that time, the National Education Association had become more active politically and had the new administration in its debt. As a consequence, federal programs again grew from $11.6 billion in the first year of the Carter administration to $15.4 billion during the fourth year. In addition to creating the Department of Education, several new programs were also enacted.

Within a year of President Carter's defeat and Ronald Reagan's ascent to the presidency, however, funding for all of these programs had been cut by 12 percent, forty-four of them had been "block granted," tuition tax credits were being advocated for parents of students in private schools, and the new Department of Education was scheduled to be abolished. What brought about such a radical change in fortune for education?

INTEREST GROUPS AND COALITION BUILDING

Before concentrating on the present, it might be useful to review the history of federal aid to education from a somewhat different perspective in order to understand this shift in support for federal education programs. In national policymaking, the leadership displayed by presidents, other elected officials, and leaders in particular fields is essential, but public opinion also must be receptive and supportive.

From the enactment of the Morrill Act to the current time, federal actions related to education have taken place when various individuals and interest groups assumed leadership during a social or economic environment that was favorable to their goals. As indicated below, the interaction of leadership and environment has continued from the early legislation, through the development of an interest in general federal aid, to an era in which interest groups have come to play an important role in the enactment and implementation of federal education legislation. As this pattern for developing federal legislation has evolved, the importance of effective leadership has become increasingly evident.

Early Legislation

The Morrill Act. Stimulated by a proposal from Jonathan Baldwin Turner, in 1853, the Illinois legislature passed a resolution asking for federal support for an industrial university in each state, with financing to be obtained through the sale of public lands. Efforts were made to seek support for this concept by sending the copies of the Illinois resolution to each state and asking the Illinois congressional representatives to support the measure in Congress. For the next several years, various efforts were made to secure support for this proposal. In 1857, Representative Justin Morrill of Vermont introduced the legislation, but the environment was not favorable because President Buchanan did not support the measure. When the bill was re-introduced by Representative Morrill in 1861, President Lincoln was in office, and there was no fear of a presidential veto. Finally, the legislation was enacted and signed in 1862 by President Lincoln (AVA 1976: 38). This legislation led to the formation of the land grant universities throughout the United States, and a tradition of using the sponsor's name in the title of the legislation was established and continued for almost a century.

Vocational Education. Events leading to the enactment of the Smith-Hughes Act in 1917 provide an additional example of the manner in which economic circumstances, or environment, can contribute to the enactment of legislation. Starting around 1890, a wide variety of education groups developed an interest in vocational education. Organizations ranging from the American Federation of Labor to the National Association of Manufacturers were conscious of the manpower needs related to the industrialization of the nation, and vocational education was perceived to be the solution to the problem (Grubb and Lazerson 1974: 7).

A coalition of individuals and organizations formed the National Society for the Promotion of Industrial Education, the predecessor organization to the American Vocational Association (AVA). The need for better-trained workers was well-recognized, but the trade unions and industrialists had differing opinions as to how these various workers should receive the appropriate vocational training. The debate continued for almost two decades, but the outbreak of World War I increased the pressures for some type of action. Pushed by the efforts of the National Society, in 1914 Congress appointed the Commission on National Aid to Vocational Education. As a result of the leadership of the various individual groups and the favorable environment, the commission's efforts led to the passage of the Smith-Lever Act in 1914 and the Smith-Hughes Act in 1917. The former legislation was sought by the agrarian interests, and the latter was designed to meet the needs of the nation during a period of industrial expansion (Grubb and Lazerson 1974: 7, 9).

Developing Interest in General Federal Aid

A continuing national interest in federal support for education resulted from the work of various national commissions, such as the

National Advisory Commission that reported to President Hoover in 1931. The commission declared that there was ample justification for providing financial aid for education to the states, provided that such action did not result in the federal government having control over the processes of education. The recommendation was that general aid for education be given rather than categorical grants for special purposes. A few years later in 1938, President Roosevelt's United States Advisory Commission on Education also endorsed the general aid approach, and again indicated that no attempt should be made to use federal aid as a means of controlling the educational content or processes in the schools (National Educational Finance Project 1971: 193–94).

Bipartisan support for federal aid was obvious during the 1940s. Senator Robert Taft of Ohio was an ardent supporter, but the critical element of presidential leadership and broad-based support in both political parties was lacking. The divisive issues of race, religion, and federal control reflected deep philosophical differences in Congress. A majority in both houses of Congress could not be assembled because of both the possibility that funds would go to segregated schools in the South or to parochial schools and also the differing positions about the degree of latitude or federal control that should be a condition of receiving funds (ACIR 1981b: 74).

Emergence of Interest Groups

Significant achievements in providing funds for education have been made since the late 1950s. As various federal aid programs have been enacted, three interest groups appear to have played a variety of leading and supportive roles in efforts to enact and maintain continued support for most federal educational efforts. First, national interest groups representing the various constituencies receiving or providing services have developed to encourage continuation of programs. Examples are the various education interest groups such as the AVA, the American Council on Education, American Federation of Teachers, the Children's Defense Fund, civil rights groups, the Council for Exceptional Children, labor organizations, and the National Education Association. As compromises were reached on such issues as whether to include parochial schools among the recipients, to address national needs, or to equalize the level of educational expenditures among states, the result has been the development of a system of federal aids that is child- rather than institutionally oriented. Rather than providing general federal aid, the direction has been to focus the funds on specific problems with the intent to provide equal access to educational opportunities for various disadvantaged persons in the American society.

The second interest group is illustrated by a network of individuals involved in the delivery or administration of federal educational programs. In some cases, they have been active in the national interest groups, and in others, they have acted independently in support of various programs. Typically, this group plays only a supportive role as consideration is given to enacting legislation and is more heavily involved in the development of regulations and procedures that determine how the programs will be conducted. The network extends from the federal program administrators, through the state educational agencies, to the local school districts and postsecondary educational institutions in which the programs are being conducted. The Council of Chief State School Officers is an illustration of an interest group that has continued to influence the course of federal education programs over the past two decades. Even though this group may not have had the power to initiate legislation, it has been influential in affecting the course of various legislative provisions and related regulations issued by the Department of Education and the previous Office of Education.

Various political figures in Congress and different administrations comprise the third component of this triumvirate that has worked together to increase the level of federal funding and involvement in education. The list of members of Congress who have been active in this effort is almost endless, but a few, such as Carl Perkins, Albert Quie, Roman Pucinski, William Ford, Edith Green, John Brademas, Hubert Humphrey, Wayne Morse, Claiborne Pell, and Jacob Javits deserve special mention. The list of persons from the various administrations includes Lawrence Derthick, Abraham Ribicoff, Wilbur Cohen, John Gardner, Francis Keppel, Harold Howe, Sidney Marland, James Allen, and especially Lyndon Johnson for his important leadership role and his commitment to education.

Even though several major pieces of educational legislation were enacted from 1948 through the 1960s, the base of public support during that period was not overwhelming for increased federal aid (ACIR 1981b: 72–3). The people appeared to be willing to follow the lead of the opinion leaders in the Congress and the administration or the various interest groups that supported federal aid to education. Success was achieved in building the coalitions needed to resolve issues related to funds for parochial or segregated schools and the federal control issues related to the categorical versus general aid conflicts.

The principal strategy was to maximize support by minimizing the potential points of conflict among various interest groups. Controversial features of legislative proposals were eliminated to reduce the opposition. Efforts were made to reach a consensus as to the programs and services that should be provided. When general agreement was reached as to the need for a specific program, the legislation could then be enacted with a reduced level of controversy (Munger and Fenno 1962: 175–76, 178–79). The result of this legislative behavior was an accumulation of categorical programs whose funding expanded or contracted in response to changing levels of support.

Recent Legislation

Leadership and the capacity to capitalize upon conditions in the "environment" continued to be major factors influencing the enactment of federal education programs in the 1950s and 1960s. Examples may be found in the circumstances that preceded the enactment of the National Defense Education Act in 1958, the Vocational Education Act of 1963, the Elementary and Secondary Education Act of 1965, and the Education for All Handicapped Children Act.

National Defense Education Act. Even prior to the report from the White House Conference on Education in 1955, President Eisenhower indicated support for the concept of federally-supported scholarships for college students. This presidential support, the backdrop of the White House Conference, and the national concern over space exploration resulting from the successful Russian Sputnik launch provided an environment of opportunity for education advocates. In this context, the leadership in the Department of Health, Education, and Welfare began preparing legislation to fund scholarships for college students to study science and engineering and programs for the improvement of guidance and counseling and instruction in defense related fields. Senator Lister Hill and Congressman

Carl Elliott also became interested in using this favorable environment as an opportunity to push legislation for these purposes as well as to provide funds for the purchase of instructional equipment and the remodeling of school facilities. This climate of leadership and interest from both the administration and Congress led to the eventual passage of the National Defense Education Act but with student loans instead of the package of college scholarships that had provided the initial impetus for the legislative proposal. Compromises were reached on the race and religion issues, and the consensus developed for national education legislation (Sundquist 1970: 326–31).

Vocational Education Act of 1963. With the election of President John F. Kennedy, the interest in federal aid for education increased, for this had been an issue of controversy during the presidential campaign. President Kennedy had supported increased federal aid and continued this effort after assuming the presidency. Even though no legislation was enacted during his tenure in office, this interest contributed to the development of a favorable environment for the leadership of President Lyndon B. Johnson.

Events leading to the enactment of the Vocational Education Act of 1963 illustrate the effect of the interaction between various groups and the contribution that receptive conditions make in the enactment of legislation. During the 1960 presidential election, John F. Kennedy indicated his support for vocational education and convened a panel to evaluate the current federal efforts on vocational education. The panel's report led to the introduction of omnibus legislation with vocational education being one component of the bill. President Kennedy continued his strong support. With assistance from the American Vocational Association, substitute legislation was proposed to overcome some objections to the original legislation. Under the leadership of Congressman Carl Perkins and Senator Wayne Morse, and with the support of the president and the professional community, the environment was favorable for action. Following considerable debate, the bill passed both houses. Unfortunately, President Kennedy was assassinated while the measure was in conference, but President Johnson signed the bill into law a few weeks after assuming office (AVA 1976: 77, 81–2).

Elementary and Secondary Education Act of 1965. A series of events set the stage for the enactment of the Elementary and Secondary Education Act of 1965 (ESEA). The nation was mourning the untimely death of a very popular president, and his successor was a master of the legislative process. Under the strong leadership of President Johnson, the course was charted and strong support was provided from the White House. He lent the prestige of the office of the president to the issue, made the legislation a major commitment, found points of compromise among various interest groups, and resolved the issue of aid to parochial schools before introducing the legislation, resulting in a bill that was enacted by Congress with minimal change (ACIR 1981a: 74).

The enactment of the ESEA is viewed as a remarkable legislative achievement attributable to an interaction of multiple circumstances (Bailey and Mosher 1968: 70-1). Not only did President Johnson have a high level of commitment to the legislation but the principal architects of the legislation were officials in the Johnson administration. The five titles of the legislation illustrated the range of compromises that were made to meet the objectives of the various interest groups. One traditional barrier to federal aid—aid to parochial schools—was overcome when compromises were reached on this issue.

Even though the programs were broad and comprehensive and the funding level was perceived to be a major breakthrough, the categorical element was maintained with the assurance that the funds would be expended on identified national priorities. An additional critical element was that the United States Supreme Court's *Brown* v. *Board of Education* (1954) decision on school desegregation was beginning to be implemented. Issues related to federal funds for segregated schools had been raised by civil rights groups and members of the traditional southern voting block in the Congress when previous federal aid efforts were proposed, but both relaxed their opposition to the ESEA proposal because they thought that the programs would provide some relief for the pressing educational problems attributable to school integration.

President Johnson's previous leadership role in Congress and the heavy Democratic majority in the Congress were invaluable assets to the president as he worked with the Congress in devising the legislative strategy that moved ESEA through the Congress within three months. America's educators found themselves being moved into new programs and different intergovernmental relationships. Concerns about the details were answered with statements that problems would be worked out during the administration of the legislation (Bailey and Mosher 1968: 70-1). As efforts were made to resolve the various problems, the influence of the education interest group consisting of a network of administrators involved in the administration of programs at the federal, state, and local levels began to develop.

Education for All Handicapped Children Act. The enactment of ESEA is in sharp contrast to the scenario surrounding the enactment of the Education for All Handicapped Children Act (EHA). The passage of this legislation was in response to the well-organized and sophisticated efforts of lobby groups for handicapped children with the collaboration of special education professionals. This legislation represents a new direction in federal education programs and is quite different from ESEA, in which categorical funds are provided for specific programs and services that contract or expand depending upon the availability of federal funds. Under EHA, various requirements, constraints, and controls have been placed on states and local school districts in their efforts to provide programs for the handicapped, but the percentage of costs for education of the handicapped supported by federal funds has remained relatively low. Faced with President Nixon's opposition to increases in federal expenditures for education, the EHA provided for graduated increases in level of funding over a period of several years. A continuing problem with the act is that funding levels for the program have not increased as provided in the legislation. This legislation indicates the extent to which federal action can influence instructional programs for a group of children and can define the rights and responsibilities of parents and states and localities in providing educational programs (ACIR 1981b: 75).

Even with these efforts to chart the course of education with various federal programs, the tendency is for the Congress, national interest groups, and federal officials to overestimate the influence that they have on the actual conduct of federal education programs. The 50 states and 16,000 local school districts still must be relied upon to administer the programs. Attitudes and conditions in these latter jurisdictions often are much more important in determining how programs will be conducted than detailed statutory provisions and regulatory requirements (Van Horn 1979: 148-50). There is little doubt that the federal government can influence the direction of educational programs to serve the handicapped and the disadvantaged, but variations and differences will remain because of the decentralized nature of the delivery system for American education.

Leadership Options

Changes in the social, economic, and political environment influence the range of options that are available to policymakers. For example, President Johnson was a staunch supporter of education, and it became a primary component in the Great Society programs. His attention to and interest in education reduced the opportunities for others to become dominant actors in the design and development of legislation. The leadership of President Johnson is considered to have contributed to the increase of the number of education programs and their funding level. This active leadership role is in contrast to the role of President Nixon, who had no special commitment to education and did not accord special recognition in the staffing of the White House or the conduct of his presidency. His interests were to have education operate at a lower cost, so the focus of the Nixon years was on program evaluation and cost containment (Thomas 1975: 228-29). Events during the first year of the Reagan administration illustrate the impact of leadership and environment as various proposals for program consolidation, block grants, and reductions in funding level have been enacted into law.

Future decisions about federal aid for education will be influenced greatly by those who emerge and assume leadership in a social and political environment that currently can best be described as conservative in its support for education. The issue of the merits of categorical versus general aid likely will continue to be a point of disagreement because of the coalitions that must be built and maintained to enact and maintain funding for education legislation. Discretionary nationally competitive categorical grants carry with them a somewhat cumbersome administrative process and appear to work against the best interests of poor states and local school districts that do not have either the fiscal resources or the staff time and resident expertise to design the programs and prepare the applications (Quie 1970: 401). However, the counterpoint is that federal funds should be directed toward critical national needs in education that are not being met effectively with existing programs and revenues for education (Brademas 1970: 403). Programs such as ESEA Title I and EHA do not have the discretionary competitive features that pose problems with traditional categorical programs, but they do require that the federal funds be used to provide programs and services for specific target populations. They offer an intermediate position between the extreme categorical programs and unrestricted general aid.

The block grant consolidation in the Education Consolidation and Improvement Act of 1981 might be viewed as another step in the evolution of federal aid to education, for this act shifted the locus for priority setting from the federal level to states and localities. However, some observers fear that this act may be the first step in a carefully orchestrated effort by the federal government to eliminate all funds for education and to withdraw from any type of direct federal involvement, leaving funding for education totally to states and localities. Will leadership and environment mesh to bring about new federal initiatives or to accelerate the recent movement toward deemphasizing the federal role in education?

CHANGING CONDITIONS

Just as in the past policy was determined on the basis both of general factors in society and of individual leadership, so it was in the first year of the Reagan administration, and so it will continue to be. In order to understand why federal aid to education was so challenged in 1981, it is necessary to review the changed environment.

Political

President Reagan was successful in his first year in office although his conservative predecessors were not, because of numerous factors, several of which were blatantly political in nature. The National Education Association's endorsement of President Carter for reelection undoubtedly left a residue of ill feelings in the Republican victors, and unfortunately education in general was to feel the resulting anger. Additionally, the political right, whom President Reagan represents, had developed an agenda for action that included support for private school tuition tax credits, opposition to the Department of Education, and assaults on public schools in general. Lastly, federal education spending represented one of the more visible areas in which President Reagan personally believed the federal government had little or no role to play.

A decade ago, President Nixon held many of the same political beliefs but he did not achieve in his first year in office the success garnered by this new administration. Partly explaining this difference in achievement are two political advantages enjoyed by President Reagan but not enjoyed by his conservative predecessors. First, the Senate became Republican in 1980 for the first time in twenty-six years, giving the president ready-made control of one house of the legislative branch. On the average, all Republicans in the Senate supported the president 80 percent of the time in 1981; this was the highest level of loyalty recorded over a twenty-nine-year period (Presidential Support 1982: 18–24). This extraordinary record of support paralleled the support given by the Democrats under President Johnson in 1965. Second, Southern Democrats also crossed over to support the president to a greater degree than they had done under President Nixon. The conservative coalition of Republicans and Southern Democrats was especially effective in 1981. On those votes where the conservative coalition was obvious, the victory rate was 92 percent, the highest rate in the last twenty-four years (Conservatives 1982: 50–5).

Even more importantly, however, the Congress had recently reformed its budget process in such a fashion as to make itself more easily dominated by a powerful president. The Congressional Budget Control and Impoundment Act was passed in 1974 as a reaction to President Nixon's illegal impoundment of funds. In addition to setting limits on such impoundments, the act also established procedures for the Congress to deal with the entire federal budget as a whole instead of piecemeal as had been done for decades.

A real irony lies in the fact that one such method of congressional budget control—"reconciliation"—has been turned on the Congress by the Reagan administration to control the legislative process by having the president's entire program adopted in full and on one vote in the House of Representatives. Previously, the president's proposals would have been subject to scrutiny piece by piece with a far greater likelihood of the rejection of large portions of the program since each would have had to be judged on its merits. It is almost impossible to overemphasize the importance of this change in congressional procedure for President Reagan's success in his first year. Other presidents have been as popular and as powerful as this one in the beginnings of their terms, but President Reagan had available a powerful parliamentary advantage enjoyed by none of his predecessors.

In 1982 there is less popular support for the president, and the Congress may be less inclined to follow his lead by means of an "up or down" vote on his whole program. As with the genie out of the bottle, however, it may be difficult for the Congress in the years ahead to be as independent of the executive branch as in the recent past because this parliamentary device has been created to control a fractious legislative body. Reconciliation is to be used as a way to control Congress.

Administrative

Additional reasons for the president's success may be found in the state of federal education programs themselves. By 1980 there were clearly too many of these programs (i.e., well over a hundred, depending on the method used for counting). In addition, Congress and the Carter administration had not only avoided trying to eliminate some of the least important programs, but they had not even found a way to stop creating new ones each time the federal education laws were up for renewal. The Education Amendments of 1976 created eleven programs; the Amendments of 1978 created nineteen; and the Amendments of 1980 created eight.

The programs also were too complicated to administer. Each time laws came up for renewal, new requirements were inserted on top of the existing requirements. The executive branch added to these difficulties by including even further new requirements in the regulations issued to implement the programs.

In 1980 Congressman Carl Perkins, Chairman of the House Committee on Education and Labor, led Congress in disapproving four sets of regulations issued by the U.S. Office of Education and then by the new Department of Education. In the view of Congress, these regulations added new requirements to programs when these requirements were not in the laws creating these programs or in the intent of the legislators.

Chairman Perkins, the most steadfast and dogged proponent of federal aid to education in the Congress, even stated his belief that federal programs were losing their local support due to their complexity:

> What we are doing is causing animosity on the part of the people at the local school board levels. They feel that they are trying to do the best job possible in carrying out the intent of the law, only to find out that the General Accounting Office has said they have violated the law because they have overstepped the regulations. . . .
>
> This situation makes it more difficult to obtain funding in the U.S. Congress, and let me tell you that is one thing that has happened to us now.
>
> You are unable to get the best supporters of education to come forward and talk to their Congressmen because they are miffed about regulations, and things of that kind. We on the political scene run into that everyday. We are not asking any department anywhere along the line to get involved in politics, but we are asking the departments to stay within the true intent of the law and let the law be carried out as we intend it without putting additional burdens on the people (U.S. Congress 1979: 4, 5).

Demographic

In addition to these political and programmatic difficulties, by 1980 federal education programs were facing broader changes in society. Over a period of seven years, the Committee on Education and Labor in the House of Representatives had a vacancy on the Democratic side for three years and had one or two members who served on the committee as their second-choice major committee for four years. No new Democratic member chose to fill that vacancy in all those years even though in the 1960s and early 1970s members stood in line to join the committee.

Education had lost its political magic due to demographic shifts in society. A decade ago 44 percent of the population were parents of public school pupils. Today, that figure is down to 28 percent. As a result, fewer and fewer people have a direct stake in the schools, and more people are inclined to vote for their pocketbooks instead of the schools in their communities.

In addition to the general demographic facts showing a lessening of support for public schools, there are regional differences that could accelerate this decline of support at the federal level. The 1980 census showed a decline of about 5.1 million in the school-age population, or about 10 percent of the 1970 total, but this decline varied significantly by region: In New England, the Mideast, the Great Lakes, and the Plains regions, the declines were 14.8 percent, 17.6 percent, 16.1 percent, and 17.2 percent, respectively, while in the Southeast and Far West, the declines were under 5 percent (Sherman 1982).

This shift is especially critical for education, for the political support for federal aid to education has tended to be much stronger in the eastern parts of the United States than in the western parts. On the whole, greater declines in the East might lessen high enthusiasm for federal aid in the East, while relatively low declines in the West might not increase already tepid support for federal aid in that region. This trend may continue in the future. The school-age population by 1990 is expected to reverse the decline of the 1970s, so that in the year 2000 the number of school-age children should exceed the 1985 levels by nearly 20 percent. Again, there will be regional differences (Sherman 1982).

Growth rates for the school-age population will be higher in the southern and western regions of the country than in the North and East. Thus, by the year 2000, the Southwest and Rocky Mountains regions will be further above the national average in their proportion of school-age children, while New England and the Mideast will be further below the national average.

Consequently, future support for federal aid to education may not come from representatives of the regions that have tended to favor federal aid. At the same time, representatives of regions that have tended to be more skeptical of such aid also may not support it due to that skepticism, even though the aid would be to their benefit because of increased enrollments.

Added to this factor of fewer children is another demographic trend at the other end of the age spectrum. By 1990, one in five Americans will be over the age of fifty-five. For the first time in our history, this age group will exceed in numbers the entire elementary and secondary school population. This is especially critical, since the elderly vote more consistently than any other group in the nation and politicians tend to meet their needs.

Between 1960 and 1980, the number of people at the age of sixty-five and over increased nearly 60 percent. Their proportion of the population rose from 9.0 percent in 1960 to 11.3 percent in 1980, and by 1990, this group is expected to be 12.5 percent of the population and to remain so for the rest of the century. Obviously, this will be a powerful political force.

Other Pressures on the Budget

In addition to the challenges posed by demographic changes, education faces stronger competition for resources from other areas. Clearly, the higher costs of energy are squeezing all budgets—governmental as well as personal—and the recent national consensus for higher defense spending will squeeze other federal programs even further.

Spending for defense is increasing tremendously at the federal level. In 1980 defense spending amounted to $142.6 billion; by 1982, this amount had grown by 53.5 percent to $218.9 billion, and President Reagan is proposing an additional increase to $263 billion. If the president is successful, defense spending will have grown by 84 percent in three years; and if he is not fully successful, it will have grown well over 50 percent. Clearly, increases of this magnitude in such a short period of time in spending for one large area of the federal budget create tremendous pressures on other areas of the budget, especially when tax revenues are being drastically reduced.

Decreasing Tax Revenue

Federal aid for education is further imperiled by decreasing tax revenues at the national level. President Reagan's tax reduction bill of 1980 was the largest tax reduction in history. Most people have concentrated on the personal reductions, but corporations benefitted even more than did individuals. By taking advantage of new provisions in the tax codes, most corporations should pay little federal tax in the future.

The same bill also was weighted very heavily in favor of reducing the taxes of the richest people in society. A full 10 percent of its benefits went to 0.2 percent of the population—those who make over $200,000 a year.

Greatly reducing the taxes for the rich and practically eliminating the corporate tax will place great strains on federal resources, which is the primary reason for such huge projected budget deficits. Moreover, the existence of these deficits—although caused by reducing revenues—is being used as the pretext for cutting back further on federal spending.

Even before this recent tax bill created such problems, however, federal resources were feeling the strain. The reason for this is that the federal government was raising relatively less revenue than before. In 1968 the federal government raised 62.2 percent of all tax revenue in the country; by 1977 that amount was 58.1 percent. By way of contrast, the states increased their share from 19.8 percent to 23.7 percent and therefore were better able to fund expansions of services than was the federal government.

The ACIR (1980) stated that a crossroads had been reached regarding federal domestic assistance and that states and local governments must assume a greater financial burden in providing existing services. The ACIR concluded that federal support of domestic governmental activity had crested and was on its way down. This " cresting" occurred under President Carter and seems to be a long-term trend not rooted in the actions of any one administration. However, President Reagan has certainly given it a hefty shove by so drastically reducing federal tax revenue. Will changes take place in the political, demographic, and economic conditions that will contribute to a renewed interest in federal education programs to address national priorities or to serve the special needs of expanding target populations, or will the present trend continue?

FUTURE

Since it is unwise to try to predict the future precisely, this discussion focuses on some general principles that will help guide future action. These principles are both those general in society and those peculiar to politics.

First, basic demographic facts are having enormous effects on policy. There are fewer young children, and less emphasis is therefore being placed on their education. Concomitantly, there are more people in their twenties and thirties than ever before—due to the inevitable aging of the "baby boom" children—and therefore colleges and universities, especially community colleges that cater to adults, should do quite well.

Inevitably, less political attention will be given to elementary and secondary education simply because there will be fewer "clients" and fewer taxpaying parents demanding money for the schools. The so-called echo of the baby boom, when children of the baby boom generation have their own children, may cause a slight reversal, but demographers predict the numbers of these infants will never reach the previous numbers of students.

Another aspect of demography that will effect the schools will be the demand of the elderly for more resources to be spent on programs to meet their needs. This factor, in addition to the increasing pressures for more energy and defense spending, will exacerbate the competition for resources.

Second, the federal government is losing its overwhelming primacy in revenue raising. States and localities are now raising more revenue comparatively than the federal government, and this trend should continue; in fact, it may even accelerate due to the massive Reagan tax-cutting bill. Obviously, governments with less revenue usually mount fewer programs.

Third, the federal government is losing its image as the most efficient level of government. A recent ACIR poll showed, in fact, that the federal level of government was considered the least efficient, especially by those who are well educated and financially secure (ACIR 1981a: 6). As mentioned previously, in the area of education the great number and complexity of programs undoubtedly contributed to this reduction in support for federal programs. The first three general societal trends would seem to make propitious the Reagan program of cutbacks and phase-outs of programs, but there are several other factors at work that can bring to bear contrary pressures.

The first of these, the fourth predictive factor, is a growing concern regarding the mathematics and scientific illiteracy of American pupils, especially as compared to Japanese and Russian students. If this concern develops into a national consensus that action must be taken to protect the competitive advantage of American business and the national defense, then it is probable that federal action will be taken. A similar situation occurred in the late 1950s with concern precipitated by the Sputnik launching leading to the enactment of the National Defense Education Act of 1958.

Fifth, the political conditions leading to Reagan's success in his first year are bound to change to his disadvantage. It was extraordinary in the history of the Congress for so much power to be concentrated in this new budget procedure. Even if this budget process survives in some shape, it is probable that Congress will revert again, to a great degree, to its traditional form of decentralized power through the committee system. If the president's program has to be considered piecemeal by the various subcommittees and committees of the Congress, it is bound to be stymied in part and to be very substantially changed in part.

In particular, the prospects for the prompt enactment of the Reagan "swap" proposal are directly proportionate to the chances of Congress using the so-called reconciliation procedure, which leads to one up or down vote on the entire package. If Congress does not use such a procedure, then most of the swap will be lost in the myriad of congressional subcommittees affected by this extremely comprehensive idea.

Sixth, the state of the economy has a great effect on national action. President Reagan has staked to an unusual degree the future of his administration and of his party on improvements in the economy. If such improvements do not occur, his political support could erode swiftly. If this happens, the tactic of trying to encourage economic improvements through direct government spending could recur. Such a reversal could lead to Keynesian "pump-priming" for job training, employment, and education programs.

Seventh, members of Congress like to have their names associated with specific programs so that they can claim political credit back home for a "sound legislative record." It is difficult to claim credit for such broad assertions as reviving the economy through holding down government expenditures (especially if the economy does not revive). The history of federal programs is one of creating categorical programs to meet specific needs and, somewhat incidentally, to enable the representatives to claim specific credit. Then, when block grants are formed every now and again in order to clean up these categorical programs, the tendency over time is to recategorize or to put additional requirements on these funds so as to address specific problems (Hastings 1982: 330-32). This history seems to militate against the Reagan efforts to block grant and swap with the states.

The eighth factor is that state and local governments are also feeling fiscal pressures; therefore, the rhetoric that any cutbacks at the federal level will mean only a shift of funding to the state and local levels strains belief. Consequently, client groups may fight harder because they now realize that cuts really mean termination of programs. State and local politicians may also begin to oppose these cut-backs and block grants with reduced funding because they know that they will be the ones in the position of carrying out the elimination of programs with all the associated political flak.

The ninth factor is that the president is more conservative than the American people in terms of what he believes the role of the federal government should be. Many polls show that the majority of people see a need for national programs such as education and housing aid, whereas the president has made clear for years his position that all such programs should be the sole responsibility of state and local governments.

Lastly, the political party that controls the presidency and the Congress does make a difference in terms of what gets funded: Democrats tend to favor greater social spending than do Republicans. Whether the Republicans retain control of the Senate and whether the Republicans capture control of the House of Representatives in the elections of 1982 will make a difference in terms of federal support for education. If the Republicans retain the Senate and capture the House, it is almost a certainty that funding will be less, and if President Reagan is reelected in 1984, or if a similar person succeeds him, support for education will continue to be imperiled. Other factors also are involved, such as the degree to which teachers are organized politically and the particular time that specific programs are being discussed in Congress (with an election year being a time of more attentive listening to organized groups, such as educators).

CONCLUSION

In conclusion, the first year of the Reagan administration caused the greatest challenge to federal support for education within a decade; and in many ways, this challenge was far more successful than the earlier Nixon attack. The continued success of efforts at cutbacks in funding and elimination of programs will depend on an array of factors, all of which cannot be seen or understood at this time.

The healthy aspect of this challenge is that it has caused an examination of programs resulting in the elimination or sharp curtailment of many programs of lesser importance. The unhealthy part is that many programs that took years to develop and to become effective have been damaged through cutbacks in funding and uncertainty as to their future prospects. The next year or two will determine which, if any, federal programs remain; and their survival will depend to a very large degree on whether local teachers, administrators, and citizens believe that specific programs should remain and whether they can convey that feeling to their political representatives.

REFERENCES

Advisory Commission on Intergovernmental Relations (ACIR). 1980. *Significant Features of Fiscal Federalism: 1979-80 Edition.* Washington, D.C.

_____. 1981a. *Changing Public Attitudes on Governments and Taxes.* Washington, D.C.

_____. 1981b. *The Federal Role in the Federal System: The Dynamics of Growth.* Washington, D.C.

American Vocational Association (AVA). 1976. "200 Years of Vocational Education, 1776-1976." *American Vocational Journal* 51, no. 5 (May): 23-89.

Bailey, Stephen K., and Edith K. Mosher. 1968. *ESEA: The Office of Education Administers a Law.* Syracuse, N.Y.: Syracuse University Press.

Brademas, John. 1970. "The Case for Categorical Aid." In *The Politics of Education at the Local, State, and Federal Levels,* edited by Michael W. Kirst, pp. 403-406. Berkeley, Calif.: McCutchan Publishing Company.

Brown v. Board of Education, 347 U.S. 483 (1954).

"Conservatives Hit New High in Showdown Vote Victories." 1982. *Congressional Quarterly* 40, no. 2 (January 9): 50-5.

Grubb, W. Norton, and Marvin Lazerson. 1974. "Vocational Education in American Schooling: Historical Perspectives." *Inequality in Education* 17, no. 16 (March): 5-18.

Hastings, Anne H. 1982. "The Block Grant Record: Lessons from Experience." *Phi Delta Kappan* 63, no. 5 (January): 330-32.

Munger, Frank J., and Richard F. Fenno. 1962. *National Politics and Federal Aid to Education.* Syracuse, N.Y.: Syracuse University Press.

National Educational Finance Project. 1971. *Alternative Programs for Financing Education.* Gainesville, Fla.

National Center for Education Statistics. 1981. *Digest of Education Statistics.* Washington, D.C.: U.S. Department of Education.

"New Concepts in Aid-to-States, Communities Launched." 1973. *Congress and the Nation,* Vol. III, 1969-72. Washington, D.C.: Congressional Quarterly, 97-104.

"Presidential Support." 1982. *Congressional Quarterly* 40, no. 1 (January 2): 18-24.

Quie, Albert H. 1970. "The Case of Categorical Aid." In *The Politics of Education at the Local, State, and Federal Levels*, edited by Michael W. Kirst, pp. 399–402. Berkeley, Calif.: McCutchan Publishing Corporation.

Sherman, Joel D. 1982. "Demographic Trends, 1960–2000: Implications for School Finance." Paper presented at the Annual Meeting of the American Education Finance Association, Philadelphia, Pennsylvania, March 19–20.

Sundquist, James L. 1970. "For the Young Schools." In *The Politics of Education at the Local, State, and Federal Level*, edited by Michael W. Kirst, pp. 326–396. Berkeley, Calif.: McCutchan Publishing Corporation.

Thomas, Norman C. 1975. *Education in National Politics*. New York: David McKay Company, Inc.

U.S. Congress. House of Representatives. 1979. *Hearing on Title I, Elementary and Secondary Education Act Regulations* before the Subcommittee on Elementary, Secondary, and Vocational Education of the Committee on Education and Labor, 97th Cong., 1st Sess. on H. Res. 423 (October 16). Washington, D.C.: U.S. Government Printing Office.

Van Horn, Carl E. 1979. *Policy Implementation in the Federal System*. Lexington, Mass.: D. C. Heath and Company.

3 STATE-LEVEL POLITICS AND SCHOOL FINANCING

Susan Fuhrman *

The early 1980s is a unique time to reflect on the politics of school finance at the state level. The decade of the 1970s saw the largest growth ever in the state share of education spending: State aid to elementary and secondary education doubled, and the state share of all educational costs rose dramatically. These developments were a result of efforts of the school finance reform movement, which emphasized state acceptance of constitutional responsibility to educate all children and to free that education from dependence on local property wealth.

In the 1980s, the state will continue to be the pivotal actor in school finance but not because of the reform movement's impetus. The decrease in the federal role in education will force the states to make a number of critical choices concerning the level of funding for programs affected by federal budget cuts and the structure of programs consolidated or altered in the spirit of the "new federalism." This added responsibility comes to states at a time when education politics are undergoing a number of transitions and many states are facing severe fiscal distress.

This chapter addresses the politics of state level school finance decisions as they were in the seventies and as they are likely to be in the eighties. If the seventies can be characterized as a decade of re-

*Susan Fuhrman, Research Associate, Eagleton Institute of Politics, Rutgers University.

form, at this point the eighties must be seen as a time of uncertainty. A number of changes are occurring that will have a major impact on the state politics of school finance, but the magnitude and ultimate effect of the changes are as yet unclear. After recapitulating some of the political developments of the seventies, this chapter focuses on the trends of the early eighties and speculates about their impact on state politics and school aid.

THE 1970s: A DECADE OF REFORM

In the 1970s the school finance reform movement swept the country with hurricane force. By the count of the Education Commission of the States, twenty-eight states reformed their systems of school aid during that decade. Reform meant a great expansion in equalization programs to compensate for local property wealth disparities, the reduction of disparities in per pupil expenditures and in educational tax burden, the development of new measures of district fiscal capacity that reflect income as well as property wealth, greater attention to programs for special pupil populations, and recognition of certain district-related characteristics, such as municipal overburden (Odden and Augenblick 1980, 1981). The growth in state aid occurred primarily because states compensated for low property wealth by "leveling up" poorer districts. Only a few states chose the politically more difficult path of redistributing funds from rich to poor districts.

Emergence of General Government

The reform movement dramatically altered the politics of school aid decisions at the state level. Prior to the 1970s, school finance problems, like most education issues, were decided by educators. The educational interests, led by state department of education staff—for the most part former local educators—came to agreement on the terms of a state aid package. They presented the package to the legislature and governor who usually deferred to their opinion and ratified rather than shaped the final product. Educators formed a united front; teachers, administrators, boards, and parent groups stood together. Legislatures and governors, who in any case lacked the expertise to question the complex formula arrangements, felt that whatever the educators supported had been compromised out in advance and represented the consensus of the interested parties (Bailey et al. 1962; Iannaccone 1968; Kirst and Somers 1981).

By the beginning of the 1970s a number of changes occurred that permitted the reform movement to exert its astounding impact on educational politics. First, the legislature changed immensely as an institution. Reapportionment led to the election of younger legislators from more competitive districts. These new, less rural-oriented legislatures also were undergoing reform, expanding to full-time institutions with greatly increased capacity. The most important development was the growth of legislative staffs that enabled legislators to assess independently the claims of educators and state department officials. Second, the gubernatorial office also was strengthened. Governors increased their staffs and were benefitting from constitutional revisions granting them improved veto power, greater tenure potential, and greater budgetary control. Third, the educational interest group configuration changed drastically. A number of factors caused the united front of the educators to disintegrate. Chief among them was the growth of teacher militancy and collective bargaining. Occurring over a fifteen- to twenty-year period and at different stages in different states, the fragmentation of the educational interests combined with the growing expertise of legislators and governors to set the stage for the eclipse of the educators and the emergence of general government, particularly the legislature, as *the* education policymaker.

School finance reform was the weight that tipped the scales in terms of the emergence of general government. Finance was the education issue that legislators and governors had always cared about the most. Because of their budgetary responsibility they had to take an interest in finance, even if that interest stopped at approving the educators' consensus. When finance became *the* issue of the 1970s, it accelerated the assumption of a leadership role by legislators and governors, a role that was probably inevitable given the changes in the institutions and the interest group configuration. Reform hastened the process and greatly magnified the impact of the changes that were occurring.

The extent of the shift to general government was clear to political scientists who studied the politics of school finance reform. In every reform state, there were legislative leaders who masterminded and executed a strategy for reform resorting to all varieties of compromise and persuasion to convince their colleagues. A number of governors—for example, Askew of Florida, Milliken of Michigan, and Anderson of Minnesota—also took starring roles, making finance reform an election issue in many cases. The increasingly fragmented education interests were further paralyzed by school finance issues that divided membership into wealthy versus poor and urban versus rural districts, rendering many groups incapable of supporting any single distribution alternative even if they agreed on principles of equity. New interests such as minority and urban advocates and even farmers and businessmen often were more vocal and involved in school finance reform than the traditional education lobbies (Fuhrman et al. 1979). In some states, such as South Carolina and Washington, the prime actors were citizen coalitions that used skillful, effective public education techniques to raise the consciousness of the public and policymakers (League of Women Voters Education Fund 1978; Hannigan 1981).

Activism of State Courts and Reform Networks

School finance reform became the single most important education issue of the 1970s because of two significant developments: the activism of state courts and the emergence of a national reform network. When the school finance reform movement first began in the late 1960s and early 1970s, politically impotent reformers turned to the courts after legislatures initially failed to respond. In states where there was a school finance court case, it is doubtful whether reform would have occurred without it. In states without a case, governors and legislators feared the initiation of a suit and acted in anticipation of one. The activism of courts resulted in interesting tensions between the branches of state government.

Courts were not always clear about their intent; they were pressuring for change but not indicating precisely which type of change would be acceptable. For example, in *Serrano* v. *Priest* (1976), the California court adopted the principle of "fiscal neutrality," declaring that there should be no correlation between property wealth and school spending. However, it was never clear whether the primary goal should be equalizing expenditures among districts or equalizing taxpayer burden. The ambiguity made it that much more difficult to develop a reform coalition within the legislature (Elmore and McLaughlin 1981; Kirst 1981). The *Robinson* v. *Cahill* (1973) decision in New Jersey also was rather nebulous. As Lehne (1978) points out, the whole of the state's educational programs as well as its finance system came under review since the legislature was never sure of the extent of the court mandate.

The second major impetus to reform was the development of a national network of reformers. Led by foundation and government officials, the network was composed of scholars, graduate students, lawyers, citizen education groups, minority research and action centers, and national organizations such as the Education Commission of the States and the National Conference of State Legislatures. The reform network researched the technical issues of school finance and the political and economic issues that surrounded it, helped plaintiffs and state officials seek more equitable financing arrangements, and disseminated information to policymakers and the public. The strength, expertise, skill, and commitment of these individuals and groups provided an important stimulus to reform throughout the decade (Kelly 1978; Kirst 1979, 1981).

To summarize, the activity of the courts and reformers propelled finance reform onto the agendas of legislatures that were capable of handling the issue and anxious to be assertive in educational politics. Similarly, governors saw reform as an issue that would give them leverage in educational policy. On the other hand, traditional educational interests were not in a position to deal with finance reform; in fact, the matter often contributed to their further disarray. State departments of education were not the education policy initiators they had been in the past; legislatures took over much of the innovative leadership role, cutting their teeth on school finance reform and going on to other education issues such as minimum competency testing, new structures for local citizen input, and enhanced accountability systems.

Finally, all this activity took place in a period of relative fiscal plenty. The reform states used fiscal surpluses to "level-up" poorer districts. As has been pointed out, only a few states—Utah, Montana, and Minnesota—have recapture provisions that redistribute funds. During the 1970s, states added over $27 billion to their share of education spending, and it was this ever-expanding pot that made reform possible. As major as they are, the political developments associated with reform are overshadowed by the availability or money; without surplus funds most of the reform would not have occurred.

THE 1980s: A DECADE OF UNCERTAINTY

By the late 1970s, the supply of dollars available for education spending was shrinking. A new fiscal climate of retrenchment set the context for the transition to the 1980s. The fiscal situation is a major factor creating uncertainty about state politics and school finance, and it is aided by changing political demands for education and declining public confidence in public education. These developments combine to check the willingness of policymakers—legislators and governors—to play the leading role in education they did in the 1970s. The new times also seem to be affecting interest-group patterns. Finally, these changes are occurring at a time when states are going to have major new educational decisionmaking responsibilities as a result of the changed federal role.

Fiscal and Political Retrenchment

The change in the fiscal situation of states began to effect education spending by 1981. While real resources for public education from all sources declined in 1980, the state role continued to grow, albeit at a slower pace (Odden and Augenblick 1981). By 1981, however, there was evidence that a number of states were in real fiscal distress. Tax and expenditure limitations enacted in the 1979–81 period produced fiscal pressures in states such as California and Massachusetts. Others were suffering from severe economic difficulties, for example, Michigan and Oregon. In the majority of states, economic reserves were quite low: Although 5 percent is generally considered the minimum surplus necessary to guard against future uncertainties, in the summer of 1981, thirty-one states reported surpluses of no higher than 5 percent, and twenty-seven states projected surpluses of 3 percent or less (Gold 1981).

To add to the bad news, states were about to contend with sharp cuts in federal education spending. In some, like New Hampshire, where reliance on federal funds was very high, the cuts might end in precipitating school finance reform financed through new state taxes. In most, though, the fiscal situation will make reform extremely difficult, if not impossible. There are so many demands for the shrinking state dollar that the major school finance issue for the early 1980s may be simply finding the means to hold on to the equity gains of the 1970s.

The competition for tight dollars is taking place within education as well as between education and other social services. There will probably be increased contention between elementary and secondary education and higher education as the latter sector experiences severe enrollment declines. Even more intense is the struggle between general aid and categorical programs. There is evidence that as money tightens, categorical programs suffer at the expense of general aid. In some states, the effect on categoricals has been no more severe than on general aid: Cuts have been across the board. Yet because they were always in a favored position, protected from harm when cuts first began, the eventual necessity for special programs to shoulder their share of the damage has made their plight seem worse than it actually is. This was the case in Michigan where the economic situation is so disastrous that education has had to absorb several hundred million dollars worth of cuts with more to come.

In other states, categoricals are in fact suffering more than general aid. Thirteen states studied by the Urban Institute favored general over categorical aid in 1980 and/or 1981 budget revisions (Wolf 1981). In some states, categorical aid was cut in nominal dollars, in others in real dollars, while in a few cases the projected real increase was simply reduced. Concluding that "legislators' basic and ongoing commitment is to preserving the unrestricted basic aid to which the districts back home give priority" (Wolf 1981: 37), the Urban Institute study indicated that only special education aid, which involves direct legal constraints on spending behavior, was able to grow, though often more slowly than before. In compensatory education, real spending actually fell during 1980 and 1981, and bilingual and vocational programs also suffered (Wolf 1981: 36–41). Minnesota is a case in point. Having to trim $160 million from the 1982–83 biennial education appropriation, the legislature cut foundation aid by 9 percent and categoricals by 6.5 percent.

Retrenchment has been political as well as fiscal. As Kirst and Garms (1980) noted, citizens with a direct interest in supporting pub-

lic education—parents—are declining as a population group. Furthermore, a larger proportion of parents are composed of low-income,
black, and Hispanic, persons who are less likely to be politically
active. Upset by declining test scores, incidents of violence, poor discipline, and declining teacher quality, the public has apparently lost
much of its confidence in education. By 1980 only 35 percent of the
American public gave public schools an A or B rating (Odden and
Augenblick 1981: 21). Nonpublic enrollments, which fell during the
1970s along with school enrollment in general, are likely to rise in
the 1980s (Odden and Augenblick 1981: 38). Policymakers in many
states are beginning to face issues of regulating the growing number
of private schools.

The Policymakers Retreat

The negative set of circumstances produced by these fiscal and political trends has begun to exert an impact on education policymakers
and education politics. In marked contrast to the 1970s, legislators
are not anxious to be deeply involved in education. They are retreating because they perceive it as a depressing, no-win area where they
have no new programs or initiatives to distribute to constituents. All
they can bring home are cuts, and that is far from appealing.

A fifty-state study of legislative education leadership, conducted
at the Eagleton Institute (Rosenthal and Fuhrman 1981; Fuhrman
and Rosenthal 1981) revealed that for the past fifteen years most of
education policy, including finance reform, was made by a single,
unusually committed group of legislators. In most states, there was
a generation of legislative education leaders who entered the legislature with a background in education, typically as school board or
PTA members, and stayed with the field throughout their entire
lengthy tenure. They served on education committees and appropriations committees, often on both at the same time, and took their
colleagues with them from one major educational innovation to another—from collective bargaining to finance reform to minimum
competency testing to school improvement. This generation was
about to depart the legislature at the beginning of the 1980s. Sixteen
percent of the leaders surveyed said that 1979–80 would be their
last term, another 33 percent indicated they would serve only one

additional term (Rosenthal and Fuhrman 1981: 36). It is not yet clear who, if anyone, will replace this group of leaders. Many education committee chairmen indicated that they had difficulty recruiting new members to their committees and that other policy areas were more sexy or appealing. As one legislator said, "there are no goodies to hand out like years ago" (Rosenthal and Fuhrman 1981: 104).

The difficulty in attracting legislators to education may be symptomatic of a larger problem. Legislators may be retreating from specialization in general. The newer breed of legislators is very ambitious politically and more apt to shift from one policy area to another to capture the public's eye. To such a legislator, the legislature is something more than a place where he can do some good for his constituents and the state: It is also a rung on a career ladder. Such legislators are much less willing than their predecessors to stay with one field throughout their legislative tenure, and that tenure is likely to be shorter than in the past.

The attractiveness of education as a specialty may be a particular problem now, however, because legislators see education as a highly contentious area. They are discouraged by what they perceive as vicious in-fighting among the interests. In some states, the fragmentation of the interests—the hostility between teachers and administrators and school boards, between the traditional interests and those formed around categorical programs, between the statewide organizations and the geographically based subgroups—has gone so far that legislators distrust all groups, discount any group demand as self-interested, and are inclined to stay away from the entire field. Even veteran education legislators are turned off by the in-fighting. It is increasingly difficult to take a stand on behalf of "education"; there is no agreement on what such a stand should be. It may be that the largest single group to involve themselves in education in today's legislatures are themselves former or current teachers, and they may have trouble getting their colleagues to accept their motivations as unselfish.

To some extent, legislators have the freedom to indulge their skepticism of groups because they have their own education staffs and are in less need of the information they get from lobbyists. In virtually every state there are experienced, sophisticated staffers who specialize in education, many in school finance specifically. These staffers will be the repository of legislative expertise in education as the generation of legislative education leaders departs. They already free the legislators they serve from dependence on state department or lobbyist information. While raw data on school finance is typically collected by state departments, the legislature performs its own independent analysis in more and more states.

Another trend within legislatures that will have an impact on the politics of school finance in the 1980s is the increasing power of appropriations committees in education. Almost a fifth of the legislative education leaders identified in the Eagleton study served on fiscal committees only and not on education committees (Rosenthal and Fuhrman 1981:14). More and more policy is being made in these money committees. They are doing more than deciding on the level of funding: They are designing formulas and attaching policy language, such as accountability procedures, to budget bills. The prominence of these committees is naturally related to the importance of school finance in the 1970s. Legislators serving on appropriations may have gotten their introduction to education through finance issues and kept their interest, expanding their purview into areas more traditionally the domain of substantive education committees. The intense involvement of fiscal committees increases the likelihood that school finance decisions will be integrated with other educational policy matters. On a less positive note for education, the domination of the money committees means that more education decisions are being made by legislators who are not necessarily education specialists—legislators who are most aware of the need to balance education demands with the need for other services. No other group of legislators is more cognizant of the trade-offs between services or of fiscal constraints.

Governors, like legislators, are showing less interest in education than they did in the 1970s. Governors traditionally involve themselves in education only sporadically. The myth that education is apolitical persists to the point that governors see their education responsibilities, other than in a budgetary sense, as fulfilled once they have appointed the necessary boards and commissioners. Only when they can enhance their political capital do they take stands on particular education issues. School finance reform was such an issue, particularly in the early 1970s. The negative fiscal and political circumstances surrounding education are now powerful deterrents to gubernatorial involvement.

Whither Reform

These changes in the legislature and the retreat of the governors do not augur well for finance reform. Reform has always been shepherded through by a dedicated corps of legislative education leaders who tried session after session until they accomplished their goal. It is now less likely that there will be such persevering individuals devoted to the cause of education. Yet school finance, if not reform, will remain a critical issue. In 1979, 76 percent of legislative education staff leaders still worked "a lot" on school finance issues (Rosenthal and Fuhrman 1981: 53).

The failing economy and the need for states to compete for industrial development are incentives to focus on finance, of course. A number of governors called for increased education aid in their 1982 state of the state messages: California's Brown and Colorado's Lamm spoke of the state's need to prepare children for a high technology society, while the governor of Mississippi spoke of the relationship between education and economic development. There are some states where reform has yet to take place, and conditions are ripe: As indicated, New Hampshire will suffer so severely from federal cuts it may have to commit more state money to education, and a school finance court case has just been filed. There are court mandates in Maryland, Wyoming, Arkansas, and West Virginia.

Most likely to reform are those states in good fiscal health.[1] Oklahoma recently passed a reform law; Wyoming, Texas, Nevada, and Nebraska are others thinking about reform. The states with enough money to contemplate reform are generally western states with mineral wealth. A major issue in those states will be how to address districts of varying size. Nebraska is considering district reorganization; reducing the large number of school districts by consolidating the smallest districts would considerably improve equity. Arkansas and Oklahoma are concerned about adequately compensating for district size differentials through their finance formulas.

These reform-ripe states also will face the challenge of developing the technical capability to institute reform. The reforms of the 1970s generally came after years of consideration by legislative committees, special commissions, and task forces. These groups served as arenas where compromises were eventually hammered out before presentation to the entire legislature. The commissions also were classrooms where legislators, group representatives, and public members learned the mechanics of school finance and were taught, usually by consultants, to use simulations to predict the impact of alternative reform options. The states that now have the money to reform do not have long histories of reform efforts and they lack the technical expertise produced by those years of deliberation. They are only now beginning to learn about simulations, ways to measure equity, and other technical issues. Therefore, even with the dollars to implement reform and even if the political will exists, it may take some time before reforms actually take place in these states.

Educational Interest Groups and Retrenchment

Perhaps the most interesting political development of the 1980s will be changes in interest group activity. The logical, even the imperative, course of action for groups—given what is known about policymakers' aversion to in-fighting and given greater competition between education and other services—would be to end their bitter fragmentation and rebuild a coalition in support of public education. Since the parent base of supporters is shrinking, educators also would be wise to reach out beyond traditional supporters of education to business and other interests. Whether such new coalitions will emerge is uncertain.

A new "general aid collective" was organized in the late 1970s in California. It included the traditional statewide education interests— such as teachers and administrators—and geographically based interests. It excluded the single-interest groups focusing on the handicapped, bilingual, and other special needs students. This attempt to provide a united front was very successful, largely because it did not seek total commitment of member organizations but merely "agreed not to disagree." When the group—called the Tuesday Night Group because of the time of its Sacramento meetings—could reach a consensus it did. It never pressed for full agreement or evidence of member organization support (Kirst and Somers 1981). However, as Elmore and McLaughlin (1981: 294–96) pointed out in their case study of the California school finance story, the only issue the group could agree on was more money for education. Even after Proposition 13 was passed, the state surplus meant that side payments could be made to all the component interests to keep them together. When "more money" is not available, can such a collective persist? Can a collective form around protecting education from cuts or seeing that education holds its own relative to other services? Such a collective would seem to be the only way to truly protect education, but it would require a degree of "statesmanship" on the part of lobbyists "representing the interests of education against other local government responsibilities and in reconciling competing concerns within the education sector" (Elmore and McLaughlin 1981: 295).

Such statesmanship may be difficult to develop. In Minnesota, the educational interest groups formed a united front at the beginning of the fall 1981 special budget cutting session. However, the coalition very rapidly fell apart in the face of proposals to make differential rather than across-the-board cuts in education. Finally, about the only thing educators could agree on was that if they were going to get fewer state dollars they wanted fewer mandates along with them.[2]

Certainly the single-interest groups formed around categorical programs will have to reassess their strategy under conditions of fiscal retrenchment. As Elmore and McLaughlin (1981) noted, when money is tight, the likeliest legislation will be omnibus bills that treat trade-offs between and within service areas. Single-interest groups will need to communicate with other education interests to form integrated packages rather than present their claims directly to individual legislators as in the past. To some extent, the single-interest groups must deal with a backlash to their tremendous success at the state level over the past ten years. Certainly it will be hard to shelter special programs as programs for the average student are cut, despite court mandates and legal protections for special needs students. Finally, a real question mark about the future of special-interest groups is raised by the recent actions of the federal government in devolving greater responsibility for special needs pupils to the state level.

The New Federalism

The Education Consolidation and Improvement Act of 1981 consolidates twenty-eight education programs into block grants administered by the states and includes changes in the regulation of compensatory education aid, formerly Title I. The consolidation and deregulation actions should focus attention on the state level. The obvious impact of a reduction of federal dollars for special programs, a lessening of federal restrictions surrounding the use of program funds, and the block grant movement would be the intensification of special-interest group activity in state capitols. Special needs groups would be expected to enhance their state capacity and presence, seeking to replace the lost federal clout with state dollars and service and accountability mandates. Furthermore, such stepped-up activity should aggravate the competition between the general and special aid forces. While state special needs programs grew enormously during the early and mid-1970s, many of them developed as they did because of corresponding federal programs. For example, special education programs at the state level have all been redesigned to conform to P.L. 94–142. The federal government was the leader when it came to special populations while the state was the sole provider of general aid. Now general and special aid are truly in the same arena, and the politics should reflect that.

However, a number of factors make a prediction of increased state-level special needs lobbying and intensified competition uncertain. As indicated, hard fiscal and political times may overcome competitive tendencies and force new coalitions. New cooperative actions on behalf of public education may be the only way for education to hold its own relative to other services. Moreover, some states may decide to transfer decisionmaking responsibility—and interest-group attention—down to the locals by block granting to the local education agency (LEA) level. A few states have already moved in this direction with their state categorical programs and would probably follow suit if they gained more discretion with federal money. In its 1980 revision of school finance, Arizona placed all its categorical aid through the operating formula. Mandates to provide certain special programs remain, but districts may use discretion in allocating funding among programs. Utah has a Special Purpose Options program under which aid for fourteen programs including compensatory, gifted, and bilingual education is combined. The amount of funding to districts is determined on a program-by-program basis, but LEAs may use the funds for any single program or combination of programs or services.

The argument for state-level consolidation is similar to the claims made for federal block grants: Power is being devolved to a level of government more familiar with needs and better able to operate flexibly. However, in Arizona, and perhaps elsewhere as well, a major impetus behind consolidation was the desire to diffuse interest-group activity at the state level and to focus attention on local school boards. Arizona legislators may have been influenced by unpleasant memories associated with an earlier revision of special education aid. When the state began to mandate services for the handicapped and greatly increased its aid to 90 percent of excess costs, districts began to identify as learning disabled many children previously served in remedial programs. The state was overwhelmed with demand. A number of policymakers apparently deliberately sought to insulate themselves from such claims for service by allowing the districts to become the arbiter of special program allocations.[2]

What states do about block grants also will influence other aspects of education politics. Some legislatures, having grown used to a major and often a leading role in education policymaking, have moved quickly to assure that they have a say in the use of federal block grant funds. In the past most federal funds escaped legislative control despite efforts in the late 1970s to institute reappropriation procedures. In most cases reappropriation was no more than a formal acceptance of existing funding and usage levels. Little, if any, modification resulted from legislative action. However, with more discretion devolving to the state level, these legislatures want to make sure that they are not preempted by the executive from deciding on the use of consolidated funds. In 1981 almost half of the state legislatures enacted laws increasing their involvement in the oversight of federal funds. In a number of legislatures, special or existing committees were granted authority over block grants. For example, Connecticut, Louisiana, Maine, Nevada, North Carolina, Oklahoma, and Tennessee passed legislation requiring committee review of block grant expenditures (Yondorf and Benker 1982).

Since most legislatures are not always in session and since their agendas are increasingly crowded, it would not be surprising if block grants worked to the relative advantage of state departments of education. The enhanced policymaking, auditing, and evaluation authority resulting from blocks will pose a difficult challenge to departments suffering from personnel losses as a result of federal and state budget cuts. However, state departments of education have undergone significant modernization and improvement in operations in recent years that make them better able than in the past to accept added responsibility. The majority have greatly augmented their data gathering and analytic capabilities. A number have revised their strategies and even their structures to be more sensitive to implementation problems at the local level. McLaughlin and McDonnell's recent study of state education agencies (SEA) reveals that many are improving opportunities for local input to and participation in policy-making; reorganizing technical assistance around functional areas, such as reading or math, rather than around narrow federal/state programs; and regionalizing services so as to work with locals more effectively (McLaughlin 1981).

These improvements in state education agency operations have yet to impress many legislators who express great cynicism about agency function and capability. They complain about overbureaucratization, lack of leadership, and staff mediocrity. It seems that a number of legislatures "regard the department with varying degrees of dislike" (Rosenthal and Fuhrman 1981: 64). Whether a devolution of increased authority to the state will lead to greater animosity or greater harmony between these major education actors is just one of the elements that makes this new decade the uncertain era it is.

POLICYMAKERS AND EDUCATORS: IS IT ALL CYCLICAL?

In the 1970s, general government, particularly legislators, dominated education policymaking. School finance reform and most other education issues were initiated, developed, and enacted in a complex set of politics with legislators, governors, and nontraditional interests in the forefront and educational interest groups and state departments in the background.

While the political configurations of the 1980s are difficult to forecast, perhaps there will be a shift back to a renewed role for educators. Retrenchment and conflict are turning legislators and governors away from education at a time when state departments will probably benefit from enhanced discretion passed along by Washington. The interest groups may see the imperative to regroup, realign, and rediscover the strength in union they once had. If states do devolve more discretion over special programs onto the locals, local school boards—and perhaps the courts—would be the focus of intensified activity by single-interest groups, and statewide educational interests could concentrate on the essential task of protecting education vis-à-vis other services.

When state level economies improve significantly, legislatures and governors may renew their interest in education and begin to initiate and innovate once more. In the interim, it is entirely possible that educational policymaking in the early eighties will once again be the province of the educators although never so exclusively as in the past. The decade of school finance reform has left its impact by opening the politics of education to more players, and that impact is indelible.

NOTES TO CHAPTER 3

1. Material on reforming states is based on information supplied by The Education Finance Center, Education Commission of the States, January 1982.
2. Based on interviews with state officials October 1981 through January 1982.

REFERENCES

Bailey, S., R. Frost; P. Marsh; and R. Wood. 1962. *Schoolmen and Politics.* Syracuse, N.Y.: Syracuse University Press.

Elmore, Richard, and Milbrey McLaughlin. 1981. *Reform and Retrenchment: The Politics of California School Finance Reform.* Santa Monica, Calif.: The Rand Corporation.

Fuhrman, S.; J. Berke; M. Kirst; and M. Usdan. 1979. *State Education Politics: The Case of School Finance Reform.* Denver, Colo.: Education Commission of the States.

Fuhrman, Susan, and Alan Rosenthal, eds. 1981. *Shaping Education Policy in the States.* Washington, D.C.: Institute for Educational Leadership.

Gold, Steve. 1981. "Mid-1981 Fiscal Survey of the States." Denver, Colo.: National Conference of State Legislatures, Legislative Finance Paper No. 6.

Hannigan, Janet. 1981. "Politics of School Finance Reform in Washington." Unpublished paper, Education Policy Research Institute, Educational Testing Service, Princeton, N.J.

Iannaccone, Lawrence. 1967. *Politics in Education.* New York: Center for Applied Research.

Kelly, James A. 1978. "The New Politics of Education Finance." Paper presented to the Chief State School Officers, South Padre Island, Texas, August 1, 1978.

Kirst, Michael. 1979. "The New Politics of State Education Finance." *Phi Delta Kappan* 60, no. 6 (February): 427–32.

_____. 1981. "The State Role in Education Policy Innovation." Stanford University: Institute for Research on Educational Finance and Governance, Policy Paper No. 81–C1.

Kirst, Michael, and Walter Garms. 1980. "The Political Environment of School Finance Policy in the 1980s." In *School Finance Policies and Practices: The 1980s: A Decade of Conflict*, edited by James Guthrie, pp. 47–75. Cambridge, Mass.: Ballinger Publishing Co.

Kirst, Michael, and Stephan A. Somers. 1981. "California Educational Interest Groups." *Education and Urban Society* 13, no. 2 (February): 235–36.

League of Women Voters Education Fund. 1978. *Campaigning for Fair School Finance: Cases in Point*. Washington, D.C.

Lehne, Richard. 1978. *The Quest for Justice*. New York: Longman, Inc.

McLaughlin, Milbrey. 1981. "State Policy and Local Change." Paper prepared for seminar on the Education Commission of the States Governance Center. Denver, Colorado, May 1, 1981.

Odden, Allan, and John Augenblick. 1980. *School Finance Reform in the States: 1980*. Denver, Colo.: Education Commission of the States.

_____. 1981. *School Finance Reform in the States: 1981*. Denver, Colo. Education Commission of the States.

Robinson v. Cahill, 303 A.2d 273 (1973).

Rosenthal, Alan, and Susan Fuhrman. 1981. *Legislative Education Leadership in the States*. Washington, D.C.: Institute for Educational Leadership.

Serrano v. Priest, 135 Cal. Rptr. 345 (1976).

Wolf, Alison. 1981. "State Spending on Education and Levels of Educational Services." Washington, D.C.: The Urban Institute. Mimeo.

Yondorf, Barbara, and Karen Benker. 1982. "Block Grants: A New Chance for State Legislatures to Oversee Federal Funds." Denver, Colo.: National Conference of State Legislatures, Legislative Finance Paper No. 15.

4 THE COURTS AND SCHOOL FINANCE REFORM
An Expected Utility Model

Tyll van Geel*

Between the late 1960s and the early 1980s court suits were brought in twenty-four states challenging the constitutionality of the states' systems for financing education. In eight states, courts upheld the constitutionality of the systems; in five states the highest court ruled that the system of finance did not meet the state's constitutional requirements; in five states trial courts ruled the systems unconstitutional; in one state the highest court ruled that the system is probably unconstitutional and remanded the case for trial. Currently, decisions or trials are pending in five states. Beyond this, new rounds of litigation are being undertaken, or contemplated, in four states in which the highest state court has already declared the system unconstitutional.[1]

It is interesting to study this judicial involvement in the formation of educational finance policy for a number of reasons beyond satisfying curiosity about whether these particular examples of judicial action have made a difference. A study of the judicial role unavoidably also must raise more general questions about the state policy formation and implementation process with a view toward modeling that process in order to make predictions regarding policy change. In this connection, more can be learned about the source, nature, ex-

*Tyll van Geel, Professor, Graduate School of Education and Human Development, University of Rochester.

71

tent, and conditions surrounding the influence of the judiciary. Thus, the study of the judicial role in shaping educational finance systems raises questions about when and to what degree constitutional government works. More broadly, it teaches something about one problem of social order.

This chapter probes these questions. In the first section, one question is raised: Why have suits challenging school finance systems been brought in almost one-half of the states? In the second section, a theoretical perspective is proposed for dealing with two additional questions: Is there any a priori reason to expect that a judicial decree in a given state is a *necessary condition* for reform and/or that the issuance of a judicial decree ordering reform is a *sufficient condition* for bringing about real reform or only symbolic reform? The limited empirical work on the politics of school finance reform is reviewed in the third section with the dual purpose of testing the theory outlined in the previous section and presenting the conclusions of the researchers. The last section includes a brief conclusion.

VARIABILITY IN WHERE SUITS ARE BROUGHT

As noted, efforts to reform school finance systems by means of the judiciary have been made in about one-half of the states. What accounts for the effort to use courts in this way? One obvious answer is that individual families and taxpayers who were frustrated with the existing school finance system in their state brought suit to seek rectification of the perceived inequalities and injustices in that system. While there is probably considerable truth in that response, it is an incomplete one. If inequalities were at the root of the use of courts, suits would have been brought in all states in which there were significant inequalities in the educational finance system. An examination of Tables 4-1 through 4-4 reveals, however, the absence of such strong relationships: That is, the existence of inequity in a school finance system does not cause reformers to resort to the courts. One relationship that is discernible is that the mean correlation coefficient for states in which winning suits have been brought is higher than the mean correlation coefficient for states in which no suits have been brought. Since the correlation coefficient measures the relationship between expenditures per pupil and property values, this suggests that suits are more likely to be brought in states in which individuals feel aggrieved as taxpayers and that the primary purpose

Table 4-1.   States in Which the Highest State Court Has Ruled
the School Finance System Unconstitutional.[2]

	Coefficient of Variation	Gini Index	Correlation Coefficient	Simple Wealth Elasticity
California	14.0	7.1	0.63	0.18
Connecticut	18.6	10.3	0.70	0.39
New Jersey	15.1	8.4	0.55	0.19
Washington	18.4	10.2	0.40	0.20
Wyoming	15.0	8.1	0.81	0.20
Mean	16.22	8.82	0.62	0.23

Table 4-2.   States in Which the Highest State Court Has Ruled
the School Finance System Constitutional.

	Coefficient of Variation	Gini Index	Correlation Coefficient	Simple Wealth Elasticity
Arizona	14.0	6.4	0.50	0.18
Idaho	14.7	7.7	0.42	0.14
Louisiana	12.0	6.8	-0.03	0.01
Ohio	22.9	12.8	0.58	0.37
Oregon	11.4	6.4	0.38	0.17
Pennsylvania	20.9	11.7	0.65	0.28
Georgia	19.4	10.8	0.38	0.22
Texas[a]	18.1	9.3	0.64	0.17
Mean	16.68	8.99	0.44	0.19

a. The U.S. Supreme Court ruled in *Rodriguez* v. *San Antonio Independent School District* (1973) that the school finance system of Texas did not violate the equal protection clause of the fourteenth amendment of the U.S. Constitution.

of the suits is to obtain property tax relief. But note that the mean correlation coefficient in Table 4-2 is lower than in Table 4-4, throwing even this modest evidence into doubt. Perhaps all that can be said is that suits are more likely to be won in states with a higher correlation coefficient than in states with a lower correlation coefficient (see Tables 4-1 and 4-2). Yet, if this were so, one would have expected suits to have been brought in such states as Kentucky,

Table 4-3. States in Which Litigation Has Begun but Has Not Yet Terminated with a Ruling from the State's Highest Court.

	Coefficient of Variation	Gini Index	Correlation Coefficient	Simple Wealth Elasticity
Arkansas	18.1	10.0	0.74	0.28
Colorado	17.6	9.4	0.63	0.31
Kansas	14.4	7.4	0.73	0.23
Maryland	14.7	8.0	0.60	0.18
Massachusetts	24.9	12.5	0.24	0.23
New Hampshire	13.9	7.7	0.61	0.37
New York	19.8	10.6	0.71	0.33
Oklahoma	17.2	7.9	0.80	0.19
South Dakota	18.0	9.1	0.68	0.36
West Virginia	9.7	5.5	0.63	0.21
Wisconsin	14.4	8.1	0.09	0.10
Mean	16.61	8.75	0.59	0.23

Michigan, Nebraska, Nevada, Rhode Island, Utah, and Virginia. In short, the safest conclusion seems to be that the data reveal no meaningful relationships between equity (no matter how measured) and the initiation of suits.

An examination of the tables also reveals that the existence of gross inequalities is not even a necessary condition for reformers to resort to the courts. For example, suits have been brought in Oregon (Table 4-2) and West Virginia (Table 4-3), and neither state ranks high on the measures of inequity except in the case of West Virginia, with a correlation coefficient of 0.63.

If the courts are used not simply by aggrieved families and taxpayers seeking redress, why are they used? Another possible explanation is found by examining the parties who have brought these suits: In roughly one-half of the cases the first named plaintiff is not an individual child or taxpayer but a governmental entity such as a school board.[3] What this suggests is that locally elected officials have seen the advantage of such litigation. On the one hand, these local officials can be seen as altruistically looking after the best interests of their constituencies. On the other, they can be seen as viewing litigation as part of a reelection strategy; that is, the suit demonstrates

Table 4-4.   States in Which No Suits Have Been Brought Challenging
the School Finance System as Unconstitutional.

	Coefficient of Variation	Gini Index	Correlation Coefficient	Simple Wealth Elasticity
Alabama	12.2	6.8	0.58	0.18
Alaska[a]	23.0	10.9	-0.06	-0.08
Delaware	22.6	11.7	0.57	0.37
Florida[a]	12.1	6.7	0.51	0.21
Hawaii				
Illinois[a]	17.4	9.7	0.33	0.13
Indiana	15.7	8.8	0.69	0.28
Iowa	7.3	4.0	0.47	0.01
Kentucky	21.0	11.1	0.81	0.28
Maine[a]	15.0	8.2	0.37	0.16
Michigan	20.5	10.6	0.67	0.26
Minnesota	18.6	9.9	0.13	0.19
Mississippi	14.6	8.0	0.85	0.19
Missouri[b]	23.4	12.2	0.75	0.32
Montana[a]	NA	NA	NA	NA
Nebraska	18.1	8.7	0.76	0.45
Nevada	7.5	2.0	0.92	0.25
New Mexico	13.2	5.9	0.32	0.07
North Carolina	12.1	6.6	0.50	0.18
North Dakota	16.2	8.3	0.24	0.12
Rhode Island	13.6	7.7	0.63	0.39
South Carolina	13.6	7.4	0.60	0.41
Tennessee	22.7	12.8	0.42	0.18
Utah	9.7	4.7	0.78	0.05
Vermont	16.5	9.2	0.62	0.36
Virginia	24.3	12.7	0.72	0.43
Mean	16.29	8.53	0.55	0.22

a. Litigation has touched on particular aspects of the school finance system. In Maine, Wisconsin, and Montana, the challenge was to an aspect of a reform of the system intended to bring about greater equality in educational expenditures among the districts.

b. Case voluntarily dismissed by plaintiffs following passage of reform legislation.

to the local voters that the official is attempting to rectify local tax and budget difficulties. Evidence from a case study of the politics surrounding *Robinson* v. *Cahill* (1973) in New Jersey supports this conjecture (Lehne 1978). In addition, a number of other case studies show that school finance reform litigation has been promoted by a national network of reform-oriented organizations, lawyers, and professional consultants who also may not be involved for purely altruistic or sincerely held ideological reasons. Thus, one might argue that courts have been brought into school finance reform for three reasons: first, as a mechanism for resolving the genuine and sincerely felt grievances of individual families and taxpayers; second, as part of the political strategy of locally elected officials to retain their offices; and third, as a way of achieving the goals of a variety of reformers.

The difficulty with all of these explanations, however, is that they do not account for the fact that only half of the states have experienced judicial challenges. If suits are advantageous to politicians, one would expect legal challenges to have occurred in most states. Perhaps part of the answer lies in the fact that legislatures in Florida, Illinois, Maine, Missouri, New Mexico, South Carolina, and Wisconsin have voluntarily attempted to improve the equity of their systems, thereby eliminating both the need for such suits and the opportunity to gain political advantage by bringing them (Fuhrman 1979). Still, there remain many states where suits, if filed, would be expected to overcome inequity or to advance political fortunes. A number of explanations might explain the absence of suits in these states: The legislative route to reform has remained open and promising in some states; the expectation of a legal victory is less in some states than in others; or, in the states in which suits have not been brought, the statistical measures of inequity make the systems appear inequitable but in actual operation they deliver resources in such a way (e.g., through categorical grants) as to satisfy what otherwise might be grievances that could lead to legal action.

Also, it might be argued that a judicial strategy of reform has not been adopted in some states because the political advantage of such a suit would not be sufficient, given the preexisting distribution of political resources, to overcome opposition to reform. That is, a victory in the courts would not sufficiently add to the reformers' political resources to enable them to bring about more than perhaps a symbolic reform. The next section of this chapter discusses a theory regarding the influence of the judiciary and places this last hypothesis in its proper framework.

THE INFLUENCE OF THE JUDICIARY:
A THEORETICAL PERSPECTIVE

When the judiciary has declared a state's system for financing education to be unconstitutional, it raises a question about the circumstances under which this decree will or will not be implemented by the state's legislature. One approach to answering this question is through a priori reasoning about the relationship among the variables that affect legislative decisionmaking, including a judicial order. This kind of reasoning requires the construction of a model of the legislative process that allows consideration of the unique contribution of a judicial decree to the legislative process while holding other variables constant (an idea expressed by the phrase "ceteris paribus"—other things being equal). The model can be studied in an attempt to predict the effect of a judicial decree on the legislative process. Even if the model has elements that appear unrealistic, as long as it is internally consistent (logically deduced from first premises) and useful, it is acceptable. If the model is unrealistic yet meets these criteria, it is appropriate to say that the political process operates "as if" it were actually like the model in all respects.

In the discussion of the model, it is assumed that the judicial order requires a new pattern in the distribution of expenditures among school districts, which can be achieved only by taking money from some districts and giving it to others or by raising extra money for schools and distributing this new money only to certain districts. Under this assumption, implementation of the judicial order will produce a set of "winners" and "losers."

Several other assumptions are made about the judicial opinion in order to be able to assess its effect in a reasonably "clean" or parsimonious way. First, it is assumed the judicial opinion is sufficiently clear that the political process following the issuance of the opinion avoids debates as to the intent of the court, its real goals, and whether the court really meant what it said or whether it was actually seeking a reform not adequately articulated in the opinion itself. (In reality this problem has marked the politics surrounding the implementation of judicial opinions striking down school finance systems.) Second, it is assumed the opinion itself does not require reform of the state's system for raising revenues for public schools; that is, the opinion is not, for example, concerned with the constitutionality of the property tax per se. The fact that the issue of how revenues for education are to be raised may come up in the debate over the implementation of the court order is another matter.

Given the above assumptions, a three-part question is posed. Is there an a priori reason to expect that a judicial decree in a given state is a *necessary condition* for:

1. speeding up legislative action that, but for the judicial decree, would have occurred at a later date?
2. legislative action that has only the appearance of reform, that is, only appears to reduce inequities (however defined)?
3. legislative action that in fact reduces inequities in more than a trivial way?

The answer to all three parts of the question appears to be "no." To arrive at this answer it is necessary to explicate a theory of policy-making using expected utility theory.

Generally speaking, expected utility theory says that people choose between courses of action by examining the expected utilities of the available options and then selecting the course that has the highest expected utility. Note, what is examined is not merely utility but "expected utility," which means the rational decisionmaker interested in maximizing utility compares courses of action in terms of a simple calculation such as: $E(U) = p(U)$. In other words, the expected utility of an action is equal to the probability of the outcome occurring, p, times the perceived utility of that outcome for the person making the decision. One course of action may, if it succeeds, yield a higher utility than another, but the probability of its success may be less; it is therefore possible that the course of action with the higher utility has the lower expected utility, making it irrational to choose that option. Important refinements of this basic model can be made.[4]

Political actors also can be understood as choosing among their options in terms of an expected utility calculation. For example, given the option of choosing to pursue a change in a particular policy or not, the actor will gauge his or her utility for the outcomes associated with the courses of action (utility of the status quo versus utility of the preferred policy) and then calculate the perceived probabilities attached to the two courses of action. (It is assumed that maintaining the status quo is perceived as virtually certain; thus the crucial question is the probability of achieving the desired reform.) The perception of the probability of success in seeking reform is best operationalized in terms of an assessment of the distribution of political resources among those who want reform and those who oppose a change from the status quo. Of course, the side with the larger proportion of the resources is perceived as having the greater perceived chance of success. (The resources involved include money, proportion of population in support of one's position, votes on other issues that can be "delivered" to one's potential allies, access to the media, and so forth. It also is likely that the greater the proportion of resources, the greater the chances for bringing about a reform.)

One important resource that political actors can utilize is a legitimate claim-right, that is a claim-right that has been legitimated by the judiciary as a legal right. It can be assumed such a claim-right is an important resource to the extent three conditions (hereafter, Conditions) are operable: (1) A large proportion of the populace of the state shares the belief that legitimated claim-rights should be recognized. Perhaps they share this belief because they, in their self-interest, want their legitimated claim-rights to be recognized and understand the only way to achieve this is by recognizing other people's claim-rights. (2) It is believed this claim-right should be recognized because not to do so would damage the institution of the judiciary, and it is in everyone's self-interest to maintain the judiciary as an effective branch of government. This condition entails the further belief that the judiciary is doing a good job overall—that it is a valuable institution of government even if it occassionally renders opinions that run counter to one's immediate or short-term self-interest. (3) Related to the second condition is a third condition, which is a more general version of condition two—this claim-right should be recognized because not to do so would damage the legitimacy of the existing system of constitutional government, and it is in one's self-interest not to inflict such damage on the existing governmental arrangement.

From the above it follows that for a judicial decree establishing a legitimate claim-right to be a *necessary* condition for achieving school finance reform, the legitimated claim-right would have to be such an important political resource that those interested in achieving reform would absolutely require it before they could conclude that the expected utility of attempting to seek most reforms was higher than not seeking reform. But such a conclusion discounts too heavily all the other resources that actors may have that might lead them to think that the expected utility of action designed to achieve reform was relatively higher than inaction. For example, the view that judicial action is a necessary condition for reform would lead to the conclusion that the new majority of a recently reapportioned legislature would not, in the absence of judicial decree or the threat of one, take steps to pursue their own self-interest and change what had been an "inequitable" system into one that was more equitable and favorable to their constituents. In any event, there is evidence that a judicial decree is not a necessary condition for reform. First, there has been a long history of reform in school finance systems that at least has paid lip service to the importance of improving equity in its various forms.[5] Second, there are recent examples of voluntary reform in the absence of a judicial decree in Florida, Illinois, Maine, Missouri, New Mexico, South Carolina, and Wisconsin (Fuhrman 1979).

A more difficult three-part question is whether the issuance of a judicial decree is a *sufficient condition* for:

1. speeding up legislative action that, but for the judicial decree would have occurred at a later date?
2. legislative action that has only the appearance of an equity-based reform?
3. legislative action that in fact reduces inequities?

Again, to answer this question expected utility analysis is applied.

In order for a judicial decree to be a sufficient condition for the reform of a school finance system, certain other conditions would have to exist. First, the judicial decision granting one group a legitimated claim-right would in fact have to increase the proportion of political resources available to that group to the point that they perceive that it would be rational to attempt to seek a reform of the finance system. Second, this group's assessment of its expected utility would have to be correct, that is, it does have sufficient resources to push through the reform (or could now obtain enough with the aid of allies). If the group really has been advantaged by the judicial decree, then it could be expected that the issue of school finance reform would indeed be placed on the legislative agenda and that *at least* a symbolic reform would be adopted.

What follows is an analysis designed to illuminate this basic insight. Several assumptions are made at the outset. First, it is assumed that at the time of the judicial decree a majority of the legislature supports the status quo; if there is to be a change in policy, some members of the majority will have to change their minds or be defeated at the polls by people who prefer a change in policy. This assumption implies that the status quo is supported by people and/or groups with a greater proportion of the resources than those who, at the time of the original legislative choice, preferred a different policy. This restriction eliminates from consideration the situation in which the existing system may simply have remained in place because of the inattention of the legislature as it concentrated its time on other policy issues despite the fact a latent majority for change existed.

Second, it is assumed that people who seek legislative office desire to win at least a bare majority of the votes in the next election and therefore attempt to take policy positions that are favored by a majority of the voters. That is, they produce policy positions in order to win votes. Moreover, since the primary goal is winning votes, if achieving a majority in the next election requires deception regarding the full implications of positions, candidates will engage in deception. It also follows that if there is to be a change in policy because of the judicial decree, the decree will have to have an impact on the constituency of these elected officials, an impact that leads to the formation of a new legislative majority in favor of reform.

Third, it is also assumed that the candidate's position on the issue of school finance reform is an important factor in the decision of members of the constituency whether or not to vote for a candidate. Fourth, it is assumed that the members of a legislator's constituency, including interest groups, are also interested in maximizing their own self-interest. That is, the constituency of each school district prefers to keep the state aid they have rather than lose any (or all of it); they prefer to keep the quality of schools at the same or less cost to themselves or to improve the quality of their schools at the same or lower cost or at somebody else's expense. Similarly, it is assumed the constituency prefers not to pay higher taxes to support schools in other school districts.

Fifth, it is assumed the legislature is made up of representatives from four types of legislative districts. (The precise proportion of the legislators from each type of district cannot be estimated a priori.) First, Type 1 legislative districts are comprised predominantly of school districts that would benefit from the implementation of the principle(s) promulgated in a judicial decree ordering reform of the school finance system. Implementation of the judicial order would mean these school districts would be "winners." This does not mean these school districts would not also be advantaged or disadvantaged if other aspects of the system, not specifically addressed by the judicial order, were changed; the constituency (and legislator) from these districts therefore may favor reform in one respect but oppose other reforms, or favor yet additional reforms. Second, Type 2 legislative districts are comprised predominantly of school districts that benefit from that aspect of the existing school finance system ruled unconstitutional. Compliance with the judicial order means these districts would be "losers," and legislators from these districts will be impelled, ceteris paribus, to vote for continuation of the aspect of the present system (the status quo) toward which the judicial order is directed. Again, this does not mean the population of these districts would not favor other reforms in the finance system. In any event, all candidates in either a Type 1 or a Type 2 legislative district will share the same view on that issue of school finance reform addressed by the judiciary because not to express those preferences would mean sure electoral defeat.

The third group of legislative districts (Type 3) consists of those school districts where implementation of the decree is not a salient issue because of insufficient gains or losses. These districts, however, may have other issues that are salient but are not addressed in the judicial order—for example, increased aid for school construction or reform of a categorical aid program. Thus, these legislators may join one or the other side in an ensuing struggle in exchange for support for policy gains they prefer. Finally, it is assumed that a fourth group of legislative districts (Type 4) exists, comprising various combinations of the school districts found in Types 1, 2, and 3 legislative districts. Some of these Type 4 districts may be represented by legislators who, because of electoral pressure, support the status quo; others may support reform or be indifferent about the issue. Candidates for elective office in Type 4 districts may very well oppose each other on the basic reform issue as each candidate calculates differently where the electoral advantage lies.

In addition to legislators, the governor, the chief state school officer, and/or the state controller may become significant participants in the reform process. If all of these officials are elected, their incentive also will be to deliver policies that maximize their chances for reelection. Of course, their constituency will include all three types of school districts discussed above, and like the legislative representatives from Type 4 legislative districts, these officials will be forced to engage in a careful calculation as to where the electoral advantage lies.

It is worth stressing that the judicial order may point toward a reform that few legislators had sought. If most legislators' priorities for reform have been different from the reform won in the courts, the judicial decision may come down in a political context that requires mobilization of support for the opinion if the decision is to have any chance of being implemented.

Given these different types of legislative districts and the other assumptions made above, the question becomes whether, ceteris paribus, a judicial decree is sufficient to change the preferences of the constituencies in these three types of school districts to such a degree that there emerges in the legislature a new majority in favor of a reform of the status quo. This question can best be approached in light of two different sets of circumstances: (1) It is assumed that any reform must be accomplished with existing resources; a change in the finance system, therefore, requires an actual redistribution of resources from some school districts to others; (2) after exploring reform under fixed resources, this restriction is lifted and legislative reaction is examined in light of expanding resources.

Reform with Fixed Resources

This analysis examines the possible impact of a judicial decree on the activities and policy positions of legislators from the four types of legislative districts and the governor.[6]

Type 1 Districts. It is assumed that before the judiciary spoke, legislators from Type 1 districts were not actively pursuing the kind of reform mandated by the judiciary or that the pursuit was modest in its expenditure of time and resources. These legislators were not more actively engaged because the constituency's expected utility calculation had not resulted in placing a high priority on the use of political resources for seeking this policy change. Thus, the question becomes whether a judicial decree is a sufficient condition for changing the expected utility calculation of the constituents of a Type 1 district.

If it is assumed that the population of the state, the representatives, and the governor hold to the Conditions discussed earlier, it can be anticipated that the constituents of Type 1 districts would conclude that their proportion of the political resources available for this issue would have increased. In other words, the judicial decree will have given the constituency and their representatives a new resource, the claim-right, which gives the legislators from these districts an increased advantage in the legislative process.

The constituents of Type 1 districts, perceiving that their legislators now have a greater share of the resources available in the legislative arena, can rationally raise their expectations as to what their legislative representatives can obtain for them. That is, with this increase in resources, the perceived chances, ceteris paribus, of winning an improvement in policy will have improved, and it now makes more sense than before to attempt to achieve such a policy reform. If the judicial decree has actually shifted what had been a disadvantage in resources to an advantage, then the constituencies would expect even more—an all-out effort to achieve reform. Whether the decree transformed what had been a relative disadvantage into a genuine advantage depends, of course, in part on the extent of the disadvantage Type 1 districts were under before the judicial decree. If the disadvantage were great enough, the judicial decree could make up some of the disadvantage but not all. The stronger the Conditions noted earlier, the more the judicial decree will represent a significant gain:

1.0   The more the anticipated reform is a departure from the status quo (the greater the anticipated gain in utility) and/or the more the judicial decree has transformed what had been a disadvantage in resources to an advantage, the more these constituents and their representatives have an incentive to actively work for a significant reform and to avoid bargaining. Indeed, under these conditions legislators from Type 1 districts will be expected to play "hard-ball" politics to achieve reform, that is, to use threats, pressure, and sanctions to obtain reform.[7]

1.1   The less the anticipated reform is a departure from the status quo (the less there is to be gained) and/or the less the judicial decree has resulted in a real shift in the proportion of resources held, the more these constituents and their representatives have an incentive to bargain and to settle for a reform that may depart only slightly, if at all, from a symbolic reform.

1.2 The more the estimates discussed in proposition 1.0 are correct, the more likely it is that legislators from Type 1 legislative districts will in fact be successful in the legislature.

The calculations of the amount of resources available must include not only what each side has directly under its own control but also those resources allies—for example, those legislators who represent Type 3 legislative districts and the governor—might bring to each side in the struggle. Whether the attempt to gain allies is successful depends upon a number of additional factors. Perhaps the most important factor is whether the Type 1 constituency and their representative can offer something to the potential allies in exchange for their support on this issue—for example, support on another issue salient to the Type 3 legislator and others. Support from allies also may depend on the extent Type 1 legislative districts share a set of common interests with potential allies; that is, particular Type 3 legislators would prefer to see Type 1 legislators gain in this struggle because they generally share common interests on other issues that are not shared with Type 2 legislators and their constituencies. The affiliation need not be truly positive; as long as the potential ally has less in common with the Type 2 legislators than with the Type 1 legislators, the Type 1 legislators may be able to count on some support from Type 3 legislators and others. These Type 3 legislators and others fit the adage "my enemies' enemy is my friend" (Bueno de Mesquita 1981).

Hence, even if the judicial decree does not have the effect of changing a disadvantage to an advantage for Type 1 legislators, the behavior of Type 3 legislators and others can affect the expected utility calculations of the Type 1 legislator:

2.0 The more Type 1 districts and their legislators receive support from others, the less important will be the effect of the judicial decree on the expected utility calculations of Type 1 districts.

2.1 The more support Type 1 districts and their legislators receive from others, the more likely it is that legislators from Type 1 districts will fight for achieving more than a symbolic reform.

As allies are gained by Type 1 legislators, the issues placed on the agenda will become more complex. Legislators from Type 1 districts may be working not only to achieve the kind of reform ordered by the judiciary but also, for example, a new categorical aid program or tax reform their allies want.

2.2   The more Type 1 districts seek reform with the aid of allies, the more they will be engaged in attempting to include as part of the reform effort changes external to the judicial order. The more allies Type 1 districts gain, the more likely they will win a reform that includes their primary concern.

Obtaining this support from allies is not costless; Type 1 legislators and their constituencies may be faced with the need to lower their potential net gain in order to make side payments to their allies. Because working with allies reduces the net benefits one might obtain, Type 1 legislators will try to minimize the number of allies.

Because of the expectations of the constituency in Type 1 districts, the individual legislator will have a strong incentive to try to deliver the reform seemingly promised by the judiciary. This task would not be as difficult if the limitation of fixed resources could be lifted. With expanded resources, allies could be given side payments, and the full expected net gains from the reform could be realized. If the constraint of fixed resources were lifted by increasing taxes for education, however, the net benefit for the district from the reform would be reduced compared to what might have been obtained in a reform effort that redistributed wealth without the aid of allies and the side payments. Thus, the elected representative may have his or her own incentive to raise taxes for education, make side payments to allies, and achieve the reform but hide the full implications of the tax increase from the constituency—that is, advertise the reform as yielding the full net gain that would have occurred if taxes had not been raised:

3.0   Legislators from Type 1 districts have an incentive to achieve the reform seemingly promised by the judicial decree by increasing state taxes in such a way that it appears to their constituents they will obtain a reform worth as much as a reform achieved without allies, without side payments, and without a rise in taxes for education.

Type 2 Districts. With the issuance of a judicial decree, one would expect the constituents of Type 2 districts and their representatives to conclude that their proportion of the relevant political resources has declined. That is, they will perceive that the proponents of reform will have a greater probability of success in an effort to reform the school finance system. However, the impact of this perception on their preferences for what their elected representative should do depends on several other factors.

If the constituents of Type 2 districts hold an overwhelming advantage in resources prior to the judicial decision, it is unlikely that after the issuance of the decree they will perceive themselves as potential losers in a legislative struggle over reform. Despite the mandate, they will have little incentive to bargain for the best deal but instead will use rough political tactics to hold reform to a minimum. It also follows that the more these constituents expect to lose from reform (the greater the possible departure from the status quo), the more adamant they will be about resisting reform, even if they perceive that the probabilities of their succeeding have been greatly reduced. But it also has been assumed these constituents hold to the Conditions noted earlier; hence it follows that the issuance of a judicial decree could have the following effects:

4.0   The more the anticipated reform is a departure from the status quo (the greater the anticipated loss of utility) and/or the less the judicial decree has transformed what had been an advantage in resources to a disadvantage, the less incentive these constituents have to see their representatives bargain; they would prefer their representatives to fight for only a symbolic reform.

4.1   The less the anticipated reform is a departure from the status quo (the less the anticipated loss of utility) and/or the greater the extent to which the judicial decree has resulted in a real shift in advantage in terms of political resources, the more these constituents have an incentive to have their representatives bargain; they will tend to want to seek a compromise that is the least departure from a purely symbolic reform that can be achieved. In preferring that their representatives bargain, these constituents prefer that the tactics of "hard-ball" politics be eschewed—for example, the use of threats, sanctions, counter-attacks, and so forth. Hard ball politics is a relatively more expensive method of resolving a conflict than bargaining.

As noted earlier, the calculation of the amount of resources available to those in favor and those opposed to reform must include not only what each side has directly under its own control but also those resources allies might bring to each side in the dispute—for example, those legislators who represent Type 3 legislative districts and others:

5.0   The more support Type 2 districts and their legislators obtain from others, the less important will be the effect of the judicial decree in the expected utility calculations of Type 2 districts.

5.1   The more support Type 2 districts and their legislators obtain from others, the more likely it is that legislators from a Type 2 district will fight for holding to a mere symbolic reform.

At the same time as allies are gained in exchange for support on other issues of importance to the allies, the more complex the issues will become before the legislature. Legislators from Type 2 districts may not only be working to limit the kind of reform ordered by the judiciary but also, for example, to pass a new categorical aid program or a tax reform their allies want.

6.0   The more Type 2 districts attempt to defend against reform with the support of allies, the more they will be engaged in attempting to place new and perhaps unrelated issues on the agenda of the legislature for decision.

As the overall effort at reform becomes more complicated and as both sides gain strength (and therefore have less incentive to bargain), it will take a greater length of time to achieve a legislative enactment that settles the issues. It is conceivable that the political process precipitated by the judicial decree could stretch over a period of several years if the sides were sufficiently balanced in resources that both sides calculate that continuation of the struggle is likely to lead to success.

As noted earlier, obtaining support from allies is not costless; thus Type 2 legislators and their constituencies may be faced with a dilemma—to avoid the loss of resources they have to spend resources. They may be confronted with the following set of choices in order of preference (that is, in order of least net cost): (a) a symbolic change in the status quo; (b) a symbolic change plus modest extra costs associated with making side payments to others; or (c) a meaningful reform as sought by those seeking implementation of the judicial order. In these circumstances if (a) appears impossible to achieve, then (b) would be the preferred strategy. However, if (a) is impossible to achieve and if (b) and (c) are both equally costly, then the legislator from a Type 2 district faces a new problem.

Another strategy the constituents and legislators from Type 2 districts may pursue is lifting the fixed-resource constraint and using the extra money raised to increase the resources of the districts that seek compliance with the judicial decree. Leveling-up, instead of leveling-down, could represent a plausible strategy assuming three propositions are true: (a) The constituency of Type 2 districts resent and resist having to do with less in absolute terms at a given time (T_2) than they had at an earlier time (T_1); (b) the defenders of the status quo are not heavily committed to maintaining the existence of relative inequalities per se; what they resist most is an absolute loss of resources; and (c) the defenders of the status quo dislike an absolute reduction of resources held at a given time (T_1) more than sharing inequitably in new resources made available at T_2, even if the inequitable sharing in the new resources reduces in T_2 the relative inequalities in existence at T_1.

As an empirical matter the last two propositions are especially shaky; with equal assurance one could claim that many people are committed to maintaining their relative advantage over others— especially preserving the relative educational advantage of their children over other children—and that people resent not sharing equally in newly found resources to which they are as much "entitled" as others. Thus, the more accurate these later counterpropositions, the more inaccurate the claim that leveling-up would be an "easy" course for defenders of the status quo to adopt. In contrast to the uncertainty about the empirical basis for (b) and (c), there is a basis for assessing (a). Economists have successfully hypothesized that people prefer more to less; thus an absolute reduction in resources would be resisted. Besides, it appears to be a widely shared norm that a reform that places some people in a better position at the expense of other people is presumptively wrong, whereas a reform that places at least one person in a better position and no one in a worse position, ceteris paribus, is to be preferred. Leveling-down violates this norm, whereas leveling-up arguably does not, at least if one assumes that reducing inequalities itself is not a harm. But even if it is assumed that leveling-up is perceived as a harm, it seems safe to say the perception of harm is less than occurs under leveling-down. In sum, leveling-down is almost certainly to be resisted, but one cannot be sure whether a strategy of leveling-up would be embraced warmly. To the extent it is reasonable to assume people want to maintain advantages for their children, it seems reasonable that even a policy of leveling-up will be resisted but perhaps with less intensity than the policy of leveling-down.

In any event, leveling-up is not likely to be costless to the constituency in Type 2 districts, and if this claim is true, leveling-up becomes even more problematic as a preferred strategy for the constituency. But it should be noted that the legislator from the Type 2 legislative district may be attracted to a leveling-up strategy to avoid leveling-down, especially if the costs of that strategy can be hidden from the constituency. Thus, one may anticipate that the legislator will work on behalf of a leveling-up strategy that is represented to the constituency as involving lower costs for the constituency than is in fact the case. In other words, the legislator from a Type 2 district may seek to increase state taxes for education in covert ways. Alternatively, the legislator may openly support a new state tax— such as an income tax—in order to support a leveling-up program, while proclaiming (falsely) to the constituency that the new tax will not represent a net tax increase because the increase will be offset by a reduction in local property taxes.

Type 3 Districts. These legislative districts by definition predominantly comprise school districts that will not be benefited or harmed in a substantial way by a reform consistent with the principles of the judicial order. However, these constituents and their representatives will go through a calculation to determine the sort of support they might get for their preferred policies in exchange for supplying their support on the school finance reform issue. The choices these potential allies make could be crucial to the question of the proportion of resources available to legislators from Types 1 and 2 districts and hence to their expected utility calculations, their choices, and their behavior.

As was the case with legislators from Types 1 and 2 districts, these legislators also may see an advantage in lifting the fixed-resource constraint; they also may support new taxes for education to help pay for the reform they want most. As was the case with legislators from Types 1 and 2 districts, however, these legislators will attempt to create the appearance that the net gains they seek are larger than they are in reality.

Type 4 Districts. These legislative districts by definition comprise various combinations of school district types that are found in the other legislative districts. Whatever the combination, it is assumed that there is no clear preponderance of the population from one type of school district since, if this were the case, the mixed legislative district would in effect be either a Type 1, 2, or 3 district. Accordingly, the internal politics of these districts will be dynamic, with candidates for the legislature possibly adopting differing positions on the reform issue because they estimate differently which policy position will garner the most votes.

Assessing the impact of a judicial decree on the internal politics of these districts involves a complex analysis because Type 4 districts can consist of different combinations of constituencies, as revealed in Table 4-5. Reading down the columns, it can be seen that Type 4B legislative districts are represented by an elected representative who favors the status quo and that comprise group Types II, V, and VIII. That the elected representative favors the status quo must mean, according to the assumptions, that a majority in the district favors that position, but it is also assumed that these Type 4 legislative districts are not dominated by a single type of school district as were Types 1 through 3 legislative districts. Hence, it follows that the electoral outcome in Type 4B must be the result of a combination of votes cast by Types II and VIII groups. (A similar analysis could be made of the electoral politics of Types 4A and 4C.)

The interest here is in the effect that a judicial decree would have upon the legislative elections in district Types 4A, 4B, and 4C and ultimately the choice made in the legislature. Turning first to Type 4B, a judicial decree would adversely affect group Type V just as it would adversely affect legislative district Type 2. That is, group Type V, under a judicial decree, could experience a reduction in its proportion of the political resources in the district, a change that could, in a close case, turn what had been an advantage to a disadvantage vis-à-vis group Type II. Such a change in fortunes could in turn have an effect on the position taken by the legislative representative, moving that person from a position supporting the status quo to a position in support of reform or to a position of neutrality. Such a change in

Table 4-5. Impact of a Judicial Decree on the Internal Politics of Type 4 Districts.

	Type 4A Elected Representative Has Favored Reform	Type 4B Elected Representative Has Favored Status Quo	Type 4C Elected Representative Has Not Taken a Strong Stand on Either Side
Constituency in Type 1 School District = Constituency Type 1	Group Type 1 = Constituency Type 1 living in a Type 4A legislative district.	Group Type II = Constituency Type 1 living in a Type 4B legislative district.	Group Type III = Constituency Type 1 living in a Type 4C legislative district.
Constituency in Type 2 School District = Constituency Type 2	Group Type IV = Constituency Type 2 living in a Type 4A legislative district.	Group Type V = Constituency Type 2 living in a Type 4B legislative district.	Group Type VI = Constituency Type 2 living in a Type 4C legislative district.
Constituency in Type 3 School District = Constituency Type 3	Group Type VII = Constituency Type 3 living in a Type 4A legislative district.	Group Type VIII = Constituency Type 3 living in a Type 4B legislative district.	Group Type IX = Constituency Type 3 living in a Type 4C legislative district.

position in enough legislative districts would obviously affect the likely outcome of the legislative struggle.

A similar sort of analysis could be undertaken for Types 4A and 4C legislative districts, but to keep matters from becoming more complicated, only inferences based on an expected utility analysis for Type 4B are stated:

7.0 The more the anticipated reform is a departure from the status quo (the greater the anticipated loss) and/or the less the judicial decree has transformed what had been an advantage in resources for Type V, the less desire group Type V will have to see its representative from the Type 4B district bargain; they would accept only a symbolic reform.

7.1   The less the anticipated reform is a departure from the status quo (the less the anticipated loss of utility) and/or the greater the extent to which the judicial decree has resulted in a real shift in advantage from group Type V within the Type 4B district, the more likely it is the representative will move away from defending the status quo.

8.0   The more the anticipated reform is a departure from the status quo (the greater the anticipated gain in utility) and/or the more the judicial decree has transformed what had been a disadvantage for group Type II to an advantage, the more this group will have an incentive to take political action to garner support for meaningful reform.

8.1   The less the anticipated reform is a departure from the status quo (the less there is to be gained) and/or the less the judicial decree has resulted in a real shift in the proportion of resources held by group Type II, the more incentive group Type II will have to bargain and seek a reform that departs only slightly, if at all, from a symbolic reform.

The calculations for both group Types II and V will be affected by the allies they are able to obtain within legislative district Type 4B for the reasons noted in connection with the discussion of Type 1 and Type 2 legislative districts.

What the actual outcome of these intradistrict struggles will be, in terms of the activities and positions taken by the representatives from these districts, cannot be estimated a priori. Whether a judicial decree would be a sufficient condition to bring about a change in the policy preferences expressed by the elected representatives will depend on such factors as the strength of the Conditions in the district, the distribution of resources prior to the judicial decree, and the choices potential allies make.

The Governor. The governor faces the same political problem a legislator elected from a Type 4 legislative district faces since the governor's electoral district (the entire state) comprises Types 1 through 3 school districts. Because it is assumed that at the time of the judicial decision a majority of the legislators favor the status quo and that a sufficiently large portion of the state's population favors the status quo, then it also must be assumed that the governor favors the status quo. But if it is now assumed that the governor shares with the populace of the state a belief in the Conditions, it follows that the

judicial decision would have the effect of moving the governor toward the position of favoring a symbolic reform—but only a symbolic reform. The governor's position would shift further in favor of
a more substantial reform only if the judicial decree leads to such an
increase in activism on behalf of reform that the governor calculates
it as an advantage to join that side of the struggle. At the same time,
the governor is not likely to want to so seriously harm those who
would lose in a reform effort that they would become implacably
opposed to him in future elections; the governor will have an incentive to hold the reform to modest proportions and/or to lift the fixed
resource limitation to bring about greater equity by leveling-up and/
or by providing the losers with compensation in the form of other
policy changes. Of course, lifting the fixed resource constraint itself
is not costless; like the legislators, the governor will have a strong
incentive to mislead the state's population as to the true costs of
expanding the resources available for education.

9.0   The more the anticipated reform is a departure from the status
      quo (the greater the anticipated loss for the losing school dis-
      tricts) and/or the less the judicial decree has transformed what
      had been an advantage in resources for the potential losers, the
      less these potential losers have an incentive to see their gov-
      ernor bargain; they would prefer that the governor fight and
      accept only a symbolic reform.

9.1   The less the anticipated reform is a departure from the status
      quo (the less the anticipated loss of utility) and/or the greater
      the extent to which the judicial decree has resulted in a shift
      in advantage from the potential losers to the potential winners,
      the more the governor will move away from defending the
      status quo.

10.0 The more the anticipated reform is a departure from the status
      quo (the greater the anticipated gain in utility for winning dis-
      tricts) and/or the more the judicial decree has transformed
      what had been a disadvantage for the potential gainers to an
      advantage, the more these potential gainers will have an incen-
      tive to take political action to persuade the governor to take a
      position in favor of meaningful reform.

Finally, it should be added that the interest on the part of all parties
in seeking the governor's assistance rests on the fact that the gov-

ernor has resources that could make a crucial difference in the legislative struggle over the reform addressed by the court as well as other issues raised in the bargaining process.

In this section under a condition of fixed-resources, the circumstances were examined in which a judicial decree could be a sufficient condition for placing an issue of school finance reform on the legislative agenda, a sufficient condition for leading to a mere symbolic reform, or a sufficient condition for precipitating real reform. In addition, the propositions suggested under what circumstances the participants in the struggle would rationally conclude they could use hard-ball politics or would have an incentive to bargain. Discussion also included the business of building a coalition for reform with the assistance of allies, the cost associated with reliance on allies, and the implications for kinds of reform when allies are involved. The analysis showed that there will be a tendency to expand the reform agenda to include a wide range of issues, including the raising of new taxes in order to lift the fixed-resource constraint.

Reform with Expanding Resources

The restriction of fixed resources is dropped, and now it is assumed that judicial action occurs at a time when, for reasons having nothing to do with the judicial decree or the effort to implement the decree, resources available for education are expanding. For example, the state may be experiencing sudden financial growth, or the federal government may have increased the amount of financial aid flowing into the state, or considerable savings in another of the state's programs may enable a shift of resources from that area to education.

Arguably, the central effect of lifting the assumption that resources for education are fixed is that it becomes easy for defenders of the status quo to acknowledge the legitimated claim-right by leveling-up as opposed to leveling-down. As noted earlier in the discussion of Type 1 legislative districts and their representatives, this argument rests on certain assumptions, not all of which have solid empirical footing. It was concluded that leveling-up will be resisted but with less intensity than the policy of leveling-down; it represents a path of least resistance, especially if the actual costs of leveling-up are hidden from both the potential losers and potential winners of the effort to comply with the judicial order.

A judicial order requiring increased equity in school finance in a period of expanding resources would thus be satisfied by a policy of leveling-up; but because leveling-up itself is not costless and for other reasons discussed earlier, one would expect potential losers to resist total leveling-up. The stronger the operation of the Conditions, however, the more leveling-up will be acceptable as a price that must be paid for adherence to the Conditions. Even if the Conditions are strongly held, it can be anticipated that a policy of wholly leveling-up would be resisted as a policy that unnecessarily goes too far. In sum, in a period of expanding resources a judicial order is likely to result in something more than a symbolic change but something less than the elimination of the existing relative inequalities.

Furthermore, as noted, the process of pushing toward implementation of the decree is likely to involve the gathering of allies to help in the effort to support and oppose implementation—allies that may have their own reform agenda. Besides, with the availability of expanded resources for education, this in itself will be an incentive for all participants to seek their preferred additional reforms. The result is likely to be the undertaking of a multiple set of reforms, some of which necessarily will detract from full implementation of the judicial decree because they use resources that otherwise could have been used for this purpose. Thus, the outcome of the reform effort is likely to be a combination of more than symbolic compliance with the judicial decree plus other costly reforms not addressed in the judicial decree.

THE INFLUENCE OF THE JUDICIARY: EMPIRICAL PERSPECTIVES

This section of the chapter analyzes three case studies of the politics of school finance conducted in the shadow of judicial orders. The inquiry will be directed toward the dual purpose of testing the theory outlined in the previous section and informing the reader of the conclusions of these researchers insofar as they shed additional light on the question of the influence of the judiciary.

California

Elmore and McLaughlin (1981) conducted the most complete case study of the politics of school reform in California, tracing the story from the filing of the complaint in *Serrano* v. *Priest* in 1968 to the 1980s. Briefly, the chronology of events in California is recounted: Prior to 1968 the political effort to equalize the distribution of resources among school districts met with little success, leading a group of reform-minded lawyers and others to develop a suit challenging the substantial disparities in per pupil expenditures among school districts. The complaint was filed on August 23, 1968 and dismissed by the superior court in January 1969; an unsuccessful appeal was taken to the appeals court, which in turn was followed by an appeal by the original plaintiffs to the California Supreme Court. On August 30, 1971, the California Supreme Court gave the plaintiffs their first and major victory (*Serrano I*), ruling that the state's system for financing education was unconstitutional, assuming the facts as alleged by the plaintiffs were correct; the case was remanded for trial. Before the case was heard by the superior court, the U.S. Supreme Court ruled on March 21, 1973, in *Rodriguez* v. *San Antonio Independent School District*, that the legal theory used in *Serrano* was not a correct interpretation of the federal Constitution and that therefore the school finance system of Texas was not in violation of the fourteenth amendment. Events also moved forward in California with the passage of SB-90 on December 1, 1972, a law that embodied a reform of the finance system and that had some equalizing effects. On April 11, 1974, the trial in *Serrano* was completed, and Judge Jefferson issued an opinion stating that the decision in *Rodriguez* made no difference because the California system of finance was in violation of the state's own constitution and this violation existed despite the reforms of SB-90. He imposed a six-year deadline for compliance (1980) and required that any new finance system must yield expenditures per pupil that varied no more than $100 among school districts. An appeal directly to the California Supreme Court followed, and on December 30, 1976, the court upheld the trial court's opinion and order (*Serrano II*). In the intervening two years between the trial court opinion and the final supreme court opinion little legislative action occurred; however, a new governor was elected, Edmund G. Brown, and a new legislature was installed in January 1975. In anticipation of the California Supreme Court opinion, work began on plans for complying with *Serrano II*; and, following the issuance of the opinion, a complex political process ensued, ultimately producing a new piece of reform legislation, SB-65, on September 2, 1977. This is as far as the events will be related except to note that in June 1980 suit was once again filed in California charging that the new system of finance still did not comply with *Serrano II* because the inequities had not yet been reduced to less than $100 per pupil.

The analysis of these events by Elmore and McLaughlin was not intended to be, nor could a case study be, a test of the kind of theory outlined in this chapter; nevertheless most of what they discovered is not inconsistent with the theory. They found that *Serrano I* did spawn a reform effort where there had been no meaningful reform effort for decades: *Serrano I* placed reform on the political agenda, transforming an ideological issue into a legal mandate. They also concluded that the modest reform of SB-90 was adopted at a time when there was no real increase in resources available for education; thus, the strategy adopted was to increase the state sales tax to support a program of leveling-up the poorer districts while imposing an almost meaningless cap on the possible rise in expenditures by the high-spending districts. This modest reform, which itself was ultimately found to be unconstitutional in *Serrano II*, was necessarily adopted in the face of then Governor Ronald Reagan's opposition to real equalization. Yet the researchers also concluded that without *Serrano I* SB-90 would not have addressed expenditure equalization at all. Turning to SB-65, the researchers found that it was passed in a period when state surpluses were increasing because of a rising economy and at a time when the new governor favored compliance with *Serrano I* and *II*. They also found that SB-65 went further but not the full way toward compliance with *Serrano I* and *II*. Finally, Elmore and McLaughlin found that SB-65 included much more than just steps to comply with *Serrano I* and *II* but represented a complex change in educational policy that resulted from bargaining among proponents of compliance and their would-be allies.

Three other important points made in the Elmore and McLaughlin analysis should be highlighted. First, the *Serrano* decisions demanded a reform on the basis of a principle—fiscal neutrality—about which there was, for reasons not explicated in the case study, considerable confusion. Substantial discussion was devoted to sorting this question out.

Second, the principle of fiscal neutrality, before *Serrano I* announced it, had not been a rallying flag for those interested in seeking educational reform. Once it was announced, however, it did gather supporters who pushed for compliance as well as for those other reforms they had been seeking all along. The allies of those seeking compliance added their own demands, thus expanding the total reform effort into something more complex than envisioned by the judiciary.

Third, Elmore and McLaughlin made a statement at one point that appears to contradict the theory:

> [A]lthough the Court decision modified the legislative agenda and secured an audience for school finance reform proposals, that was the only aspect of the problem it changed. It did not alter the underlying political forces that would constrain legislative response, nor did it generate a politically consequential constituency for reform (1981: 156).

The contradiction with the theory emerges if one stresses the portion of the statement that claims that the decision did not "alter the underlying political forces," suggesting the decision did not affect a reallocation of political resources. But that claim itself seems implausible in light of their other findings: that *Serrano* altered the agenda, that *Serrano* made a difference in the formulation of SB–90, and that prior to *Serrano I* reform efforts had failed. It appears, then, that *Serrano* did alter the distribution of political resources to an extent and did, therefore, affect legislative behavior.

New Jersey

The primary analysis of events in New Jersey is by Lehne (1978), who provided an in-depth description and analysis of the process leading up to the filing of the complaint in *Robinson* v. *Cahill* (1973) and the political process that followed. The chronology of events goes as follows. The complaint was filed on February 13, 1970, at the behest of locally elected officials in Jersey City. The trial judge's opinion striking down the state's system of finance was issued on January 19, 1972, appealed to the state's highest court, and affirmed on April 3, 1973, on the ground that the existing system was inconsistent with the state's obligation under the state's constitution to provide for a "thorough and efficient" system of education. In a subsequent opinion issued on June 19, the court ordered legislative compliance to be completed by December 31, 1974. In January 1974, a new governor took office, Brendan Byrne, and he, his staff, and the legislature set to work on developing legislation to meet the judicial decree. By the end of the year when the court's deadline fell due, no legislation had succeeded in passing both houses of the legislature. On January 23, 1975, the New Jersey Supreme Court extended the time for compliance until October 1 because it would be "chaotic . . . [for] many school districts to effect financial changes for the . . . [upcoming] school year at this late date and on such short notice" (Lehne 1978: 135). Four months later the court acted again, ordering that $300 million in state minimum support aid for local school districts be redistributed in such a way that the poorer districts would receive more money and the affluent districts less. That fall, on September 29, reform legislation was finally passed, and even though the new law was not funded, the supreme court found on January 30, 1976, that on its face the new law was constitutional. In February new hearings were scheduled by the court. One month later the state assembly on March 15 and 16 passed a bill establishing the state's first income tax to fund the new school finance legislation. In the face of the likelihood that the state senate would not pass the tax bill, on May 13 the court ordered all spending for public schools to cease on July 1, 1976: New Jersey's public schools had to close unless the legislature acted. On June 30, a federal district court refused to intervene, and on July 1 the schools closed; on July 7 the assembly passed a new tax package, which the Senate also adopted on July 9, ending the constitutional crisis.

While Lehne's analysis of these events was not intended to provide a test of the theory outlined earlier, his findings are not inconsistent with the theory. His central finding was that the *Robinson* v. *Cahill* decision placed school finance reform on the agenda of the legislature—a finding he made based solely on the obvious fact that the legislature had not addressed school finance reform earlier. In the face of fixed resources, the New Jersey legislature increased taxes to enable it to adopt a policy of leveling-up. Lehne found the decision triggered consideration of a wide range of issues because various participants in the political process attempted to hitch their own agendas to the reform ordered by the court. He found people were torn between opposing the judiciary on policy grounds and not wanting to subvert the New Jersey Supreme Court; he ultimately concluded that it was policy preferences that dominated people's reactions and not respect for the courts. Similarly, he found that as long as the school districts of legislators were not financially hurt by specific proposals to deal with *Robinson*, their evaluations of the ruling were not closely related to its impact on their constituencies. He observed that the actual logic employed by the court in support of the decision was unimportant in contributing or detracting from the effect of the opinion. Finally, he observed that the effect of the reform itself seemed to have been marginal, even with regard to Jersey City, in terms of increased state aid and that after reform substantial disparities remained among the school districts of New Jersey in the amount of money spent per pupil.

It also should be mentioned that Lehne (1978) presented other evidence that may be construed as inconsistent with the theory but is ultimately simply puzzling because of the inconsistencies in the evidence. This evidence is found in two public opinion polls and the codified results of interviews with a sample of members of the state's senate and assembly (Lehne 1978). For example, the data showed that the richer and more educated a person was the more likely he or she was to approve of *Robinson* (even though the case clearly implied a redistribution of wealth) and that people in cities who seemed to stand to gain from the opinion disapproved of the opinion by a 52 percent to 27 percent margin with 22 percent undecided. Also, individuals preferred that state aid be distributed evenly rather than going to poorer school districts but would approve of such a reform if a court ordered it. However, these same individuals also, by a small margin, disapproved of the *Robinson* opinion and would not approve of a court order requiring them to raise their own taxes to pay for schools in poor and disadvantaged communities. A similar sort of puzzle is found in the data from interviews with legislators. Despite overall public disapproval of the opinion, 62 percent of the legislators polled approved of the opinion but 96 percent thought the whole school finance question should not be settled by the courts.

Washington

Gale's (1981) research provided a description of the events in Washington state surrounding the decision in *Seattle School District No. 1 v. Washington* (1978). Again, the basic chronology begins with the fact that prior to judicial action no real change in the school finance system had occurred since 1965 despite the fact that increasing numbers of school districts were having difficulty raising revenues by means of the special local levies on which they had to rely. Following the decision in *Serrano I*, administrators in Northshore School District began preparation of a case challenging the state system on the same theory as articulated in *Serrano I*; the state supreme court in 1973 sustained the system in the face of the challenge (*Northshore School District v. Kinnear* 1974). Unsuccessful political efforts to reform the system of finance continued as the difficulties facing local districts in raising money mounted. The Seattle school board, faced with an especially difficult financial situation, filed suit in 1976, and the decision striking down the system on a theory different from the *Northshore* case was issued on January 14, 1977. Among other things, the court ordered the system changed so that local tax levies would not be the basic source of revenue for the basic education program. On June 20, 1977, the state legislature by an almost unanimous vote in both houses adopted reform legislation. Full funding of the reform was to be phased in over a period of years. In September 1978 the state supreme court upheld the trial court opinion, and in 1979 the state achieved full state funding of the reform bill, a year earlier than planned.

As with the other studies, this one was not designed as a test of the theory, yet there is evidence in the analysis of the events not inconsistent with the theory. Gale found resistance among legislators to the original trial court opinion but also found the sentiment of several people in leadership positions was that the court was telling them what they knew they had to do anyway. The nearly unanimous vote on the basic reform legislation appears to have been the result of a careful packaging of a variety of reforms (including special education, vocational education, and education of the gifted) with a carefully crafted basic distribution formula. The new law specifies the basic program that all local districts must offer, funds this basic program according to a funding formula, and permits districts to raise extra money locally via special levies within certain limits. These limits could have strongly held down spending in high spending districts if it were not for a grandfather clause that permits a district to request more levy money than allowed under the limit if it is necessary to make its state money and levy money equal to last year's state and levy money plus 4 percent. (More recent legislation changed the 4 percent figure to 6 percent.) The new legislation worked to level-up the lower spending districts because of the funding formula but at the same time in effect allowed high-spending districts to continue spending large amounts because of the grandfather clause. The crucial ingredient making it possible to reform quickly by leveling-up, however, was the existence of a state fiscal surplus because of increased revenues from a sales tax fanned by inflation. Gale's analysis of the political process in Washington, unlike the other studies, does not include data or insights that seem to contradict the theory outlined earlier.

CONCLUSION

This chapter indicates that much has yet to be learned about the variability in the pattern of where suits challenging school finance systems are brought. More generally, additional research is needed about when people will use a judicial strategy to obtain reform. Second, to explain precisely the influence of the judiciary on school finance reform, or on the reform of any policy controlled by the state legislature, a general model of politics or policymaking is required. The building of such models—especially models that take into account the influence of the judiciary—is a relatively new enterprise in political science, and what has been outlined here represents a very early step in the process of constructing such models. Indeed, the model outlined, in order to become truly useful, needs to be reduced to mathematical form with variables that are measurable. Only then can the real testing of such a model be undertaken using data from historical experiences with reforms. Nevertheless, this chapter represents a first effort to move in that direction, with the hope that if this initial step has been sufficiently well executed, others will become intrigued by the possibility of constructing useful models of the political process.

NOTES TO CHAPTER 4

1. *Upholding constitutionality*: see Table 4-2 in text; *highest court finds system unconstitutional*: see Table 4-1 in text; *trial courts ruling system unconstitutional*: Arkansas, Colorado, Kansas, Maryland, New York; *highest court remands case for trial*: West Virginia; *pending litigation*: Massachusetts, Oklahoma, South Dakota, Wisconsin, New Hampshire; *new rounds*: California, Connecticut, New Jersey, Washington (Lawyers' Committee 1980).

2. These tables are adapted from Odden and Augenblick (1981). The coefficient of variation is the standard deviation divided by the mean; it states the percentage variation in expenditures per pupil about the average. The Gini Index indicates the degree of variation from perfect equality. For both figures values close to zero indicate equality, and values closer to one indicate inequality (Odden and Augenblick 1981: 7). The correlation coefficient indicates the relationship between expenditures per pupil and local property wealth per pupil. A value closer to zero indicates a less precise relationship. Simple wealth elasticity shows the percentage increase in expenditures per pupil associated with a 1.0 percent increase in property wealth per pupil. This reflects the magnitude of the relationship. An elasticity close to zero indicates the school district expenditures do not change much with changes in wealth; a great elasticity indicates that higher district expenditures tend to be found in higher wealth districts (Odden and Augenblick 1981: 8–9).

3. See Lawyers' Committee (1980). A review of the information in the Lawyers' Committee publication does not reveal the extent to which school districts joined in suits brought originally by taxpayers and/or children and their parents. For example, several cities joined the plaintiffs in *Serrano* v. *Priest* (1971) (see Elmore and McLaughlin 1981).

4. Through expected utility one can make predictions about the behavior or choices people make. For example, assume Jane has two courses of action available to her (X, Y). Also assume that these courses of action will lead to either of three outcomes (a, b, c.). Further assume that Jane prefers a to b, and b to c; and that if she chooses action X she will obtain b for certain, i.e., the chances of obtaining b equal 1; but if she chooses action Y she has a 0.5 chance of realizing her least preferred outcome c, and a 0.5 chance of realizing outcome a. It is also assumed that Jane is interested in choosing the alternative course of action that will maximize her utility. Thus, it would be irrational for Jane to choose the option that would yield the lower amount of utility. Stated differently, a necessary (and possibly sufficient condition) for the choice of either X or Y is that it be the option with the highest expected utility. Which option would it be rational for Jane to choose and which option would it be irrational for her to choose? The following provides a start toward an answer:

$$E(U_x) = P_b(U_b) \qquad (4.1)$$

$$E(U_y) = P_a(U_a) + (1 - P_a)(U_c) \qquad (4.2)$$

where

$$E(U_x) \quad = \text{ expected utility of action } X$$

$$E(U_y) \quad = \text{ expected utility of action } Y$$

P_b = probability that outcome b will occur if action X is chosen

P_a = probability that outcome a will occur if action Y is chosen

$(1 - P_a)$ = probability that outcome c will occur if action Y is chosen

U_b = utility of outcome b to Jane

U_a = utility of outcome a to Jane

U_c = utility of outcome c to Jane

The condition for adopting either X or Y is that the expected utility for that option is greater than for the other option. The condition for the adoption of X is that:

$$E(U_x) > E(U_y)$$

Now if the utility for Jane of outcome b is 6 and if it is certain to occur if option X is chosen (i.e., $P_b = 1$), then 1 is substituted for P_b and 6 for U_b in [1] and $E(U_x) = 6$ is concluded. And if U_a equals 12 and U_c equals 4 and if P_a equals 0.5 and $(1 - P_a)$ equals 0.5, then it follows that $E(U_y)$ equals 8. Hence, it would be irrational for Jane to choose X; thus it can be predicted that she will choose Y.

5. For much of this century efforts have been made to promote the adoption of legislation that would improve the equity (defined in various ways) of educational finance systems (see Benson 1961: Chapter 6). Many of these proposed formulas (e.g., percentage equalizing) have been in fact adopted by states. But it is also well known that state legislatures have modified these formulas in various ways; thus whether the formulas as modified have tended to equalize is a question that requires empirical study. Unfortunately the study of the actual effects of educational finance legislation is a very recent phenomenon; in other words, statistical analyses of the type found in Tables 4-1 through 4-4 are not available for the first half of the century. Hence, the most that can be said is that at least ostensibly efforts have been made to improve the equity of school finance systems; whether those efforts were a sham prior to rise in judicial activism is not known.

6. An enormous intellectual debt is owed to Bueno de Mesquita (1981). The model developed here follows closely in important respects the model Bueno de Mesquita has developed for predicting when nations will go to war to achieve their objectives. This seminal work should be read by all political scientists interested in seeing how political science can be made truly scientific.

7. This proposition and many of the others in the text follow logically from the assumptions made in the text and from the formulas discussed in note

4. For example, if one examines formula (4.1) it can be seen that the higher the value of P_b and/or (U_b) the higher will be the value of $E(U_x)$, and the higher the value of $E(U_x)$ the greater the incentive to choose option X.

REFERENCES

Benson, Charles. 1961. *The Economics of Public Education*. Boston: Houghton Mifflin Company.

Bueno de Mesquita, B. 1981. *The War Trap*. New Haven, Conn.: Yale University Press.

Elmore, Richard, and Milbrey McLaughlin. 1981. *Reform and Retrenchment: The Politics of California School Finance Reform*. Santa Monica, Calif.: The Rand Corporation.

Fuhrman, Susan. 1979. *State Education Politics: The Case of School Finance Reform*. Denver, Colo.: Education Commission of the States.

Gale, Diane. 1981. "The Politics of School Finance Reform in Washington State 1975–1979." Ph.D. dissertation, University of Washington.

Lawyers' Committee for Civil Rights Under Law. 1980. *Update on State-wide School Finance Cases*. Washington, D.C.

Lehne, Richard. 1978. *The Quest for Justice*. New York: Longman, Inc.

Northshore School Dist. No. 417 v. Kinnear, 530 P.2d 178 (Wash. 1974).

Odden, Allan, and John Augenblick. 1981. *School Finance Reform in the States: 1981*. Denver, Colo.: Education Commission of the States.

Robinson v. Cahill, 303 A.2d 273 (1973).

Rodriguez v. San Antonio Independent School District, 411 U.S. 1 (1973).

Seattle School District No. 1 of King County, Washington v. State of Washington, 585 P.2d 71 (1978).

Serrano v. Priest, 487 P.2d 1241 (1971), (*Serrano I*); *subsequent opinion*, 557 P.2d 929 (1976), (*Serrano II*); *rehearing denied*, January 27, 1977; *as modified* February 1, 1977.

5 ANALYZING THE IMPACT OF SCHOOL FINANCE REFORM

Patricia R. Brown*
Richard F. Elmore**

Between 1971 and 1981, twenty-eight states enacted school finance reform measures—fifteen states between 1971 and 1973, twenty-five by 1977. Reform was accompanied by court cases in twelve of the twenty-eight reform states; fiscal surpluses were present in eighteen of the twenty-eight at the time of enactment (Odden 1981: 16, 39). By any standard, this is a considerable amount of reform (see Table 5-1). A review of the studies of the diffusion of innovation among states reveals that the mean rate of diffusion for so-called state preserve policies is about sixteen years for the first 25 percent of the states and twenty-four years for the first 50 percent (Welch and Thompson 1980; Walker 1969; Gray 1973). Judged strictly by the volume of activity, then, school finance reform occurred at more than twice the expected rate.

But when the term "impact" is used in school finance reform, it means something more than the volume of activity. Reformers presumably had some purpose, or set of purposes, in mind. The impact of reform should be judged by how closely results match these purposes. The conventional wisdom is that school finance reform was

*Patricia R. Brown, Assistant Professor, Department of Political Science, University of California, Berkeley.
**Richard F. Elmore, Associate Professor, Graduate School of Public Affairs, and Associate Director, Institute for Public Policy and Management, University of Washington, Seattle.

107

Table 5-1. School Finance Reform Activity, 1971–81.

Year	States per Year	Cumulative Total	States
1971	2	2	Iowa, Minnesota
1973	13	15	California, Colorado, Florida, Illinois, Kansas, Maine, Maryland, Michigan, Montana, New Mexico, North Dakota, Utah, Wisconsin
1974	3	18	Arizona, Connecticut, Virginia
1975	3	21	Indiana, Ohio, Texas
1976	1	22	New Jersey
1977	3	25	Missouri, Tennessee, Washington
1979	2	27	Massachusetts, South Carolina
1981	1	28	Oklahoma

Source: Odden (1981: 16).

"about" equity, defined both as reducing absolute disparities in expenditure levels and tax rates among school districts and reducing the relationship between wealth and expenditures. For most analysts of school finance policy, the success or failure of reform hinges on whether state school financing systems are more or less equal, by these standards of equity, after reform than they were before. Much has been written about the measurement of equity and the performance of school financing systems by these measures (Berne and Stiefel 1978; Friedman and Wiseman 1978; Garms 1979; Garms, Guthrie, and Pierce 1978; Sherman 1981).

The approach presented in this chapter is somewhat different from these analyses. Equity is treated as one of several objectives that influenced the construction of school finance reform measures and as one of several outcomes against which the impact of reform should be judged. The authors describe a model of political choice that can be used to understand the trade-offs that state policymakers faced and hence the outcomes that could be expected to follow from reform. The approach is hypothetical, using the authors' research as well as the research of others to extract propositions about the impact of reform. The rationale for this approach grows out of the authors' analysis of the problems of using equity measures to assess the impact of reform and their understanding of how states actually went about the process of reform.

THE PURSUIT OF ELUSIVE EQUITY

It is correct to say that school finance reform was "about" equity only in the sense that the *in*equities of school financing systems were what inspired reformers to act. The intellectual, legal, and political roots of school finance reform lie in studies designed to expose those inequities and devise alternative bases for financing systems (Wise 1967; Horowitz and Nietring 1968; Kirp 1968; Coons, Clune, and Sugarman 1970; Elmore and McLaughlin 1982: 13–69). So it is entirely consistent with the motives of reformers to analyze the impacts of reform measures using equity criteria.

On the other hand, reform measures were not constructed entirely by reformers. The arguments of reformers served as the stimulus for debate, but the actual content of reform measures was determined by bargaining among political interests with a stake in school finance. The objectives of political actors cannot be characterized as easily as those who stimulated discussions of reform. Nor can the exact combination of political actors working on reform in a given state be easily characterized; conditions varied considerably across states. So while it is consistent with the intent of reformers to think of equity as the objective of reform, it is not consistent with what is known about the process of reform.

There are at least five reasons why focusing on equity to the exclusion of other outcome measures may not give an accurate picture of the impact of school finance reform:

1. Reformers Themselves Did Not Agree on What Equity Meant

The major disagreement among advocates of reform was over whether the objective of reform was "equal fiscal opportunities" or "equal fiscal outcomes" (Carroll 1979b: 3-4). The former would accept some undefined level of disparities in tax rates and expenditures as long as voters who chose to tax themselves at the same level would receive the same return in revenues, thus reducing the relationship between wealth and expenditures (Coons, Clune, and Sugarman 1970). The latter views reduction of tax and expenditure disparities as the main objective of reform, independent of the preferences of local voters (Kirp 1968). As Friedman and Wiseman (1978: 200) argued, these two points of departure produce contradictory results. Often reformers held both objectives simultaneously, and both were written into court decisions and legislation, making it difficult to determine precisely what constituted progress toward "equalization" of financing systems. Furthermore, the two positions contained contradictory views of the role of local choice in the determination of expenditures and tax rates. Equal fiscal opportunities meant for its advocates a more equitable financing system with no loss of local control. Equal fiscal outcomes meant for its advocates that the preferences of local voters and policymakers should be overridden in the interest of larger objectives.

2. The Equity Effects of Reform Have Varied Widely, Depending on the Content of Reform Measures, the Index of Equity Used, and the Period of Time Analyzed

Given contradictory equity goals, it is not surprising that the "success" of reform depends in large part on how one chooses to define and measure impact. In an early multistate study, L. Brown et al. (1978: 208-209) found that ten of nineteen reform states had reduced expenditure disparities between 1971 and 1975 but that four of these still had among the highest disparities in the country; thirteen had reduced wealth-related expenditures by at least 5 percent; but only eight had made "at least some progress" toward both objectives. Later studies confirmed these mixed results. Carroll's (1979b: 15, 17) five-state study found little reduction in revenue and expenditure disparities among districts but a significant reduction in tax rate disparities. Hickrod, Chaudhari, and Lundeen (1980: 196) found in a three-state study uneven effects on tax and expenditure disparities, consistent reductions in wealth-related expenditure disparities, but mixed effects when these disparities were controlled for tax effort. Studying the impact of reform in five states over several years, P. Brown (1981: 227-229) found varying impacts of reform on expenditure and tax disparities within the same state depending on the year of analysis because of gradual implementation of reform measures and adjustments made after the results of reform were known. Some of these differences are methodological artifacts; some are not. But an obvious conclusion one might draw from such results is that the impact of reform measures might vary widely because the measures themselves were designed to do very different things, depending on the conditions that attended their passage (P. Brown 1981).

3. The Process of Reform Revealed Conflicts Between Equity Objectives and the Special Needs of Individuals and School Systems

Early analyses of equity assumed a coincidence between "wealth neutrality" and "income neutrality"; school finance systems designed to eliminate property wealth as a determinant of expenditures were assumed by reformers also to equalize expenditures as a function of family income. Helping poor schools was the same as helping poor children (Wise 1967; Kirp 1968; Coons, Clune, and Sugarman 1970). The discovery that district property wealth and family income were imperfectly correlated resulted in measures designed to soften the impact of reform on districts with relatively high property wealth and low incomes—namely, large cities (Cohen 1974). In addition, cities were found to have greater revenue needs and greater competition among municipal services for existing revenue (Garms, Guthrie, and Pierce 1978; Goertz 1981; Sjogren 1981). Overall, cities tended to spend more per pupil on education, tax themselves at a lower rate, and have higher-than-average property values. The result was that reform measures based on the principle of wealth neutrality penalized them, in absolute terms or relative to other districts (Garms, Guthrie, and Pierce 1978: 393, 405). As the problems of cities became apparent, other special cases emerged based on cost differentials, scale, and sparsity (see Chambers 1981). School finance formulas became littered with exceptions to the general distribution criteria and special categories of support to soften the effect of reform. These adjustments of equity objectives to fiscal and social realities may have resulted in school financing systems that are more "rational" by some standard but not necessarily more "equitable" by the criteria of reformers.

4. Much of the Actual Debate in State Legislatures Over the Content of Reform Proposals Had Little to Do With Equity

In some states—notably Kansas, Minnesota, Wisconsin, Ohio, and California—reform measures were considered as parts of larger revenue packages (Fuhrman 1978: 161; Elmore and McLaughlin 1982: 75–112). In those states, a large part of the debate centered on allocation of revenues among *functions* of government rather than among units of government. In virtually all states, education finance reformers were forced to fight for a share of state revenues before they could debate equity issues. In some states, broad questions of institutional reform and accountability were introduced into school finance reform debates, focusing attention on how revenues were being *used* in addition to how they were being raised and distributed (Fuhrman 1978: 165; Elmore and McLaughlin 1982: 113–168). In still other states, the main debate was about the state's responsibility for some minimum share of educational expenditure, and equity was a subsidiary issue (Lehne 1978; Gale 1981).

Perhaps most importantly, reform debates raised the issue of tax relief in ways that often conflicted with the objectives of reformers. L. Brown et al. (1978) found that in eleven of nineteen reform states finance reform was accompanied by tax relief. "The reform laws," they observed, "provided new state money which was in part channeled to property tax relief," but in eight of those states "per pupil expenditures declined relative to the national average, suggesting that property tax relief occurred at the expense of the educational program" (1978: 210–11).

5. There Was a Distinct Shift in Both the Pace and Content of School Finance Reform After 1973—the Net Effect Reducing the Equity of Reform Measures

Two factors seem to have precipitated this shift in emphasis. The first was the U.S. Supreme Court's refusal to enter the school finance field in *Rodriguez v. San Antonio* (1973). The second was an economic downturn that reduced fiscal surpluses available at the state level to finance new reform measures (Fuhrman 1978: 167). Reforms introduced after 1973 were much more diverse in their objectives and much less tied to simple equity arguments.

To say that school finance reform was "about" equity is, in other words, a useful but not entirely accurate characterization. The closer one gets to the process of reform in specific states, the more elusive equity seems and the more complex are the values and objectives operating on reform proposals. This is not an argument against assessing the impact of school finance reform by equity criteria but rather an argument for taking a closer, more systematic look at the trade-offs confronting policymakers in the construction of reform measures. The expected impact of reform ought to be based in part on what policymakers were trying to accomplish as well as on what reformers thought they ought to accomplish.

MULTIPLE OBJECTIVES, MULTIPLE TRADE-OFFS

The model that best captures the process of school finance reform is one that posits multiple objectives, multiple trade-offs, and constraints, rather than the simple maximization model implicit in evaluations based solely on equity criteria. Inequalities of tax rates and expenditures and their wealth-relatedness created the occasion for reform in many states, but the reconstruction of school financing systems opened up a broader range of interdependent choices with impacts beyond equity. The choice facing policymakers was not simply whether to equalize, or by how much, but how to allocate scarce resources among multiple objectives—some competing, some complementary, some equity-enhancing, and others not. The determinants of these allocation decisions were political; that is, how the decisions were made depended on who was involved and how they represented their interest.

School finance policy is actually a bundle of three discrete subpolicies, each with its own set of trade-offs: *Revenue policies* prescribe the sources from which school funds are to be derived; *expenditure policies* prescribe the purposes, functions, and distribution criteria for state-level educational expenditures; and *governance poli-*

cies prescribe the division of authority between states and localities. One set of subpolicies cannot be changed without affecting the others in some way. Changing the mix of revenue sources used to finance education affects both the amount of revenue available to fund new programs and the proportional share of revenues derived from state and local sources. Altering the program mix at the state level, by adding new programs or changing the proportional allocation of funds among existing programs, can result in shifts among revenue sources and changes in distribution of authority between states and localities. Increasing the state share of educational expenditures can result in a shift of political effort from the local to the state level, where revenue and expenditure decisions become increasingly important.

The exact form in which revenue, expenditure, and governance issues arise in the construction of school finance reform measures is determined by the extent of tax and expenditure inequities, the legal and fiscal constraints under which policymakers operate, and the mix of interest groups represented. The combination of these factors is unique to each state and sets up a series of trade-offs for policymakers. The resolution of these trade-offs determines the content of reform measures—or the outputs of the political process.

The near-term impacts of school finance reform should be a relatively close approximation to these outputs since the implementation of school financing systems requires relatively few discretionary choices. In other words, observations in the first few years after reform should reveal outcomes that come very close to the "real" objectives of reform, as opposed to the announced objectives of reformers. These outcomes represent what it is possible to achieve, given initial conditions and the play of interest group politics. The outcomes are "very close" to representing the real objectives of reform because reform measures frequently include phase-in provisions and grandfather clauses designed to soften the short-term impact of reform and gradually bring the system into alignment with reform objectives.

Long-term impacts are another matter, however. Certain parameters—property values, assessment practices, personal and corporate income, enrollment, and costs—that are treated as fixed in the short term are subject to change over the long term, altering the performance of financing systems in ways that bear no relationship to policymakers' initial objectives. States with financing systems that relied on a "computational tax rate" to determine the state's share of local expenditures found, for example, that escalating property values and improved assessment practices were dramatically shifting tax burdens from the state to the local level. Many state financing systems contained no allowance for the likelihood that enrollments might decline while costs might continue to escalate or that the relationship between enrollment and costs might vary considerably from one period of time to another. Shifts in enrollment and costs resulted in unanticipated revenue shortfalls for some districts. One would expect the longer-term impacts of reform measures to differ from short-term impacts, other things being equal, by the degree that reforms are sensitive to changes in these parameters. One would also expect impacts to be less and less tied to policymakers' objectives the further one gets from the passage of reform measures when parameters change.

But other things are not always equal in the relationship between short- and long-term impacts; policymakers and interest groups may decide to take an active hand in shaping long-term impacts. To the degree that coalitions that formed around initial reform measures remain stable and active in the face of shifting parameters, one would expect marginal adjustments to be made in the content of school finance policy that would bring longer-term impacts into alignment with policymakers' original objectives. On the other hand, coalitions change over time too, resulting in changes of objectives. So longer-term impacts may differ from short-term impacts, not just as a function of changes in parameters but also as a function of active intervention of new coalitions.

The elements of this model are presented in Table 5-2. Stated briefly, the model predicts that the near-term impact of school finance reform in a given state is a function of a set of initial conditions or constraints and a set of politically-determined trade-offs. The longer-term impact is a function of the sensitivity of reform measures to changes in certain parameters and the stability of reform coalitions.

EXPLAINING IMPACTS

The impacts of school finance reform are highly conditional and variable from state to state. The structure of the model in Table 5-2 suggests why this is true. Reform may originate in arguments

Table 5-2. Constraints, Trade-Offs, Impacts.

Constraints	Trade-Offs	Short-Term Impacts	Parameters	Long-Term Impacts
Court decisions	*Revenue*	*Equity*	Enrollment	*Equity*
Revenue surplus	Tax equity v. tax relief	Expenditure disparities	Property values	*Program Structure*
	Income v. property wealth	Tax rate disparities	Assessment practices	*State-Local Relations*
Interest group organization	Reward effort v. reward wealth	Wealth neutrality	Personal and corporate income	
		Income neutrality	Costs	
Tax structure	*Expenditure*		Coalitions	
	General aid v. targeted expenditures	*Program Structure*		
Disparities in effort, wealth, and expenditure	Wealth neutrality v. equalization	General aid		
	Level-up v. level-down	Special formula provisions		
		Targeted support		
	Governance			
	State expenditure controls v. local determination	*State-Local Relations*		
	State tax limitation v. local determination	State-local share		
	State expenditure categories v. local determination	Expenditure controls		
	On v. off the bargaining table	Tax limitations		
	State v. local share of total expenditures	Program controls		
		Stability, moderate change		

about equity, but it is consummated in political choices that are constrained by prior conditions and made by people with widely varying interests. The exact combination of prior conditions and political interests working on a reform measure is different in each state, but the patterns are similar enough across states to allow for general descriptions. Analysts of school finance policy tend to focus on a narrow band of constraints, choices, and impacts, assuming that equity is the only question before policymakers. Hence, the tendency of analysts is to declare reforms unsuccessful on the basis of single measures of impact or to dispute assessments of success or failure with evidence from individual states. The challenge of explaining impacts lies in neither of these extremes. Instead, it lies in understanding how policymakers manage the array of choices opened up by school finance reform and how these choices add up to changes in tax and expenditure equity, program structure, and state–local relations. It can be speculated that, despite the variability among states, there are some general patterns in the management of these choices and that one can talk about impacts of reform without resorting to single measures or explanations that treat every state as unique. Some existing evidence on how state policymakers handled reform are reviewed and then an attempt is made to distill from that analysis some general propositions that explain impacts.

Constraints, Initial Conditions

Constraints set the initial conditions for politically feasible reform proposals. When school finance reform is forced onto the political agenda, either by litigation or political entrepreneurship, certain limits are set on what constitutes a "reasonable" or "responsible" proposal. Those limits are determined by the dictates of existing law, the amount of money available to finance reform, the organized political interest groups whose preferences must be taken into account, the array of revenue sources that can be used for educational purposes, and existing disparities in tax effort, wealth, and expenditures.

  Court decisions are the most commonly acknowledged set of initial conditions, although, as noted earlier, they stimulated less than half the reform measures. While the influence of courts may be overstated, one would expect court decisions, where they occur, to focus attention on certain aspects of the prereform system and hence to affect the mix of equity objectives and other objectives in the construction of reform proposals (see Chapter 4 in this book). School finance court decisions have been of three types: tax equity decisions, like *Serrano* v. *Priest*; state responsibility decisions, like *Robinson* v. *Cahill*; and special interest decisions, like *Levittown* v. *Nyquist* (Levin 1977: 1). *Serrano*-type cases emphasize inequities of tax burdens and expenditures stemming from variations in property wealth and lead toward remedies that require fiscally neutral financing systems. Most of the pre-*Rodriguez* decisions followed some variant of this logic. State responsibility decisions, like *Robinson*, emphasize the state's obligation to provide adequate funding, described by the "thorough and efficient" standard in New Jersey (Lehne 1978) and the "fully sufficient" standard in Washington State (Gale 1981: 89). These decisions focused attention on the level of the state's contribution as well as expenditure disparities and fiscal neutrality. Special interest decisions, like *Levittown*, are in some respects a backlash against the insensitivity of earlier decisions to the claims of urban school districts (Levin 1977). In *Levittown*, municipal overburden was the central issue.

The shifting legal base of school finance court decisions represents both a search for basic principles and an attempt to adapt reform to differences in the language of state constitutions. The main political consequence of this shifting base, however, is that decisions were framed differently and competing outcomes were given different values in different states.

Tax structures and revenue surpluses work in tandem to determine how much discretionary revenue is available to allocate among reform objectives. A diversified tax structure provides more opportunities to shift educational expenditures among revenue sources. A relatively elastic tax structure permits states to generate surplus revenues during times of economic growth that can be used to fund reform. During the early 1970s many states saw substantial increases in revenue from economic growth and federal revenue sharing. But this situation began to change dramatically in the middle to late 1970s, making it more difficult not only to initiate reforms but also to meet the escalating costs of reforms already undertaken. California and Connecticut provide contrasting examples of these effects. Reform in California took place during a period of exceptional economic growth, with an extraordinarily diversified and elastic tax structure.

A progressive income tax and tight property assessment practices fueled a large growth in state revenues. California's reform resulted in an increase in the state's share of educational expenditures of 41.5 percent, from 36.5 percent in 1971 to 77.8 percent in 1979 (ACIR 1980: 36). Connecticut, on the other hand, began its reform with a narrow and relatively inelastic tax structure (no state income tax), during a period when economic growth had started to slow. There was no revenue surplus with which to finance reform. Hence, the reform enacted provided for a guaranteed tax base but emphasized local control of expenditure decisions. Between 1971 and 1979 the state's share of educational expenditures declined by 5.6 percent, from 39.5 percent to 33.9 percent (ACIR 1980; Odden 1981: 19–20).

Compounding tax and revenue constraints are the base-line disparities in effort, wealth, and expenditure among school districts within states. These disparities effectively determine the cost of leveling up, and they vary widely from state to state (Johns, Alexander, and Stollar 1979; Levin, Muller, Scanlon, and Cohen 1972). States like California, Texas, New York, and Michigan, with wide variations in property wealth, face more difficult reform problems than states like Florida and Utah, where wealth is more uniformly distributed across school districts. In some states the prereform finance system greatly reduced disparities in expenditures from wealth and tax effort, while in others state aid had little effect. These conditions raise the ante on how much the state must offer to achieve a proportional reduction in tax and expenditure disparities. Hence, a state like Colorado, with large initial wealth and expenditure disparities, can produce a relatively large proportional reduction in those disparities, without lowering them into the range that reform advocates regard as acceptable (P. Brown 1981). In states like Utah and Florida, where initial disparities are low, a relatively small state contribution can produce a result that is regarded as acceptable (P. Brown 1981). The constraints imposed by initial disparities coupled with those imposed by tax structure and revenue surpluses effectively limit the proportional reduction in disparities that policymakers can achieve without leveling down or recapturing revenues from wealthy districts. Seven states incorporated some type of recapture mechanism in their reforms—California, Massachusetts, Minnesota, Montana, Utah, Wisconsin, and Maine—but two (Maine and Wisconsin) later repealed them (Odden 1981: 24).

Finally, interest group structure acts as a constraint in the sense that it determines whose views must be taken into account in the construction of reform proposals. In many states, the overlap between school finance reform and state fiscal policy in general broadened the number and type of groups involved in the process of constructing reform measures. Traditionally, education interest groups had dominated state education policy. Where interest group participation broadened to include business and tax relief advocates, fiscal questions tended to compete with or dominate educational policy questions. Tax relief and expenditure controls became entangled with equity questions. In California, for example, Governor Reagan insisted on making school finance reform part of a larger revenue and tax package. This meant that business, agriculture, and taxpayer groups were amply represented in the construction of the reform, in addition to educational interests. The reform measure that emerged from this debate put strong expenditure limits on school systems without producing a high degree of equalization. In the next round of reform, educational interest groups succeeded in breaking school finance issues away from general revenue and tax questions, and the resulting reform produced more equalization and a broad array of special support provisions (Elmore and McLaughlin 1982).

In Colorado a coalition of business groups lobbied for both tax relief and limitations on educational expenditures, which led to budget limitations that reinforced existing inequities. Agricultural interests in Kansas, led by the Kansas Farm Bureau, opposed heavy reliance on property taxes as an index of district wealth and succeeded in including taxable income as part of the statutory definition of district wealth. The Kansas reform also imposed strict budget controls (P. Brown 1981). Strong pressure for property tax relief from business and taxpayer groups in these and other states resulted in decreased reliance on local property taxes, across-the-board aid to all districts, and an increase in state support that had only limited effects on tax and expenditure equity (see Geske and Rossmiller 1977, on Wisconsin; Byron 1978, on Indiana).

Education interest groups had little direct incentive to support equalization measures, since their memberships cut across all types of districts. Teacher groups tended to lobby for increased state aid without emphasizing equity. School boards and school administrators tended to lobby first for increased state expenditures and increased local control and then for equalization measures that did not threaten the interests of their diverse membership. Leveling up and "something for everyone" tended to be the bywords of these organizations.

The exact content of reform proposals and the manner in which reform was introduced to the political agenda of states were heavily influenced by initial conditions in those states. These initial conditions imposed certain limits that effectively defined what was considered to be a responsible, politically feasible proposal. And these definitions of "responsible" and "politically feasible" did not always accord with what advocates of reform regarded as necessary to remedy the inequities of existing school finance systems.

Objectives, Trade-Offs

Constructing a reform package is a process of active bargaining and partisan mutual adjustment. A given set of initial conditions produces an array of interest groups that express their objectives, at some point in the bargaining process, in terms of concrete statutory language. Policymakers, who are formally charged with deciding among objectives, are confronted with a series of trade-offs. Some sets of objectives present policymakers with zero-sum trade-offs. Each dollar allocated to tax relief, for example, is a dollar that cannot be used to level up. Some objectives complement each other. Tax relief for the most heavily burdened districts, coupled with increased state aid to raise expenditures in those districts, serves both tax relief and equity objectives. Still other sets of objectives are independent enough of each other to allow for positive sum trade-offs. Leveling up through the general aid system serves the objective of teachers to put more unrestricted funds on the bargaining table, at the same time it serves to reduce expenditure disparities.

The trade-offs presented in Table 5-2 are for illustrative purposes and are not intended to exhaust the full range of possibilities confronting policymakers. The basic idea is that trade-offs arise in distinguishable but interdependent packages that correspond to revenue, expenditure, and governance policies. In the revenue area, the essential trade-offs have to do with (1) the degree to which reform is designed to equalize tax burdens or simply to reduce them; (2) the degree to which educational revenues are to be derived from income or from property; and (3) the degree to which tax systems should reward effort or wealth. Notice that each side of a trade-off corresponds to a distinguishable interest that is likely to be represented in the construction of a reform measure. Expenditure trade-offs have to do with (1) the degree to which state support is to be channeled to the local level through unrestricted general aid or through programs that target local expenditures on certain functions or groups; (2) the degree to which state support is designed to provide equal rewards for equal effort or simply to reduce expenditure disparities; and (3) the degree to which state support is designed to bring low-spending districts up or to hold high-spending districts down. Governance trade-offs deal with the division of responsibility between states and localities in tax, expenditure, and program content decisions, as well as the state's influence over the distribution of power between labor and management in local bargaining decisions. Here the basic issue is the degree to which state interests are distinguishable from local interests and the degree to which the former should be translated into explicit controls over local discretion.

Representing the construction of reform measures as a series of interdependent trade-offs focuses attention on two important aspects of school finance reform. First, it underscores the point that reform is not a simple maximization problem in which the success of policymakers can be evaluated by single outcome measures like wealth neutrality or expenditure and tax disparities. In fact, the range of objectives that potentially comes into play during the construction of reform measures is far broader than the simple maximization model suggests. School finance policy is like a house of cards; removing one piece for inspection and reconstruction potentially means revising the relationship among all pieces. Second, the range of objectives and trade-offs confronting policymakers is determined by the range of interests represented and by the constraints imposed through revenues, tax structure, and prior law. What appears to be a simple "dilution" of equity objectives by competing political interests is actually a much more complex series of interdependent choices, in which equity is one of a number of competing objectives. The sum of changes in the relationship between states and localities across revenue, expenditure, and governance may be much greater than the changes discernible through equity outcomes.

In some states, like Florida, South Carolina, and Utah, initial reform proposals were constructed by school finance experts from the state department of education or from outside the state. These experts tended to take their cues from national reference groups that emphasized reduction of tax and expenditure disparities, the promotion of wealth neutrality as the governing principle of school finance, and allowances for differences in student needs. In these cases, the interests of school finance experts set the agenda for early discussions, but the play of political interests through the legislative process expanded that agenda to include other objectives. Odden (1981: 39) found evidence of involvement by individuals associated with a "national network" of school finance reformers in eleven of twenty-eight reform states and evidence of executive or legislative task forces on school finance reform in all reform states.

The interplay of reformers' objectives with other interests is amply illustrated by the case of Florida, where equalization proved to be a strong force in reshaping the school financing system. During the 1960s, the Florida legislature, led by Representative Terrell Sessums of Tampa, used public concern over rising tax rates, unequal assessment practices, and unequal tax rates to build a reform coalition around school finance. As pressure for tax relief mounted during the 1960s, the legislature imposed "millage caps" that limited local school districts' ability to raise revenues, forcing them to turn to the state for support. Once backing for reform was widespread, Governor Askew appointed a blue-ribbon commission. School finance experts were hired to assist the commission in developing a reform proposal. The product of the commission was a sophisticated financing system based on pupil needs with a narrow range of local tax discretion and a high level of state support. The package was met with approval by most school districts, but Miami and Fort Lauderdale, among other urban districts, protested their loss of state revenue under the proposal and demanded cost-of-living allowances in the formula as the price for their support. Over time, then, policymakers managed to deal with tax relief, expenditure equalization, and urban differentials, but the net effect was less-than-optimal from the perspective of reformers (P. Brown 1981: 88–167).

California provides another example of attention to multiple objectives. The *Serrano* decision legitimized a small group of legislative and executive branch reformers who had been calling attention to expenditure and tax inequities for a number of years. Low-wealth, low-expenditure school districts, however, were not strongly represented in the formulation of proposals. Once the terms of the reform package began to be negotiated, educational interest groups coalesced around the one objective they could all agree upon: increased expenditures for education. Hence, debate did not center on equalization but on the allocation of state revenue surpluses to targeted assistance and increases in the foundation level for general aid. Both California governors who worked on school finance reform— Ronald Reagan and Jerry Brown—saw it less as an opportunity for equalization than as a vehicle for fiscal control and accountability in the school system. Wilson Riles, California's strong and politically sophisticated chief state school officer, viewed equalization as one of three equally important objectives—the other two being assistance targeted on students with special needs and school-level planning. The leading advocates of equalization and wealth neutrality were staff in the Assembly, the Governor's Department of Revenue, and the Legislative Analyst's Office—so-called *Serrano* Hawks. Leading members of the Assembly, including long-time reform advocate Leroy Greene of Sacramento, backed equalization, but couched their position in terms of increased support for education overall and a host of categorical programs addressed to students with special needs and organizational reform. Senators were moderate in their support of equity objectives and overtly opposed to large increases in educational expenditures. The result of this mix of interests was an enormous omnibus bill, which included large increases in foundation support, moderate equalization based on the principle of guaranteed yield, a small recapture provision for districts at the extreme high end of wealth and expenditures, large amounts of money directed at special student populations, and an ambitious organizational reform program based on the principle of school-based planning. The projected cost of the measure was $4.5 billion over three years, an amount that cut deeply into the state's revenue surplus and precluded any serious property tax relief. Within a year of its passage, the school finance provisions of the bill were obliterated by the passage of Proposition 13 (Elmore and McLaughlin 1982: 113–68).

Where supporters of tax relief, tax equity, and expenditure equalization met head-on, as in Kansas, the trade-offs attending reform were very complex. The Kansas Association of School Boards and the Kansas Farm Bureau led the movement for reform, but their objectives were quite distinct and contradictory. Education lobbyists in Kansas, as elsewhere, were concerned mainly about the level of state support for education and the differential costs facing districts. Focusing their attention on wealth and enrollment disparities, the school boards association developed a sophisticated formula allowing for different expenditure levels depending on size and wealth. The farmers, on the other hand, focused their attention on reducing reliance on property taxes. Their proposal included increasing the state's share of educational expenditures, limiting local expenditures, and substituting taxable income for assessed property valuation as the measure of district wealth. The legislature forged a compromise between these two sets of interests, using tax equity as its guiding principle. A higher state guarantee gave tax relief to the most heavily-burdened districts and increased expenditures in the poorest districts. The percentage of taxable income used to compute district wealth was increased, but the property tax was not eliminated, hence balancing rural and urban interests. Variable expenditure limits slowed the rate of growth in school expenditures, while allowing low expenditure districts to move gradually up to the level of other districts in the same enrollment category. Hence, competing, often contradictory, interests were meshed into a single system: tax relief, increased state share, adjustments of expenditure to scale, and equalization (P. Brown 1981: 88–167).

Equally interesting are instances in which the politics were more lopsided. Michigan, for example, was one state that opted for an "equal yield" approach that emphasized local control at the expense of virtually all other objectives, including equalization. Under the Burseley plan, the state's role was defined as producing equal fiscal opportunities by equalizing revenue yield per tax mill, so that a one-mill levy in Grand Rapids would raise the same amount of revenue per pupil as a one-mill levy in Lansing. Districts raising more than the state guarantee, however, were virtually unrestricted in their expenditures. Further, districts were encouraged to raise local taxes to improve educational quality. In the early years of its operation, this preference for local control resulted in an actual increase in disparities in tax rates and expenditures among Michigan school districts (P. Brown 1981: 277).

School finance systems, as these examples indicate, are not simply mechanisms for raising and distributing revenue. They also are ways of expressing the state's political and administrative role in education and signaling to local political constituencies how their interests are represented in state capitols. Opening up school finance for political scrutiny entails addressing the full range of policy questions related to the state role in education, not just those dealing with equalization. Furthermore, the trade-offs that policymakers are forced to confront in the process of reconstructing school finance systems are not "controlled" either by reformers or by policymakers themselves. Which trade-offs are posed in which way is a function of the structure and skill of interest groups. As the interest groups operating on school finance reform became more diverse and differentiated, the number of trade-offs pushed before state policymakers increased, as did the complexity of the resulting reform measures. To say that equity objectives were "diluted" by competing objectives in the process of reform is, to some degree, a misstatement of how reform occurs, since it implies that equity is the sole criterion upon which reasonable people should evaluate school finance systems. The process is less one of dilution than it is of finding an optimal mix of several objectives, each of which represents some critical ingredient of revenue, expenditure, and governance policies. If one is interested only in questions of equity, as most reformers are, then any mix of objectives seems to be a dilution. If one is interested in the full range of revenue, expenditure, and governance questions raised by school finance, as state policymakers of necessity are forced to be, then there is no choice but to find the politically feasible mix.

Roughly coincidental with the upsurge in school finance reform, two major changes occurred in the structure of interest group politics around education that affected the way reform occurred. The first of these was the breakup of the National Education Association (NEA) in the late 1960s and early 1970s, which resulted in a split between administrators and teachers at the state level. The NEA's militant pro-teacher position was reflected in both political action and collective bargaining. At the state level, its main consequence was the dissipation of what had previously been a united front of education interests in state-level politics. The second major change was the growing political sophistication of large urban school systems, which came to see themselves as having political interests much different from other systems. Their heavy reliance on federal and state assistance to augment local tax bases led them to organize independent lobbying efforts in Washington, D.C., and state capitols.

The effects of these political shifts were twofold. First, they turned what had previously been a relatively narrow, technically dominated policy area into one that was highly politicized. Second, they resulted in an alignment of political interests that bore no relationship whatever to the equity objectives of school finance reformers.

Before 1970 in California, for example, most school finance policy questions were handled routinely by deferring to the judgment of Oscar Anderson, the lobbyist for the NEA-affiliated California Teachers Association, and Ron Cox, the state education department's school finance expert. By the mid-1970s, it was impossible to construct a school finance measure without the concurrence of at least three large teacher organizations, one administrators' association, one association of school boards, two service employee organizations, six large urban school districts, and two organizations representing high and low wealth districts. These were only the education interests. At various times business, agricultural, and taxpayer organizations also figured in school finance negotiations. In order to somewhat structure this array of interests, leading education lobbyists created a loose organization called the "Tuesday Night Group" to serve as a negotiating and bargaining arena for educational interests (Elmore and McLaughlin 1982).

Although the situation in other states was not so complex as that in California, splits between teachers and administrators and between large and small districts played a role in most reform debates. Teacher groups tended to support large increases in untargeted state aid that could be easily translated into salary increases at the local level. Administrators vacillated between the local autonomy entailed in untargeted aid and their desire to keep state aid off the bargaining table through targeting of expenditures. Urban districts, both property-rich and property-poor, tended to coalesce around targeted programs that would relieve the pressure of high-cost pupils. Smaller districts tended to coalesce around increases in untargeted support. The very smallest districts, however, tended to pull loose from others and argue, like the urban districts, for special state subsidies—in their case designed to compensate for diseconomies of sparsity.

This splintering of educational interests made the construction of reform coalitions difficult. Not surprisingly, the politics of reform focused less on the questions of equalization and wealth neutrality that troubled reform advocates and more on constructing a package of side-payments sufficient to bind an increasingly divided education lobby together. These side-payments took the form of revisions of the general aid formula to account for high-cost pupils and sparsity, phased introduction of reforms and grandfather clauses to soften the immediate impact of reform, targeted assistance programs outside the general aid formula to compensate for special needs and keep money off the bargaining table, and so forth. Simply stated, educational interests did not cleave neatly along wealth and expenditure lines. Hence, reform coalitions were not constructed out of beneficiaries of equalization or wealth neutrality but out of interests that cut across wealth and expenditure lines.

Conclusion: Impacts

The analysis leads to two main conclusions about the impacts of school finance reform. First, impacts must be understood in terms of the decision processes that produce them, rather than simply in terms of their approximation to abstract standards of equity. It has been argued in this chapter that the process of constructing reforms is best understood as one of allocating scarce resources among competing objectives within constraints rather than as one of maximizing performance on a single objective. Second, given the multiple objectives and trade-offs that characterize the construction of reforms, the impacts of reform are to be found not simply in equity outcomes (expenditure and tax disparities, wealth neutrality, and income neutrality) but also in the structure of state programs and in the political and administrative relationship between states and localities. The range of impacts across these categories, the magnitude of impacts within categories, and the particular mix of impacts that characterizes a given reform measure are all by-products of the initial conditions under which reform was undertaken and the array of political interests represented in the construction of reforms.

If there is a practical message in this analysis, it is that reform is more a matter of political organization than it is of principle or technical expertise. Principles of equity served to focus attention on the inadequacies of existing financing systems, but reformers were unable to agree upon a clear and consistent set of guidelines for reform. The technical expertise of reformers helped to focus the terms of debate and to express those terms in general aid distribution formulas, but reformers themselves had little influence on the way trade-offs were made in the construction of reform measures. The most influential factor in determining the content of reform measures, and hence their short-term impact, was the structure of interest groups. The major cleavages among interest groups working on school finance reform cut across, and did not reinforce, the equity objectives of reformers. The surest way to influence the mix of objectives included in a reform measure is to organize a political constituency around those objectives one regards as important. There were strong state-level constituencies for tax relief and expenditure controls outside the realm of education interest groups. Within the education lobby, there were strong constituencies for increased state expenditures and for special state programs addressed to the needs of certain kinds of districts. But there was no unambiguous constituency for equity objectives, aside from reformers. The main problem with equalization and wealth neutrality as objectives was that they did not offer strong enough inducements to override existing interest group cleavages. Teachers, administrators, and board members from low-wealth, high-tax districts did not perceive the benefits of equalization or wealth neutrality to be strong enough to pull them together into a common front. Instead, their interests as teachers, administrators, and board members tended to override their common interests as low-wealth, high-tax constituents. This was in large part due to the fact that they could trade concessions on equity objectives for progress on other, equally valued, objectives, like increased local control or more money on the bargaining table. Leveling-up was popular, where it was possible, precisely because it served a multitude of objectives, one of which was equalization. The "dilution" of equity objectives perceived by reform advocates is, in fact, the result of the durability of interest group cleavages in the face of reform.

Beyond this practical conclusion, the analysis points to a number of propositions that attempt to explain the impact of reform measures (see Table 5–3). These propositions are viewed as rebuttable, in the sense that they reflect a tentative understanding of the relationship between trade-offs and impacts, instead of a definitive summary of the empirical evidence. The propositions are organized under the headings of equity, program structure, and state-local relations. Most of the terms are self-explanatory, but some require specification. Distinctions have been drawn among general aid, special formula provisions, and targeted assistance as categories for describing state program structure (see Tron 1980; Odden and McGuire 1980; and Winslow and Peterson 1981). General aid is money that passes unrestricted from the state to the local level, special formula provisions

Table 5-3.   Impact Propositions.

---

1. Equity Impacts
   1.1 States with the largest prereform tax and expenditure disparities will show the largest proportional gains on those outcomes after reform.
   1.2 States with prereform revenue surpluses will show greater postreform tax and expenditure equalization than those without surpluses.
   1.3 States that provide tax relief, targeted assistance, and special formula provisions as part of reform measures will show less tax and expenditure equalization than those that do not.
   1.4 States that do not provide increases in targeted assistance and special formula provisions as part of reform measures will show greater wealth neutrality than those that do.
   1.5 States that provide increases in targeted assistance and special formula provisions as part of reform measures will show greater income neutrality than those that do not.
   1.6 The level of equalization, wealth neutrality, or income neutrality achieved by reform states will not vary significantly among different types of general aid distribution formulas.

2. Impacts on Program Structure
   2.1 States with prereform revenue surpluses will show a larger proportion of postreform expenditures on targeted assistance and special formula provisions than those states without prereform surpluses.
   2.2 States with highly differentiated education interest groups will show a larger proportion of postreform expenditures on targeted assistance and special formula provisions than those with undifferentiated interest groups.
   2.3 States with targeted assistance programs and special formula provisions that antedate reform will allocate a larger share of state expenditures to those programs after reform than before.

3. Impacts on State-Local Relations
   3.1 Increases in the state share of educational expenditures in reform states will not, by themselves, increase state program control.
   3.2 Program control will increase more in those states that adopt targeted assistance programs as part of reform measures than in those that rely on general aid and special formula provisions.
   3.3 States that increase their share of educational expenditures as a result of reform will assert greater fiscal control at the local level than states that do not increase their share.
   3.4 States that adopt tax relief as part of their reform measures are more likely to impose tax and expenditure controls than those that do not.

---

are adjustments to the general aid formula for certain types of districts, and targeted assistance programs are programs separate from the general aid formula. Distinctions also have been drawn between program control and fiscal control in the propositions about state-local relations. Program control entails state-mandated activities in local school systems; fiscal control entails tax and expenditure limits imposed by state law on local districts.

The equity propositions in Table 5–3 follow the logic of the argument about the effect of initial conditions and trade-offs noted earlier. One would expect the greatest proportional change in tax and expenditure disparities to occur in those states with the greatest pre-reform disparities, even though these states usually will not fully meet a priori standards of equity. In highly unequal finance systems, simply changing the general aid formula will have dramatic equalization effects. The larger the increase in state aid as a proportion of total expenditures, the larger the equalization effects. Hence, those states that had revenue surpluses available to boost the state share can be expected to show greater equalization effects than those that did not. At some point, however, equalization becomes more difficult to achieve; that point is where marginal reductions in expenditure and tax disparities can be purchased only at the expense of other objectives that have a zero-sum relationship to equalization.

Tax relief, targeted assistance, and special formula provisions generally reduce the equalization effect of state aid, either by directly compensating for losses suffered as a result of equalization or by allocating proportional shares. Tax relief generally conflicts with both tax and expenditure equalization, since it usually takes the form of an across-the-board assumption of some share of the local tax base. Special assistance provisions for transportation, special education, vocational education, compensatory education, bilingual education, and small schools, whether introduced as special formula provisions or as targeted assistance, tend to accentuate rather than dampen expenditure differences. The larger the share of targeted assistance and special formula provisions, the greater the disequalizing effects (P. Brown 1981). To the degree that property wealth correlates positively with the indices used to distribute special aid—as it is likely to do with special education and with aid targeted on very large and very small districts—then one would also expect wealth neutrality to decline as special aid increases. But to the degree that the indices used to distribute special assistance compensate districts on the basis of concentration of low-income students (compensatory education) or on the basis of factors negatively related to income (bilingual education), then increases in special assistance should increase income neutrality. Stated in terms of interest group politics, targeted assistance and special formula provisions are ways of moderating the equalization effect of reform, of moderating the wealth neutrality effects of reform, and of increasing the income neutrality of reform.

A corollary proposition is that the *type* of formula used to distribute general aid—power equalization, foundation, or equal yield, for example—is not the decisive factor in determining the equity impacts of reform. One would not expect the equity impacts of reform to vary significantly among different types of general aid formulas because (1) the various types of formulas have been shown to be mathematically equivalent (Morgan 1974) and (2) the primary equity impacts are determined by trade-offs between general aid and special assistance provisions rather than in the construction of the general aid formula itself. Technical debates over which type of formula produces the best equity effect miss the essential political point that equity impacts are affected mainly by the effectiveness of political interests in extracting concessions to the general aid formula.

The propositions dealing with program structure in Table 5-3 follow closely from the equity propositions. The effect of reform on program structure can be expected to vary among states as a function of the availability of surplus revenues, the level of differentiation of interest groups, and the program structure that antedates reform. At any level of interest group differentiation, the presence of a fiscal surplus at the time of reform presents an invitation for competing political interests to trade among tax relief, equity, and special assistance objectives. One would expect the result of this trading to be a general increase in the complexity of program structure at the state level. Of the twenty-eight reform states identified by Odden (1981), for example, twelve instituted compensatory education programs, either through targeted assistance or special formula adjustments, and ten of those twelve had fiscal surpluses at the time of reform.

As interest group differentiation increases, the likelihood that trades will be made among tax relief, equity, and special assistance objectives increases, regardless of the presence of a fiscal surplus. So one would expect the complexity of state program structure to increase as a result of reform in those states with highly differentiated interest groups, and one would expect a larger proportion of state aid to flow through targeted assistance and special formula provisions after reform in those states than before. Likewise, a structure for targeted assistance and special concessions that antedates reform increases the likelihood that larger shares will be allocated to those programs after reform than before.

The effect of reform on state–local relations, described in Table 5–3, cannot be expected to vary systematically with increases in the state share of educational expenditures. A greater state share of expenditures does not automatically lead to greater state control of local decisions (Wirt 1980). However, if one distinguishes between program control and fiscal control, the effects of increased state expenditures can be tracked to the local level. Increases in the state share lead to state-level political pressures from tax relief advocates for tax and expenditure limitations, which over time translate into fiscal controls. In some instances, these fiscal controls were built into the reform measure itself—Kansas and Washington state are examples—and in other instances fiscal controls came as a backlash to large state expenditure increases—California is the outstanding example. The effect of fiscal controls is not so much on the *kind* of activities that local districts pursue as on the *level* of activities; so one can conceive, theoretically at least, of a system with radically decentralized program controls and highly centralized fiscal controls. Hence, long state traditions of "local control" over school programs can coexist with rather significant changes in the distribution of fiscal control. Whether the split between program and fiscal control occurs depends largely on how school administrators and boards negotiate the trade-off between a larger state share, hence less pressure on local bases, and more emphasis on targeted assistance, which brings more state program control. Obviously, the larger the proportion of special state assistance that can be built into formula adjustments, instead of targeted assistance, the less program control comes with increased state aid but the more fiscal control is likely to develop.

In terms of their expected impact on state–local relations, then, changes in the general aid formula and in special formula provisions are qualitatively different from changes in the structure of targeted assistance programs. One would expect program control to increase only as a result of increases in targeted assistance. Moreover, one would expect the long-term, if not the short-term, consequence of increases in general aid and special formula adjustments to be increased state fiscal control.

It is extraordinarily difficult to specify the differences one would expect between short-term and long-term impacts of school finance reform. But it is useful to call attention to three important issues in distinguishing short-term from long-term impacts. First, virtually every school finance reform package contained phase-in provisions and grandfather clauses designed to soften the immediate impact of reform on local school budgets. So the short-term effects, measured in terms of one or two years after reform, are not necessarily a reliable indicator of the intended impact of reform.

Second, rather substantial tax and expenditure shifts are occurring independently of school finance reform, and it is to some degree impossible to distinguish these shifts from those that are caused by reform. For example, property taxes as a proportion of total state and local tax collections have been declining steadily since 1902 — they have dropped from 82 percent to 30 percent from 1902 to the present and from 39 percent to 30 percent since 1972. At the same time, reliance on sales and income taxes has increased — from 18 percent to 23.5 percent since 1972 for sales taxes and from 14 percent to 18.5 percent for income taxes (ACIR 1980: Table 47). From 1967 to 1977 the amount of local school revenue drawn from property taxes declined from 47 percent to 42 percent at the same time that local reliance on intergovernmental revenue transfers was increasing from 44.3 percent to 50.2 percent (Behrens 1980: 22, 33). In the period 1971 to 1979 the state share of elementary and secondary education revenue increased an average of 11 percent in the states. But of the twenty-eight states that passed school finance reform measures during that period, fifteen failed to meet the average revenue increase for the period, which suggests that large shifts in fiscal responsibility for education are occurring quite independently of school finance reform (ACIR 1980: Table 26; Odden 1981: 39).

A similar shift has occurred toward targeted assistance programs throughout the states as demands from special needs populations have increased. Reform states, on average, have added five categorical programs to their education portfolio during the 1970s, while nonreform states, on average, added only three such programs. Overall, the number of state-funded targeted assistance programs increased from an average of six in 1968 to over nine in 1978, representing an increase from 13 percent to 23 percent of total state aid to education (Tron 1980). Although this shift from general aid to targeted assistance programs has been more pronounced in the reform states, it is the product of generalized demands for special programs and not just school finance reform.

All of these trends suggest that one should proceed with extreme caution in attributing major changes in equity, program structure, and state–local relations to school finance reform. In fact, school finance reform may be as much an *effect* of long-term shifts in revenue and expenditure patterns than a cause of those shifts.

Finally, it was suggested above that the long-term impact of school finance reform depends on the stability of the parameters on which funding systems are based and on the stability of the political coalitions that produced those systems. It seems unlikely that either of these will remain stable. In order for states to continue equalizing by leveling-up, they must raise state guarantee levels relative to average per pupil expenditures. As inflation drives up per pupil costs, however, the increase necessary to provide further equalization goes up an equivalent amount, making it more difficult for states to produce a real increase in equalization. In addition, contrary to the budget surpluses that many states had in the peak of the reform period, many states face severe budget problems and many face constitutional requirements for a balanced budget. This means that maintenance of the state share of educational expenditures, not to mention increases, will in many states mean zero-sum politics with other state activities—health, welfare, prisons, and so forth. These developments occur in a political climate where the number of voters with school-aged children is steadily declining, where school enrollment continues to decline or at best to stabilize, and where the real dollar costs of schooling continue to climb (Kirst and Garms 1980). None of these signs suggests stability; all suggest that the trade-offs that have characterized school finance policy will be subject to continued redefinition and renegotiation for the foreseeable future.

REFERENCES

Advisory Commission on Intergovernmental Relations (ACIR). 1980. *Significant Features of Fiscal Federalism.* Washington, D.C.

Behrens, John. 1980. "Property Taxes and Property Values: What's New About Base, Burden, and Other Mysteries." In *Public School Finance Programs, 1978–1979,* edited by Esther Tron, pp. 22–41. Washington, D.C.: Government Printing Office.

Berne, Robert, and Leanna Stiefel. 1978. "Measuring the Equity of Public Policies: The Case of Public Education." Public Policy Research Institute, Graduate School of Public Administration, New York University. Mimeo.

Brown, L.; A. Ginsburg; J. Killalea; R. Rosthal; and E. Tron. 1978. "School Finance Reform in the Seventies: Achievements and Failures." *Journal of Education Finance* 4, no. 2 (Fall): 195–212.

Brown, Patricia. 1981. "A Comparative State Study of the Politics and Impact of Education Finance Reform." Doctoral dissertation, University of Texas, Austin.

Byron, Richard. 1978. "Equalization of Educational Opportunity in Indiana." *Journal of Education Finance* 3, no. 4 (Spring): 432–42.

Carroll, Stephen. 1979a. *The Search for Equity in School Finance: Results from Five States.* Santa Monica, Calif.: The Rand Corporation.

Carroll, Stephen. 1979b. *The Search for Equity in School Finance: Summary and Conclusions.* Santa Monica, Calif.: The Rand Corporation.

Chambers, Jay. 1981. "Cost and Price Level Adjustments to State Aid for Education: A Theoretical and Empirical Review." In *Perspectives in State School Support Programs,* edited by K. Forbis Jordan and Nelda Cambron-McCabe, pp. 39–85. Cambridge, Mass.: Ballinger Publishing Company.

Cohen, David. 1974. "School Finance and Social Policy: *Serrano* and Its Progeny." In *School Finance in Transition,* edited by John Pincus, pp. 287–313. Cambridge, Mass.: Ballinger Publishing Company.

Coons, J.; W. Clune; and S. Sugarman. 1970. *Private Wealth and Public Education.* Cambridge, Mass.: Harvard University Press.

Education Commission of the States. 1981. *Revenues, Expenditures and Tax Burdens: A Comparison of the Fifty States.* Denver, Colorado.

Elmore, Richard, and Milbrey McLaughlin. 1982. *Reform and Retrenchment: The Politics of California School Finance Reform.* Cambridge, Mass.: Ballinger Publishing Company.

Friedman, Lee, and Michael Wiseman. 1978. "Understanding the Equity Consequences of School Finance Reform." *Harvard Educational Review* 48, no. 2 (May): 193–226.

Fuhrman, Susan. 1978. "The Politics and Process of School Finance Reform." *Journal of Education Finance* 4, no. 2 (Fall): 158–78.

Gale, Diana Hadden. 1981. "The Politics of School Finance Reform in Washington State." Doctoral dissertation, University of Washington, Seattle.

Garms, Walter. 1979. "Measuring the Equity of School Finance Systems." *Journal of Education Finance* 4, no. 4 (Spring): 415–35.

Garms, W.; J. Guthrie; and L. Pierce. 1978. *School Finance: The Economics and Politics of Public Education.* Englewood Cliffs, N.J.: Prentice Hall.

Geske, Terry and Richard Rossmiller. 1977. "The Politics of School Finance Reform in Wisconsin." *Journal of Education Finance* 2, no. 4 (Spring): 513–32.

Goertz, Margaret. 1981. "School Finance Reform and the Cities." In *Perspectives in State School Support Programs*, edited by K. Forbis Jordan and Nelda Cambron–McCabe, pp. 113–42. Cambridge, Mass.: Ballinger Publishing Company.

Gray, Virginia. 1973. "Innovation in the States: A Diffusion Study." *American Political Science Review* 67, no. 4 (December): 1174–85.

Hickrod, G.; R. Chaudhari; and V. Lundeen. 1980. "Progress Toward School Finance Equity Goals in Indiana, Iowa, and Illinois." *Journal of Education Finance* 6, no. 2 (Fall): 176–200.

Hodge, Michael. 1981. "Improving Finance and Governance of Education for Special Populations." In *Perspectives in State School Support Programs*, edited by K. Forbis Jordan and Nelda Cambron–McCabe, pp. 3–38. Cambridge, Mass.: Ballinger Publishing Company.

Horowitz, Harold, and Diana Nietring. 1968. "Equal Protection Aspects of Inequalities in Public Education and Public Assistance Programs from Place to Place Within a State." *UCLA Law Review* 15, no. 3 (Winter): 787–816.

Johns, R.; K. Alexander; and D. Stollar. 1969. *Status and Impact of Educational Finance Programs.* Gainesville, Fla.: National Educational Finance Project.

Kirp, David. 1968. "The Poor, the Schools and Equal Protection." *Harvard Educational Review* 38, no. 4 (Fall): 635–68.

Kirst, Michael, and Walter Garms. 1980. "The Political Environment of School Finance Policy in the 1980s." In *School Finance Policies and Practices*, edited by James Guthrie, pp. 47–75. Cambridge, Mass.: Ballinger Publishing Company.

Lehne, Richard. 1978. *The Quest for Justice.* New York: Longman.

Levin, Betsy. 1977. *State School Finance Reform: Court Mandate or Legislative Action?* Washington, D.C.: National Conference of State Legislators.

Levin, B.; T. Muller; W. Scanlon; and M. Cohen. 1972. *Public School Finance: Present Disparities and Fiscal Alternatives.* Washington, D.C.: Department of Health, Education, and Welfare.

McGuire, Kent. 1981. *State and Federal Programs for Elementary and Secondary School Students with Special Needs.* Denver, Colo.: Education Commission of the States.

Melcher, Thomas. 1981. "State Pupil Transportation Programs." In *Perspectives in State School Support Programs*, edited by K. Forbis Jordan and Nelda Cambron–McCabe, pp. 215–47. Cambridge, Mass.: Ballinger Publishing Company.

Morgan, Daniel. 1974. "The Arithmetic of 'No Wealth Discrimination.' " *Social Science Quarterly* 55, no. 2 (September): 310–30.

Odden, Allan, and Kent McGuire. 1980. *Financing Educational Services for Special Populations: The State and Federal Roles.* Denver, Colo.: Education Commission of the States.

Odden, Allan. 1981. "School Finance Reform: An Example of Redistributive Policy at the State Level." Paper presented for the School Finance Project, National Institute of Education.

San Antonio v. Rodriguez, 411 U.S. 1 (1973).

Sherman, Joel. 1981. "Equity Measurement and School Finance Litigation." *Law and Policy Quarterly* 3, no. 4 (October): 442–63.

Sjogren, Jane. 1981. "Municipal Overburden and State Aid for Education." In *Perspectives in State School Support Programs*, edited by K. Forbis Jordan and Nelda Cambron–McCabe, pp. 87–111. Cambridge, Mass.: Ballinger Publishing Company.

Tron, Esther. 1980. *Public School Finance Programs, 1978–1979.* Washington, D.C.: Government Printing Office.

Walker, Jack. 1969. "The Diffusion of Innovations Among the American States." *American Political Science Review* 63, no. 3 (September): 880–99.

Welch, Susan, and Kay Thompson. 1980. "The Impact of Federal Incentives on State Policy Innovation." *American Journal of Political Science* 24, no. 4 (November): 715–29.

Winslow, Harold, and Susan Peterson. 1981. *State Initiatives for Special Needs-Populations.* Palo Alto, Calif.: Bay Area Research Group.

Wirt, Frederick. 1980. "Does Control Follow the Dollar? School Policy, State–Local Linkages, and Political Culture." *Publius* 10, no. 2 (Spring): 69–88.

Wise, Arthur. 1967. *Rich Schools, Poor Schools: The Promise of Equal Educational Opportunity.* Chicago: The University of Chicago Press.

6 EARTHQUAKES OR TREMORS? TAX AND EXPENDITURE LIMITATIONS AND SCHOOL FINANCE

*Mary Frase Williams**

This chapter might have been entitled "The Tax Revolt and School Finance," but that would assume the answer to one of the most important issues. Is there, or was there, a national movement directed at reducing government taxes and spending that resulted in the adoption of tax and expenditure limitations in many states? Or were those adoptions the result of factors specific to individual states, or did both national and state-specific factors contribute to those adoptions?

The purpose of this chapter is to provide at least preliminary answers to two questions: (1) What has been the impact of tax and expenditure limitations (TELs) on school finance to date and (2) what is their likely impact in the future? In order to answer the second question, one has to predict the likelihood of adoptions of additional limits, which requires an examination of the politics of TELs. While the first question could be answered without reference to the politics, an understanding of the politics will provide insight into the reasons for those outcomes. The chapter is organized into three sections: The first examines the politics of the adoption of TELs, the second focuses on their impact, and the third discusses the future of TELs.

*Mary Frase Williams, Senior Research Associate, School Finance Project, United States Department of Education.

The first need is to define the phenomena and the time period to be examined. While some researchers have lumped together both tax reductions and limitations, that will not be the approach used here. The focus will be on measures, whether statutory or constitutional, that impose future constraints on the *procedures* for determining tax or expenditure levels and/or on the *levels* themselves. TELs may result in immediate reductions in tax rates or expenditures, but their more important long-term consequence is to change the rules of the game in terms of state–local finance. Such limitations are not new— they were popular during the 1930s, and many states had local limits in effect at the beginning of the 1970s. While there will be some discussion of the earlier limits, the focus here will be on limits adopted since 1970.

Two types of limits adopted in the 1970s might have affected school finance: those that pertain specifically to education and general limits that apply to state government and most or all local governments. The former apply to local school districts and tended to be adopted in the 1970s as part of school finance reform. Between 1976 and 1980, more than twenty states adopted general limits, one-third of them as the result of an initiative. These limitations were about evenly divided between constitutional and statutory measures (Austermann and Pilcher 1980; ACIR 1980).

THE ADOPTION OF STATE AND LOCAL LIMITS

Almost half of the states enacted some type of limit in the past five years. What factors contributed to these adoptions? Other limits were defeated in some of these states as well as in other states. Considerable research has been devoted to referenda on limits, but there has been little examination of the politics of legislative consideration of TELs. Therefore, this discussion of TEL politics will, of necessity, focus on referenda on limits. The discussion addresses the campaigns for limits and examines voting patterns. The literature on the latter is far more voluminous than on the former. An important theme in both discussions is the role of education.

Campaigns

Attempts to alter state–local financing patterns by use of the initiative process were not a phenomenon unique to the late 1970s. There were such attempts in the early 1970s, including many of the same states in which measures were to appear on the ballot again in the late 1970s. However, the earlier efforts in states such as California, Colorado, Michigan, and Oregon were uniformly unsuccessful, while some of the later efforts were successful.

The unsuccessful campaigns in the early 1970s had a number of common characteristics. In 1972 and 1973 a total of eight state constitutional amendments were placed on the ballot in California, Colorado, Michigan, Oregon, and Washington (all but two of them through an initiative), which would have significantly changed the state–local tax structure (Shalala, Williams, and Fishel 1973; Williams 1976). Nearly all the measures proposed significant limitations on or reductions in local property taxes. The major exception was California's Proposition 1 in 1973, proposed by Governor Reagan, which would have limited state taxes to a declining proportion of income.

All the referenda were highly complex proposals, and their complexity contributed to their defeat. Each had numerous components, and opposition coalitions were formed from groups that opposed different features of the measures. Furthermore, their complexity meant that the long-term consequences were uncertain. Opponents and proponents painted very different scenarios of their impact, with opponents in particular stressing the technical problems of the proposals. The result appeared to be that many voters were confused and in the voting booth chose the system they knew over the unknown consequences of the ballot measure.

It was generally true that many groups opposed each measure and relatively few supported them. In the case of the initiatives, those who put the measure on the ballot had failed or had not tried to build broad coalitions. The measures did not reflect negotiations and compromises designed to build support prior to the circulation of initiative petitions (at which point the measure is in its final form). In most cases education groups opposed these measures, although in Michigan a 1972 proposal was placed on the ballot by the Michigan Education Association.

In 1976 limitation measures were again on the ballot in Michigan and Colorado. Both were defeated and the factors contributing to their defeat were similar to those in 1972 and 1973: lack of resources for the proponents, nearly unanimous opposition by the "Establishment," many questions about the potential impact of the measures, and the complex and technical nature of the proposal (Williams 1979a and 1979b).

The 1978 TEL campaigns in many states have been studied. The unsuccessful campaigns in Colorado, Michigan, and Oregon had much in common with the campaigns of the early 1970s (Palaich, Kloss, and Williams 1980; Williams 1979a and 1979b). There were two limitations on the ballot in Michigan in 1978—one passed, while the other did not. The measure that was defeated, the Tisch proposal, was a complex measure whose impact was unclear and that had little backing from interest groups, public officials, and business. The education groups in Michigan opposed both limitation measures as well as a voucher proposal which was also on the ballot.

The proponent group in Colorado was also small and poorly financed, while the opposition consisted of many interest groups and public officials and was able to mount an extensive campaign. In the earlier referenda campaigns, opponents had conceded the need for changes in the state–local tax structure but had argued that the particular measure on the ballot was not the appropriate vehicle. In 1978, in the wake of a new state limit passed by the legislature, even the need for further limits was not conceded.

Like Michigan, Oregon had two limitation proposals on the ballot in 1978—one very similar to Proposition 13. After the Proposition 13-type proposal gained a place on the ballot, the state legislature passed its own tax-relief/tax-limitation measure and placed it on the ballot as well. Education groups, unions, and local officials tended to oppose the first measure while supporting the second as the lesser of two evils. The Proposition 13-clone received few endorsements from large organizations, and relatively little money was raised by the campaign. The legislative measure received the endorsement of both gubernatorial candidates, and funds were raised from organizations backing the measure. Both measures failed. Confusion may have contributed to both defeats. The measures were complex, and there were numerous charges and countercharges about what the impact of either one would be. In addition, the lack of organization and financial resources probably was a handicap to the supporters of the Proposition 13 look-alike.

Another pattern was observed in many of the unsuccessful campaigns between 1972 and 1978. Poll results early in the campaign showed majority support for the proposal. However, as the campaign continued, the proportion of voters saying they would vote yes declined, and those unsure of their vote increased. On election day many of those uncertain voters appeared to vote no (Williams 1976,

1979a, 1979b; Palaich, Kloss, and Williams 1980). The pattern of poll results suggests that as the voters heard and learned more about the measures, what had originally sounded like a good idea began to appear less desirable.

How did successful campaigns differ from unsuccessful ones? The experiences in California, Idaho, and Michigan provide some insights into this question. The Headlee proposal in Michigan is particularly interesting. That measure was a direct descendent of unsuccessful attempts in 1974 and 1976 (Williams 1979b; Palaich, Kloss, and Williams 1980). The proponents learned from those earlier defeats and revised both the proposal and their campaign strategies in ways that overcame many of the problems of the earlier attempts. Inspired by Reagan's Proposition 1 in California, a Michigan group calling itself Taxpayers United for Tax Limitation had initially tried to place a limitation aimed at curtailing state spending on the ballot in 1974 but had failed to gather enough signatures. Undaunted they tried again in 1976 and were able to place the measure on the ballot, but it was defeated, 54 to 46 percent. Before the 1978 campaign, the proposal was substantially redrafted; in that process most of the major criticisms that had surfaced during the 1976 campaign were addressed and the level of the state spending limit was raised, from 8.3 percent of state personal income to whatever percent of income state spending was at the time of adoption. That change had the effect of transforming the measure from a radical to a moderate limitation; the 8.3 percent limit of the 1976 proposal would have required a reduction in current state spending, while the 1978 measure would only curtail the growth in future state spending. Taxpayers United also acted to address the organizational and financial weaknesses of their previous campaigns. They recruited Richard Headlee, president of a small insurance company with considerable political experience and contacts in the business community, to head the organization. Headlee gave the campaign the respected, visible, and articulate spokesman it had lacked before and also provided access to campaign financing. Unlike 1974 and 1976 Taxpayers United was able to raise substantial amounts of money and to run an extensive and sophisticated media campaign. Most of the money was raised from the business community, with big contributions from several large corporations headquartered in Michigan. (A factor that may have been influential in securing corporate contributions was a change in the state's campaign financing laws in 1977 that clarified the rules applying to such contributions.)

The Headlee proposal also benefited from Proposition 13 and campaign decisions made by the opposition. There were two other measures on the Michigan ballot in November 1980 that were far more frightening to the education groups and other members of the opposition coalitions. One was a voucher proposal and the second was the Tisch proposal, a radical property-tax limitation initiated by a minor county official. The Tisch proposal had been languishing until the passage of Proposition 13, at which point momentum picked up and the necessary signatures to place it on the ballot were collected quickly. In comparison to the Tisch and Voucher proposals, the Headlee proposal seemed moderate. In particular, the limitation aspect of the Headlee proposal was seen as one with which the state could live, since the current level of state spending relative to income, which would have determined the limit, was high. Two opposition coalition groups were formed, one to oppose vouchers and the second to oppose all three measures, with some overlap in the membership of the two groups. The umbrella coalition was not formed until early October, and by default the Michigan Education Association (MEA) was responsible for the major effort against both the Tisch and Headlee proposals. The MEA decided early in the campaign to concentrate on the Tisch and Voucher proposals because they felt they had to defeat those measures. They could not live with passage of either one, whereas while they would like to see the Headlee proposal defeated, it would not be a disaster if it did pass. In addition, because of the revisions in the Headlee proposal, which had both greatly strengthened its technical merits and made it more moderate, it was much more difficult to criticize and to campaign against. Furthermore, many candidates and politicians were wary of the strength of public sentiment for tax and expenditure reductions and were reluctant to oppose all three measures on the ballot. Governor Milliken and many others opted to support the Headlee proposal and oppose the Tisch and Voucher proposals. The Michigan School Boards Association (MSBA) wavered on the Headlee proposal; the board of directors voted to support it but was later overruled by the delegate assembly.

The Headlee proposal won very narrowly at the polls (52 percent to 48 percent). In the last weeks of the campaign, the MEA changed its campaign strategy and focused more on the proposal. During the same period polls showed support for it dropping. Given the narrow margin of victory and the declining support, only slight changes in circumstances might have led to its defeat. Had the MEA campaigned more vigorously against it, or had the MSBA position been consistent, or had candidates and public officials been less afraid of the strength of the taxpayer's revolt in Michigan, the Headlee proposal might not have passed. As it was, the campaign surrounding the proposal was not marked by the handicaps that were characteristic of the unsuccessful proposals: poorly financed, a measure unrefined in the fires of negotiation and compromise, lack of support from prominent groups and individuals, and a numbers debate about the impact of the measure.

Contributing to the success of the property tax limitations in California, Idaho, and Massachusetts were specific grievances in each state about the state–local tax structure (and the property tax in particular) and a sense that the politicians had caused and/or failed to respond to those problems. In the case of California the problems centered around the combination of rapidly rising property tax bills, especially on residential property (Gold 1981a) and the growing state surplus. Polls showed the level of support dropping during the campaign, but when the assessor in Los Angeles County (and then those in other counties) released new, sharply higher assessments shortly before the election, it rekindled the enthusiasm for Proposition 13 (Baratz and Moskowitz 1978). Furthering that turnaround was the release of higher estimates of the size of the state surplus and Governor Brown's change in position on 13. While opponents tried to engage in the kind of numbers debate about the impact of the measure that had been so successful in other times and places, it did not have the same effect in this case. Opponents of the measure painted dire pictures of the service cutbacks that would result from Proposition 13, but the credibility of those predictions was not great. Contributing to such skepticism was the fact that the opponents tended to be people and groups associated with state and local government (public officials, public employees, or the beneficiaries of public programs), plus a large state surplus that could be used to offset the reductions in property taxes, the widespread feeling that taxes could be cut without reducing services, and the lack of trust in state and local officials. The situation in California at the time of Proposition 13 was unique in terms of the level of taxes and the size of the state surplus. Both factors contributed to the perception of the need for a limit. The existence of the large surplus probably contributed to the commonly held views that Proposition 13 would not lead to service reductions and that taxes could be reduced considerably without reducing services (Lipset and Schneider 1980).

Idaho and Massachusetts adopted statutory measures, rather than constitutional amendments. That may have contributed to their success in two ways. It eliminated one of the arguments made in every state where the limitation was a constitutional measure—that complex tax policy should not be written into the state constitution. In addition, it enabled the supporters of the initiative to argue that if the limitation had unanticipated or undesirable consequences, the legislature could quickly amend it, even repeal it, to remedy the problem. The latter might have been a factor in these states, since both involved considerable cutbacks in property taxes and neither state had a surplus to offset the local revenue losses. People may have been less concerned about the predictions of dire consequences in a situation where such consequences, if they materialized, could be overcome more easily and quickly. (In cases where the limit applies only to future rates of growth and is moderate in nature, or where there is a large surplus, it may matter less whether the measure is statutory or constitutional.)

Similar to California, Idaho had recent sharp increases in residential property assessments and taxes (Gold 1981a). In Idaho that had occurred not because of rapid increases in the value of property but because of changes in assessment policies and to a lesser extent because of increased local spending. However, even after these increases, Idaho could not be characterized as a state with high taxes or spending levels or high growth in the state–local sector.

In Idaho, the increases in assessments and a marked increase in the proportion of property taxes paid by residential properties (from 29 percent in 1965 to 42 percent in 1977) were the outgrowth of a state supreme court decision in the late 1960s (Palaich, Kloss, and Williams 1980). Local assessors had traditionally assessed residential property at a lower rate than other types of property. The state legislature had tried to formalize this practice in the mid 1960s, but the state supreme court ruled the statute unconstitutional. It also ordered that all property in the state be assessed at a uniform rate by 1982. Counties varied greatly in the speed with which they complied with the court order. The State Tax Commission mandated an accelerated reappraisal program in three counties in 1977. One was a large county in the Boise area where taxes rose by 28 percent on average and far more for some homeowners whose properties had been greatly underassessed. The county took advantage of the assessment increase and raised its budget approximately 50 percent in the same year. Other counties acted similarly.

Not only did some Idaho homeowners experience sharp increases in property taxes, but they also resented the state government's lack of action to provide property tax relief. A Proposition 13-type measure had been introduced in the legislature but had failed to pass. The legislature had enacted some tax relief measures, but many felt they were inadequate. The failure of the legislature to enact more comprehensive measures related to property tax relief or limitations was one reason the state's residents were receptive to the initiative. Unlike California, Idaho does not have a history of frequent use of the initiative process. Prior to 1978 only eleven initiatives had ever been placed on the ballot—and four had passed. The 60,000 signatures on the petitions for Proposition 1 were the most ever gathered on an Idaho initiative.

There was not a substantial difference in the resources and size of the campaigns of the proponents and opponents. They spent similar amounts of money. The supporters of the measure included groups such as the Idaho Property Owners Association and an apartment owners association, and the speaker of the House, who was the Republican candidate for governor. The coalition opposing the measure did not hire a staff but relied on volunteer help from the member organizations, primarily education, public employee, and local government groups. Most of the effort was devoted to grassroots campaigning where members of the organizations could be used as campaign workers. The group decided early in the campaign not to emphasize service cuts and layoffs. Their polls indicated that people were not taking such threats seriously and viewed them as "scare tactics." This meant that one element of the debate about the impact of the measure had been nearly eliminated and that the discussion of impact focused on the tax consequences of the measure. Such a definition of the campaign issues favored the supporters. "[A]nti-initiative forces had only their generalized predictions about how the measure would eventually cost homeowners more. In contrast, initiative leaders could show the number of dollars a property owner would pocket" (Palaich, Kloss, and Williams 1980: 55). Another factor that may account for the failure of the numbers debate to persuade more voters to preserve the status quo may have been a feeling that it would be Proposition 1 or nothing in terms of tax relief or limitations. Not only was there no alternative measure on the ballot, as in California, Michigan, and Oregon (which had been an explicit decision made by the anti-initiative forces that in retrospect at least some questioned), but there also was skepticism that the legislature would act if the measure failed. (However, it has not been uncommon in situations where the failure of the legislature to act has spurred an initiative to find adoption of new legislation in the wake of the defeated initiative. The resort to the initiative process may stimulate the fear in the legislature that if they do not act, the next initiative could be successful.)

Polls prior to the Idaho election showed a pattern found in many states. Support was the highest early in the campaign and gradually declined, with corresponding increases in the proportions of opponents and undecideds. Furthermore, the undecideds were likely to subsequently become opponents. However, this pattern was reversed in the last weeks of the Idaho campaign as those who originally had been undecided switched to supporting the measure, perhaps influenced by last minute ads that emphasized the amount of property taxes owners would save.

Massachusetts shared some characteristics with both Idaho and California—high taxes with the latter, a statutory measure with the former, and anger with the state legislature for failure to act to reduce property taxes with both (Tvedt 1981; Tompkins 1981). All of these factors may have contributed to the passage of Proposition 2½. Massachusetts in 1980 was characterized by a high state–local tax burden and a very heavy reliance on the property tax to finance public services. This was not a new situation. The need for realigning the state–local tax structure had been a theme articulated by many commissions, business and interest groups, and public officials for more than thirty years. A second theme that gained prominence in the 1970s was the need to limit or reduce the level of state–local taxes in order to preserve or improve the state's competitiveness relative to other states as an attractive location for commerce and industry.

Despite the recognition that the tax structure was unbalanced, the legislature over the years had failed to take long-term steps to redress the imbalance. There were increases in state taxes, but they primarily paid for new or expanded state activities. Between 1978 and 1980 the state legislature had numerous opportunities to act to limit or reduce state and local fiscal activity but failed to take any meaningful action. This failure may have created a situation where many people felt that it was Proposition 2½ or nothing. While 2½ went further in terms of cutbacks than many might have preferred, it was better than the status quo, which was the only alternative. Furthermore, since it was a statutory measure, the legislature could alleviate its impact. In the meantime the voters would have "sent a message," an unmistakable one, to the legislature.

The sponsor of Proposition 2½ was a libertarian group, Citizens for Limited Taxation (CLT), composed of small businessmen and individuals. It was later joined in the campaign by the Massachusetts High Technology Council, which represented many of the high technology firms that had become an important element in the state's economy over the past twenty years. The latter group had developed its own initiative, designed to reduce tax levels in Massachusetts and improve their ability to recruit technical personnel in a very competitive job market but had been thwarted by the legislature in placing it on the ballot. The High Technology Council contributed $250,000 to the 2½ campaign, which was very important. Even with that contribution, the sponsors were only able to afford a modest media campaign. However, there was extensive media coverage of the issue and widespread public debate, so that voters were well aware of 2½.

The opposition to Proposition 2½ was quite predictable; it consisted of education groups, good-government organizations such as the League of Women Voters, public employees, local officials, and advocacy groups. Their campaign was well financed. The Massachusetts Teachers Association (MTA) had also placed an initiative on the ballot, which would have limited the growth of property taxes and increased state aid for education. However, the MTA chose not to campaign for its own measure but to concentrate on opposition to 2½. They felt it would be better to convey a simple message to the voters—vote no on 2½. The MTA proposal was defeated 45 to 55 percent.

In many referenda on complex fiscal matters, voters appear to have chosen the known present over the uncertainty involved in the proposed changes. However, in the Massachusetts case, voters may have seen their choice as being between two knowns, an unacceptable status quo and assured property tax reductions. Tvedt (1981: 532) provided such an interpretation of voting on 2½:

> On election day, voters were asked to choose between Proposition 2½ and the status quo. Several opinion polls showed that voters supported the initiative because they felt property taxes were too high, not because they wanted smaller government or fewer services. More importantly, when given a choice, a majority preferred a moderate alternative that restricted the growth of property taxes or slightly lowered them. But this alternative was not on the ballot, and in the three years prior to the election the legislature demonstrated that it would not enact such legislation. In the end, it is likely that the known benefits of a tax cut outweighed apprehensions about unknown future service cuts. Property taxes were unacceptably high; Proposition 2½ gave voters the authority to lower them.

In summary, unsuccessful campaigns tend to share two common characteristics. The sponsors tend to be a narrowly based group that has difficulty raising the funds to run an extensive campaign, while the opposition is a broad-based coalition of groups that can draw on the treasuries, staffs, and memberships of organizations to provide the people and money necessary for a statewide campaign. In addition, the campaign revolves around the technical details of the proposal and its likely impact. This results in a numbers debate, which may convey to the voters the impression that there is great uncertainty about what would happen if the measure were adopted.

Successful campaigns also have several common elements. Coverage of the two sides of the proposal is more nearly equal, either because the sponsoring group is larger and better financed or because the media covers the campaign extensively. Another asset is a leader identified with the proposal who is something of a character and adept at obtaining media attention by his actions. Such was the case in both Idaho and California. While it was not enough to save the Tisch proposal in Michigan, it did even the odds somewhat, given that the campaign organization was very small.

Perhaps more importantly, the nature of the debate in the successful campaigns was different. Despite the fact that opponents focused on the details of the measures and their uncertain or undesirable effects, that was not the level at which the public responded to the debate. The proponents were able to keep attention focused on two much simpler issues—the need for a change and the lack of responsiveness of the state legislature to the problem. As a result the complexity and confusion that worked to the benefit of opponents to many referenda were much less of a factor in these campaigns. There may still have been an element of that in at least some of the states, as indicated by the poll results in California, Idaho, and Michigan showing support falling as the campaign progressed (as people learned more about the measure and its possible consequences). However, that trend was reversed at the end of the campaign in two of the states—in California by events that refocused attention on the central issues (i.e., the need for reform and the unacceptable nature of the status quo).

Why did the nature of the debate remain at a more general level in these states while it did not in others? One contributing factor in three of the four states (all but Michigan) may have been the acuteness of the public's sense of discontent. That discontent had two elements—it was very specific in nature and the state legislature had demonstrated (usually in several sessions) its inability or unwillingness to deal with the causes. Unhappiness about the level of taxes and the size of government is widespread at this time in history, but that has not led to the adoption of TELs, particularly strong ones, in all states that have the initiative process. What distinguished California, Idaho, and Massachusetts were very specific targets at which that discontent could be directed and that provided the basis for mobilizing people. In California and Idaho the issue was the rapid rise in residential property taxes (coupled with the large state surplus in California), and in Massachusetts it was the high level of taxes, particularly property taxes. The issues provided the fuel for the initiative process; the spark that in some sense set it off was the (in)action of the state legislatures. Had they enacted meaningful state tax reform, the potential for an explosion might have been defused. Kuttner (1980) suggested a similar combination of factors as the explanation of the "tax revolt"—public anger about unfair tax burdens, especially on homeowners, and unresponsive legislatures. In the states where initiatives were rejected, opponents tended to argue either there was need for a change, but there were better alternatives than the proposal on the ballot, or there was no need for change. Neither could be argued in these three states.

In some ways the passage of the Headlee proposal in Michigan was an anomaly; it represented passage by default. If there had been no other measures on the ballot, it is possible that it would have been defeated. If the election had been held a few days or a week later, it might not have passed. Contributing to its success was the emphasis of the MEA on the Voucher and Tisch proposals until very late in the campaign. This meant that the Headlee supporters had a relatively uncontested field in which to operate during much of the campaign. In addition the support it received from many politicians was almost by default. They were afraid to oppose all attempts to reduce the size of the public sector in the aftermath of Proposition 13, and, of the available options, the Headlee proposal was the most moderate and reasonable. In retrospect, public officials might not have had as much to fear from the public on these issues as they thought, but their fears had the effect of muting both discussion of and opposition to the proposal.

Next, the evidence related to voting behavior on TEL measures is examined. Who votes in favor (or against) TELs and why? Are the findings on voting behavior congruent with the explanations offered in this section about the campaigns in specific states?

Voting Behavior and TELs

There has been far more research and literature on voting behavior in referenda on tax and expenditure limitations than there has been on the campaigns. Given the volume of that effort and the numerous inconsistencies and contradictions in the findings, it is possible to provide only a brief overview of that literature here (see Lowery and Sigelman (1981) for a summary of this research).

Most of the studies of this topic fall into one of three categories: (1) aggregate studies of voting patterns on a single measure in one state that relate support for the measure with various characteristics of some unit of government (i.e., counties); (2) analyses of a public opinion survey conducted in a single state shortly before or after an election in which a TEL measure was on the ballot; and (3) analyses of national survey data related to TELs in general, rather than to a specific measure in an individual state. There have been relatively few comparative studies examining voting patterns in more than one state. The findings of each of these types of studies is summarized, beginning with the third one since it can be dismissed as generally irrelevant to the concerns here. However, one result that appears consistently throughout the survey data is presented first, since it provides the context within which all the other findings must be viewed.

Studies that examined *attitudes* toward public services in the late 1970s and early 1980s found very consistent patterns. In general the American public was satisfied with the level of services provided by state and local government (Ladd and Wilson 1982b; Courant, Gramlich, and Rubinfeld 1980; Lipset and Schneider 1980; Lowery and Sigelman 1981; Citrin 1979). When asked if they would like the level of public services provided to increase, decrease, or remain the same, the majority of people tended to respond "remain the same," and more said "increase" than "decrease." The major exception was welfare; when that terminology was used, people tended to respond that it should be cut, although that was not so much the reaction if some other term was used, such as social services or assistance to the needy. Among a variety of public services, people seemed more favorably disposed to public schools than to most others. They were more likely to say school services should be increased and less likely to say that if cuts must be made, they should be in education.

While people tended to be satisfied with the level of services, they also tended to be dissatisfied with taxes and the level of spending. Thus they thought taxes were high and spending should be reduced, yet they did not want decreases in services, and in fact many favored increases in services. The factor that allows these two orientations to coexist is the widespread belief that government is inefficient; that public employees are paid too much and are less productive than private sector workers; that there is widespread waste and corruption in government; and that spending could be reduced, perhaps significantly, without affecting the level of services. Ladd and Wilson (1982b) reported that in their Massachusetts sample, respondents felt that state spending could be reduced by 24 percent, local spending by 19 percent, and education spending by 13 percent without affecting the quantity and quality of services.

The 1978 election survey conducted by the University of Michigan's Survey Research Center (SRC) included a question about how people would vote on a Proposition 13-type limitation. Several researchers (Lowery and Sigelmen 1981; Hansen 1981) have used the responses to that question to analyze peoples' attitudes about the tax revolt or TELs. Unfortunately, responses to that question may be a very poor indicator of how individuals would actually vote if a TEL proposal were on the ballot in their state. At best that question may tap a general inclination to look favorably on attempts to limit taxes and spending; at worst responses may represent "nonattitudes" on

154 THE CHANGING POLITICS OF SCHOOL FINANCE

the part of many people, since they were responding off-the-cuff on an issue about which they had not thought and had little information. How an individual is likely to vote on a particular TEL measure will be a function not only of general attitudes about taxing and spending but also the nature of the limit, the fiscal situation in the state, and personal perceptions about the probable consequences of passage of the limit. The early poll results in many states that indicated high levels of support for a TEL may have reflected the same general orientation that the SRC item tapped. However, the declining levels of support as the campaign progressed represented the impact of the other considerations as people heard and read more about the limit. Thus it is not too surprising that Lowery and Sigelman (1981) concluded that the reason they could not explain more of the variance in responses to the SRC question was because it was a "style" not a "position" issue—that the tax revolt was a symbolic social movement and represented a means of expressing indirect and projective sentiments rather than economic self-interest. Such an interpretation probably is an accurate characterization of the nature of responses to the SRC question. The difficulty is that the researchers have incorrectly identified the "tax revolt" or responses to TELs with that single interview item.

In general, aggregate analyses that have tried to examine voting patterns on TELs have not been particularly successful in explaining variations in voting patterns (Lucier 1971, 1973; Levy 1975; Williams 1976; Attiyeh and Engle 1979; Morgan 1981, 1982; Freiman and Grasso 1982; Bloom 1979; MacManus 1981; Magaddino, Toma, and Toma 1980). Such analyses have two major problems—one is the danger of the ecological fallacy, and the other is that by aggregating voting decisions the extent of variation in the vote may be reduced (and the larger the unit of analysis, the more likely that is to be the case). Williams (1976) found that only political variables (percentage Democratic voting in presidential and gubernatorial elections) consistently contributed in a meaningful fashion to explaining voting on limitation measures on the ballot in five states in 1972 and 1973. A variety of fiscal and socioeconomic variables intended to test whether voting decisions were based on economic rationality or a notion of self-interest failed to show consistent impacts on the measures. Williams (1976: 30–32, 34) suggested that several characteristics of the campaigns for the measures, all of which were defeated, probably contributed to these results.

On the whole these measures we're complex and in some cases poorly drafted. A major feature of every campaign was a numbers debate, with each side producing experts who presented conflicting forecasts about the impact of the tax package on business and individuals. Therefore, the lack of a consistent pattern linking socioeconomic status or fiscal variables to voting behavior on these issues is not surprising. Comparable individuals or communities could easily reach opposite conclusions about their economic self interest in the face of the conflicting arguments.

In some respects, the voter's task in casting a ballot on such referenda parallels the problems faced in nonpartisan elections. In each case, he is presented with a complex set of stimuli without the overriding factor of political party to provide clues as to the alternative which would be most appropriate for him. Therefore, in each situation, the voter looks for other factors to guide his choice. On the referendum, especially complex and controversial ones such as these, the voter looks to other political actors with whom he identifies. He is willing to rely on the judgment of public officials such as governors or interest groups such as unions. Thus, the nature of the issues and the campaigns were probably a major reason the political variables, rather than the census and fiscal ones, were important. . . .

The large size and disparate nature of the coalitions against the proposals may also account for the contradictory impact of the census and fiscal variables. The proposals had many features and groups opposed them for a wide variety of reasons. Thus, different types of people could take the same position for widely differing reasons and similar variables could have opposite impacts if they affected people's reactions to different features of a particular referenda.

While the voter's decisions may not resemble those made under conditions of rational choice, they did in fact reveal considerable practical rationality. In the face of conflicting claims and much confusion, they rejected "a pig in a poke" and/or followed the judgments of political actors they trusted.

Two other studies (Bloom 1979; Freiman and Grasso 1982) also suggested that uncertainty about the impact of a measure may account for the lack of voting patterns that conform to expectations about economic self-interest. In both cases the researchers cite the ambiguity of measures where many of the specifics about implementation had not been specified and would have to be decided by the legislature after the measure was adopted.

In several studies researchers have analyzed survey data related to voting on TELs. Most of these have been single state studies: Massachusetts (Ladd and Wilson 1982a–1982e), California (Citrin 1979), and Michigan (Courant, Gramlich, and Rubinfeld 1980, 1981). In one study voting patterns were examined in four states (Colorado, Idaho, Michigan, and Oregon) with TEL measures on the ballot in 1978. This study was based on a survey conducted in each state shortly after the election (Palaich, Kloss, and Williams 1980). In general the findings of these studies are reasonably consistent, although slightly different sets of variables related to voter choice were used in each study.

California. Polls taken in California at the time of Proposition 13 indicated that voters felt that services would not be cut and other taxes would not rise if Proposition 13 passed (Lipson and Lavin 1979). Citrin (1979) found that the average voter in California wanted a cut in taxes but not in services and was concerned about greater efficiency. He concluded that only after the state surplus in California was reduced and Californians had to make a choice between raising taxes and cutting services would people's true preferences about taxing and spending become evident. Proposition 8 (the legislative alternative placed on the ballot to counteract 13) and Proposition 13 appeared to be perceived by voters as alternatives, since variables that increased the likelihood of a yes vote on 13 tended to have the opposite effect on 8 (a pattern also shown in results presented by Baratz and Moskowitz 1979). Both ideology and economic self-interest appeared to affect voting behavior on these measures since homeowners were more likely to vote yes on 13 and no on 8, while the reverse was true of the less educated, blacks, Democrats, and liberals. However, the explanatory power of Citrin's model is not strong; the estimated R^2 is .25 for Proposition 13 and .19 for Proposition 8.

Two reasons that Citrin may have had so little success in predicting voting behavior on these measures is that his equation lacks measures of attitudes about government spending/taxing/efficiency and of perceptions about the impact of the measures. As Williams (1976) suggested, individuals with similar characteristics can come to very different conclusions about the consequences of complex measures such as these. Furthermore, people may come to similar conclusions about the impact of a measure but evaluate those consequences quite differently depending on their opinions about the role of government.

Michigan. The analysis of Michigan voting patterns on the Headlee proposal did include indicators of a variety of political attitudes and assessments of the probable consequences of the measure (Courant, Gramlich, and Rubinfeld 1980, 1981). The results suggested that neither preferences about spending/taxing levels nor voter characteristics (e.g., income, race, age, political party, public employment) were good predictors of the vote on the Headlee proposal. However, the explanatory power of the model increased when the relationship between a voter's spending/taxing preferences and the view of the voter on the impact of the measure were taken into account. The greatest support for Headlee came from those who felt it would increase government efficiency and/or voter control over government and who also desired such increases. Also voting for it were those who wanted a smaller public sector and thought the proposal would produce that, plus a group the researchers classified as "may want free lunch." The latter group included those who did not want a smaller public sector, yet voted for the proposal despite thinking that would be the most important consequence of the Headlee proposal and others who expressed a desire for higher spending, yet voted against the proposal although they believed it would raise taxes. (Freiman (1980) suggested that Courant, Gramlich, and Rubinfeld overestimated the size of the "free lunch" group because of a lack of clarity in the wording of one question. When respondents said that the Headlee proposal would reduce taxes, they could have meant a reduction below the level that would have been otherwise, rather than an absolute reduction. The former is what the Headlee proposal was intended to achieve.) The authors draw two conclusions from their findings: Widespread support for a smaller public sector did not account for the passage of the Headlee proposal but concerns about efficiency and voter control did (Courant, Gramlich, and Rubinfeld 1981: 63–4):

> . . . [S]ome suggestive results emerge from this attempt to survey voters. One is that there does not appear to be a very widespread feeling that government is too big. More people feel that way than the converse, but the differences are not substantial and in any case not strongly related to respondents' votes on the tax limitation. Fundamentally, the tax limitation movement does not appear to be an attempt to correct spending imbalances between the public and private sectors. . . . The strongest source of support comes from those who think limitations will improve voter control of government and/or government efficiency. . . . Another strong source of support comes from those who think the amendment will reduce taxes, even though they have not reported desiring cuts in spending and taxes at that level of government. Thus

those voters appear to perceive that their own taxes will be cut without expenditures being cut, either because of supposed efficiency gains, greater uncertainty about the spending side of the budget, or the unending search for a free lunch.

Massachusetts. The most ambitious of the single-state analyses of survey results is that of Ladd and Wilson (1982a–1982e) for Massachusetts. Not only did they include measures of personal attributes, attitudes about government, and perceptions about the impact of Proposition 2½, but they also included indicators of the fiscal status of the communities in which people lived. They found that all these factors were explanatory in voting decisions on 2½. Those who were more likely to support 2½ included men, whites, the elderly, higher income, homeowners, conservatives, those desiring a smaller public sector, those less favorably disposed toward welfare recipients, and those living in communities where the greatest revenue reductions were expected as a result of 2½. Opponents were more likely to come from users of public services, Jews, the better educated, public employees and their families, renters and residents of places where pre-2½ local tax rates were the highest. These findings suggest *who* supported 2½ (Ladd and Wilson 1982d). Ladd and Wilson (1982e) also explored *why* voters supported 2½. Similar to the pattern found in the Michigan survey, responses to questions about the impact of the measure and the relation of those expectations to personal preferences were much better predictors of voting than were personal characteristics.

Consistent with findings in other studies, a concern with government waste and inefficiency was strongly related to a positive vote on 2½, especially for those who felt 2½ would increase efficiency. Not as important but still significant was the belief that 2½ would reduce taxes and spending. While a preference for less services contributed very little to the vote for 2½, those who wanted less welfare services and thought 2½ would produce that were more supportive of the measure. Those who opposed 2½ tended to fear service losses, lower school funding, and higher state taxes. As Ladd and Wilson noted (1982e: 30), "the survey results clearly indicate that the vote for Proposition 2½ was much more an attempt to obtain lower taxes and more efficient government than to reduce the level of public services." Morgan's (1981) aggregate voting analysis did not produce results that are entirely consistent with Ladd and Wilson, but he also concluded that spending reductions were not what the voters were trying to achieve.

Ladd and Wilson (1982a) also examined the role that concerns about public education played in people's decisions about 2½. Generally Massachusetts voters were satisfied with the level of education services and the way they were financed at the time of Proposition 2½. While people perceived less inefficiency in public schools than in most other public services, there still was a widespread belief that spending could be reduced substantially (15 percent or more) without reducing services. Two education-related considerations increased the probability that an individual would vote for 2½: the perception of inefficiency in school spending and the expectation that 2½ would result in more voter control over school spending (due to the elimination of the fiscal autonomy of school committees). Offsetting these factors were the people who were more likely to vote against 2½ because they felt it would decrease school spending or services. Thus, the impact of school-related factors were similar to those for all services: a concern with inefficiency rather than a desire to lower service levels. The only issue that was unique to education was the concern about control over spending levels.

The findings from the California, Michigan, and Massachusetts studies are rather consistent. However, these studies focused primarily on measures that passed. The Michigan survey also covered the Tisch proposal, but the published materials have presented relatively few findings relative to that proposal. The Massachusetts survey covered the MTA measure, Question 3, on the ballot for a portion of the sample. On that proposal, voters who thought it would lead to higher levels of school spending were more likely to support it, while those who favored school spending cuts tended to oppose it. Other expectations that contributed to a positive vote were that it would promote state tax reform, slower growth in property taxes, and slower growth in total taxes and spending. Thus it drew upon a different constituency than 2½, one that favored less growth in property and total taxes but increases in school spending. These differences reflect the differences in the two proposals. Question 3 would have limited the growth in state and local taxes and increased the state's role in financing education (Ladd and Wilson 1982a).

Four-State Study. The comparative study of TEL voting behavior in four states conducted by the Education Commission of the States

(ECS) did present analyses of patterns for both successful and unsuccessful measures (Palaich, Kloss, and Williams 1980). While some of the patterns discussed appear for all or most of the measures studied, others appear to vary with the nature of the measure or the state context. Thus the researchers concluded (1980: 57): "The implications of these findings are that the 'tax revolt' is not a monolithic movement that is sweeping the country. Voters perceive differences in the types of TEL measures and act on those perceptions. Campaigns on the TEL issue and the political culture of the state do have an effect on the outcome of the referendum."

One finding in the ECS study was a difference in voting choices on measures that would *reduce* property taxes as opposed to expenditure *limitations.* Items that tapped orientations about the role or size of government did not explain choices on the property tax measures, whereas they did play a role on the expenditure limitations. Conversely, personal attributes such as sex, education, age, and political party affiliation were more important for the proposals that would have reduced property taxes. In general, the relationships that did appear were similar in direction to those reported in other studies; the more educated, Democrats, and liberals were less likely to vote for these measures, but each of these factors was an important determinant of voting in no more than three of the six proposals studied.

The factors that were consistently important across all the measures in explaining voting decisions were two related to the impact of the proposals. Voters who felt that the proposal would reduce *their own* state and local taxes were uniformly more likely to vote for them. Similarly, those who felt the measures would have little or no impact on the provision of services also were more likely to support the proposals as opposed to those who felt the impact would be major. Thus, these results provide further evidence for the interpretation that support for these proposals was a vote for lower taxes and greater government efficiency but not for lower service levels. Those who felt that the measures would result in major service disruptions tended to oppose them.

The explanatory power of the general voting behavior model was not great in any of the states. However, additional insights into the reasons for the passage or defeat of particular proposals were gained by examining simple frequency distributions and cross-tabulations between survey items and voting on specific initiatives. In Michigan the Tisch proposal did not do as well at the polls as the Headlee, in part because people were more likely to think the Tisch would result in higher total taxes and would have major, undesirable effects on the provision of services. However, compared to responses in other states, Michigan voters were the most likely to say that the initiatives would lead to an increase in total taxes and the least likely to say that they would result in lower taxes. These perceptions may reflect the arguments by opponents to both Michigan measures that they would produce tax shifts but not tax reductions. Opponents complained that it was difficult to campaign against the Headlee proposal, because it was seen as being a reasonable and moderate measure whose primary effect would be to maintain the status quo. Responses about its impact on the provision of services indicate the problem the opponents faced: Only 22 percent believed that the Headlee proposal would have a major effect on services (in contrast to 60 percent for the Tisch). In general the survey suggested that there was not widespread dissatisfaction in Michigan about public services, which was a major reason why the "radical" Tisch measure was defeated and that even the moderate Headlee measure won by a narrow margin.

The survey revealed even less of a sense of crisis and discontent in Colorado. A major argument made by the opponents of the TEL was that it was unnecessary since the state already had an extensive set of limits that applied to schools, local governments, and the state. There were several indications from the survey that voters agreed. Colorado respondents were the least concerned about the outcome of the referenda and knew the least about it. They also were the most prone to have no opinion or to answer "don't know" to the questions about the potential impact of the measure. Furthermore, Colorado residents reported the least increases in property taxes in recent years and the greatest satisfaction with school finance. Both may reflect the impact of school finance reform in Colorado, which had produced property tax relief in the 1970s. In summary there was little indication of high levels of dissatisfaction with taxes and spending in Colorado or a felt need for further limits.

The survey evidence related to TEL voting is relatively consistent. The most important findings are that: (1) personal characteristics alone are poor predictors of voting choices on these measures; (2) support for the TEL measures is not motivated by a desire for fewer or lower levels of state and local services but rather by an interest in reducing taxes and increasing government efficiency; (3) the predictors of voting choices are based on perceptions about the impact of the measures; and (4) expectations about TEL impact vary with the nature of the measure and the state–local fiscal context. In one sense there is a national pattern to the "tax revolt," in that the same types of factors tend to contribute to a yes vote in many states. On the other hand, the phenomenon is state-specific, since the prevalence of those factors are a function of conditions within a state and the particular limit before the voters. Dissatisfaction with education or education-related issues did not explain the outcomes of TEL referenda (Ladd and Wilson 1982a; Palaich 1980; Education Finance Center 1979).

IMPACT OF LIMITATIONS

Far more has been written about the politics of TELs than about their impact. In part that reflects the fact that the limits adopted in the late 1970s have been in effect such a short period of time. In this section the research on the effects of limits is summarized. The focus is on the politics of the design and implementation of limits and how those politics have affected the observed outcomes.

Limits were components of school reform packages adopted in many states in the early 1970s. One rationale often cited for imposing such limits was that it would promote greater equity by reducing expenditure disparities among school districts. This would be the case only if poor or lower spending districts could increase spending faster than more affluent districts and if such poor districts were willing and/or able to do so. In fact the caps or limits imposed in some states were in effect disequalizing, allowing larger increases in higher spending districts, or the differential in the limits was so small that it would have taken the poor districts many years to catch up. Furthermore, many of the limits were not absolute; they provided for voter overrides or waivers, and high spending districts tended to make more use of those mechanisms (Cattanach, Lang, and Hooper 1976; Osman and Gemello 1981; Goertz and Moskowitz 1979).

In reality equity considerations do not appear to have been the primary consideration behind the adoption of limits as part of school finance reform. While scholars and reformers may have advocated changes in state aid systems to increase equity, what made such changes politically attractive to state legislatures was the issue of property tax relief, and limits were often adopted as part of reform packages to promote that goal. Two concerns that troubled legislatures about such reforms were their cost and ensuring that at least a substantial portion of the new state aid actually went to property tax relief. In the past legislators had seen large increases in state school aid, which were intended to reduce local property taxes, devoted almost entirely to increasing expenditures. Thus limits on expenditure or revenue growth were a means of both placing some constraints on increases in aid under reform and promoting property tax relief.

The conclusions of researchers who have examined the impact of limits on expenditures and equity in school finance have been varied. Those who have commented upon the impact of limits in specific states, such as Wisconsin (Hansen and Nelson 1978), New Jersey (Goertz and Moskowitz 1979; Bureau of Government Research 1980) and Colorado (Odden 1978), have concluded that the limits in those states have not promoted equalization of expenditures. In fact, they have probably hindered the achievement of that goal but may have promoted other goals such as property tax relief, limiting the growth in state school aid, and reducing expenditure growth. Studies that have examined all the states or a subset of "reform" states (Wilken and Callahan 1978; Brown et al. 1978; Winkler 1979; Cattanach, Lang, and Hooper 1976) have come to varying conclusions about the impact of limits on expenditure disparities. In general it would appear that the effects of education limits vary across states, probably as a function of both the nature of the limit and the situation in which the limit is imposed.

California is the state for which there is the most information both about impact and the politics of implementation of a general limit, yet it really is not yet clear what the long-run effects of Proposition 13 will be. Through the first three years of its implementation, the existence of a state surplus cushioned its effects as the state was able to provide large increases in state aid to local governments, including school districts, to offset much of the decline in property tax revenues. That surplus was gradually reduced, and the state now faces budget deficits, due in part to the state of the economy and the indexing of the state income tax.

Schools were the unit of local government that was most severely affected by Proposition 13 because they were highly dependent on property taxes and had fewer options for raising local revenues from other sources (see Elmore and McLaughlin 1982). Legislative leaders, in putting together the state bailout package in the summer of 1978, decided that no type of local government was to bear a disproportionate share of reductions in revenues. That decision meant that the potential that Proposition 13 represented for radically reducing expenditure disparities and for complete compliance with *Serrano* would not be realized. Leveling up expenditures in low-spending districts would have required so much additional state aid that education would have received more than its "fair share" of the bailout funds. Leveling down expenditures in high spending districts was neither politically feasible nor felt to be educationally sound because it would have led to considerable disruption in educational programs and because high spending districts included some where costs were high or that had high proportions of students requiring high-cost services. Another consequence of Proposition 13 was that it changed the politics of education and school finance in the state legislature. Before education had been considered in isolation; the only concern was what did education need. It then became a zero-sum game, and all functions were considered in relation to one another. More aid for education meant less for someone else.

The result of the politics involved in the bailout was that education received its "fair share" of the first-year bailout money—53 percent as opposed to 52 percent of lost property tax revenues. The state share of state–local education revenues rose substantially from less than 50 percent to more than 70 percent. On average, schools suffered a 10 percent reduction in revenues below what they otherwise would have had in 1978–79. The extent of reduction was not uniform but rather on a sliding scale from 91 to 85 percent inversely related to a district's expenditure level. (For a majority of districts, 1978–79 revenues were greater than those in 1977–78). The result was a greater and more rapid reduction in expenditure disparities than would have occurred under AB 65, the legislature's school finance package adopted in 1977, which was rendered obsolete by Proposition 13. In addition Proposition 13 eliminated tax rate disparities because there was now an uniform property tax rate throughout the state; the issue of taxpayer equity had been resolved. Ironically the bulk of property tax relief due to Proposition 13 accrued to owners of business and commercial property rather than to homeowners.

The permanent bailout package adopted in 1979 was similar to the one-year measure and restored stability to local planning and budget processes (Lipson and Lavin 1979). In the long-term measure, remaining property taxes were reallocated away from schools to other local governments, and more state aid was provided for education. This resulted in a further increase in the state share of funding and made schools more subject to swings in state revenue collections and state budget decisions. There were fewer state "strings" attached to the permanent bill than there had been in the first-year bailout.

Speich and Weiner (1980), in examining the impact of Proposition 13 on schools in the first year, concluded that the effects were not major ones and in some sense were primarily psychological. Two of the consequences they cited were greater uncertainty about the future and declines in employee morale. Contributing to both effects was the fact that the legislature's initial response was only for a single year, which left everyone unsure as to what the future would hold. Despite concerns that the large increase in state funding would be accompanied by substantial increases in state control over local decisions, that generally was not the case. While there were specific instances of increased state constraints or mandates, they were isolated exceptions to the general pattern of leaving decisions about expenditures and programs to local officials. Speich and Weiner suggested that the current system—where revenue-raising is highly centralized but decisions about expenditures are decentralized—is likely to persist in California. In part this is because the potential political costs to legislators and other state officials of becoming more involved are too great, given the nature of the problems in education and the lack of attractive solutions to them.

The ways in which California school districts coped with revenue reductions or slower revenue growth are what one would expect given the research on fiscal stress and retrenchment (Speich and Weiner 1980; Katz 1979; May and Meltsner 1981). Nonpersonnel and deferrable expenditures were curtailed; purchases of supplies, library books, and textbooks tended to be cut, as were maintenance and capital outlay expenditures. Support services tended to be cut in preference to instructional services. While there were personnel reductions, it is difficult to assess to what extent they were due to declining enrollments or Proposition 13. One means of increasing revenues utilized in many districts was to raise fees, such as for school lunches. Just as the state legislature did not use the construction of the bailout bill as an opportunity for considering fundamental changes in programs or priorities, neither did school districts. Reactions tended to involve short-range strategies designed to minimize the disruption to the status quo.

Idaho adopted a property tax limitation (Proposition 1) in 1978 modeled closely after Proposition 13 and a limit on state spending in 1980. It was anticipated that the impact of Proposition 1 would be substantial since Idaho, unlike California, did not have a large state surplus that could be used to cushion its impact. However, Proposition 1 was a statutory initiative, and the legislature took several steps that greatly softened its impact (Bishop 1982; Fox 1982). One decision by the legislature was to defer the implementation of the limit until 1980. In addition, the nature of the limit was revised. Proposition 1 originally included both a 1 percent limit on property taxes (as a proportion of assessed valuation) and a 2 percent limit on annual increases in assessments, but ceilings on the growth of property taxes were substituted by the legislature. In the first year, levies were frozen at their current level and in the second year a 4 percent increase was allowed. The level of levy increases has since been raised to 5 percent, and that limit can be overriden with voter approval. The school districts that have tended to vote supplemental levies have been those that traditionally have been high effort or high expenditure districts. The state has also increased state aid to education to make up for the lost local revenues, which has resulted in a higher state share.

Massachusetts passed Proposition 2½ in 1980, so that at most only the first wave of impacts can be seen. The Massachusetts Municipal Association (1982) has published the results of a survey of communities on the impact of 2½. Education and recreation tended to be the local services cut the most, and police and fire were the least affected. One factor contributing to education bearing a disproportionate share of the cuts was that in small communities other types of services often had so few personnel and such small budgets that it was difficult to make cuts that would not severely affect service levels. Another such factor was declining enrollments. Another analysis (Bradbury and Ladd 1982) also suggested that cuts in local school budgets were greater than those for other services. Areas of education that tended to be cut included cultural enrichment programs, athletics, and small classes (Ruhf 1981). School closings have been accelerated, there have been staff reductions, class sizes have increased as have teacher and administrative work loads, and expenditures have been reduced in the typical areas of maintenance and supplies.

Bradbury and Ladd (1982) also analyzed the impact of Proposition 2½ on expenditure disparities in the state and the state's reaction to the problems created by the measure. Virtually every community in the state will suffer some revenue loss as the result of 2½, either because of the property tax limits or the reduction in the motor vehicle excise tax, but the losses would be greatest in larger communities, in those with high tax rates and high spending levels. Prior to 2½ there were large variations in spending among Massachusetts towns and cities; these spending differences tended to reflect differences in property wealth, and 2½ would exacerbate both problems. In the future locally-raised revenues will be even more a function of property wealth than they were before because localities will have lost the opportunity to tax themselves at higher levels to compensate for a low tax base, high service needs, or stronger preferences for public services.

While there was no requirement in 2½ that the state cushion its impact, most people expected the state would take some remedial action. The state response differed from California's in several significant ways. One important factor affecting the state's response to 2½ was the lack of a large state surplus to provide funds for a local bailout. Funds had to come either from reductions in other parts of the state's budget or from increases in revenues, and the latter was never seriously considered in the light of the margin of victory for 2½. Thus the development of a bailout measure was more painful and the magnitude of the assistance smaller relative to the local revenue losses than had been the case in California. A substantial reduction in the number of state employees and elimination of funding for some state agencies occurred. While early proposals had concentrated the reductions in state spending for human services, that was not the case in the final budget, which contained cuts in all areas. The total new aid to localities amounted to less than half the estimated loss in local revenues.

The local aid package designed in the legislature did not seek to preserve the pre-2½ status quo. There was an early proposal dubbed the "Share the Pain Bill" that proposed a method of distribution similar to the one chosen in California, that is, in proportion to the estimated revenue losses. However, one objection to such an approach was that it would undermine what the voters had intended—to force reductions in spending in places where it was most extravagant. In addition such an approach would widen revenue and expenditure disparities among communities; it would build on the old disparities based on differences in property wealth and in fact would contribute to greater disparities in the same direction. Thus another goal of several of the proposed state aid packages was to alleviate some of the old inequities by more nearly equalizing revenues among communities. In the end the equalization rationale was the one that was reflected in the aid package. The projected impact of the net revenue losses after 2½ is that expenditure disparities will be reduced (Bradbury and Ladd 1982).

However, Bradbury and Ladd (1982) suggested that 2½ will have the opposite effect on education expenditures. Preliminary data for a sample of school districts indicated that cuts in education budgets have been proportionately less in communities spending more per pupil. Similarly, cuts in instructional expenditures and in teaching staff appeared to be smaller in high spending districts. Morgan (1982) suggested that school budget cuts have been greater in property-poor and urban communities, as has the number of school closings. The differences in education and total spending patterns reflect another way in which Massachusetts differed from California. In the former the bailout money was general aid to local governments, and it was at the local level that decisions were made about the distribution of losses among services. In California many of those decisions were made at the state level, due to the prevalence of special districts and the fiscal independence of the school districts.

Another reason that education may have suffered greater cuts than other services in Massachusetts is that 2½ also changed the local budget process for schools. Before 2½, school committees had complete control over their budgets despite the fact that they were fiscally dependent school districts. They would set their budgets, and then the city or town council had to appropriate sufficient local revenues to meet that budget. That fiscal autonomy was eliminated with 2½, so that 1981–82 is the first year in which councils have been able to control the *size* of local education budgets. If council members believed that schools had been profligate in the past or that the public felt that way (and the poll data indicated that control over school budgets was a reason for supporting 2½), then they may have seen this as their chance to bring school budgets more in line. If that is the case, then the disproportionate cuts in education relative to other services may not recur.

Proposition 2½ is a statutory measure, which means that the legislature can amend (or even repeal it). The legislature enacted a package of amendments to 2½, which the original proponents of the measure supported and the governor signed in January 1982. The effect of the amendments is to weaken the impact of 2½ somewhat. The amendments make it easier to place override questions on the ballot and also relax the requirements for approval for some types of overrides. In general the overrides voted upon through early 1982 were defeated, but in part that may have been due to considerable uncertainty about the interpretation of the override provisions in the amendments.

Gold (1981b) presented case study material on the effects of limits on local spending or property taxes in fourteen states. His basic conclusion is that one cannot generalize about the effects of limits across states (and that there is relatively little research on the impact across localities within a single state) (Gold 1981b: 49, 50):

> Limitations have been of varying effectiveness in restricting property tax levies. They were very effective in Indiana and in California after Proposition 13 for all governments. They seem to have been somewhat effective in Arizona, Colorado, New Jersey, Ohio, and Washington for nonschool governments, and in Arizona, Colorado, Iowa, New Jersey, Ohio, and Wisconsin for schools. They apparently have been largely ineffective in California (before 1978), Florida, Iowa, and Wisconsin for nonschool governments. In other states sufficient information has not been obtained to make a judgment. . . .
>
> Little of the case study material sheds light on the issue of how much the limitations restricted spending. Where property taxes were restricted, localities might have been able to obtain sufficient revenue from other sources to maintain their level of spending in the absence of the limits. In New Jersey and Arizona, the only states with spending limits, there is some indication that spending has been restricted. However, generally the subject was not addressed.

Rand researchers examined spending and service delivery in ten cities in three states with limits—Kansas, New Jersey, and California (Menchik, Fernandez, and Caggiano 1981). They did not find a consistent pattern that limits reduced expenditures and services. Where there were spending reductions (whether due to limits or other reasons), services did deteriorate but often to a lesser extent than the spending reductions. Agencies tended to focus more on their primary functions and to absorb the cuts in peripheral activities. Moderate cuts also may have been accompanied by efficiency gains, but severe ones decreased efficiency. Rarely were facilities closed or consolidated, and cuts were not greater for the "less essential" services of parks, recreation, and libraries than they were for police.

The Urban Institute studied the responses of state and local governments to limitations and fiscal pressure in a number of states. Wolman and Peterson (1981) described the types of strategies that public officials pursue under conditions of fiscal pressure. They concluded that governments that were constrained by formal limits pursued the same kinds of coping strategies as did governments facing other types of fiscal pressures, except to the extent that the limits themselves foreclosed certain options. In either case governments seek to minimize the disruption to both their external environment and their internal organization. Therefore they seek solutions that will minimize opposition, both from their own employees and the public.

TELs reduce the options of local officials and bias responses toward expenditure reductions. They also tend to distort priorities and strategies. Common tactics for reducing the impact of limits include: greater use of debt financing because it tends to be outside the limit; creation of new districts and authorities that will be outside the cap or will have their own cap; and imposition of new fees and charges, often in combination with a new special district to levy them. Limits did tend to produce lower expenditures than there would have been otherwise, even for states or localities that were already fiscally pressed.

Wolman and Peterson (1981) found that education tended to fare relatively well at the local level, in part because of the relatively high levels of state and federal aid. Within the school budget, general instruction tended to be cut more than compensatory, bilingual, and special education, which receive higher levels of intergovernmental aid. Core services tended to be cut less than administration or auxiliary services. At the state level, education was treated quite differently from state to state: Education aid increased in some states where there were limits, but in Michigan, when revenue shortfalls necessitated state budget reductions, education was cut disproportionately.

Gold (1982) examined the effects of existing limits on state taxing and spending. He concluded that most have not been restrictive because the states have been operating considerably below their limits. He also argued that most state limits will not become binding in the immediate future, although a continuing contraction in the federal role could change that.

At this time it is very difficult to draw any general conclusions about the impact of recent TELs on state and local spending and taxes. One might conclude that this reflects two phenomena – the measures are too recent to be able to determine their long-term effects yet and the research to date on effects is of a fragmentary, relatively unsophisticated nature. Even when these two obstacles have been overcome, it may still be difficult to draw general conclusions because the limits themselves and the conditions in which they operate are so varied.

While the general strategies that governments use to respond to fiscal pressure may be similar, the specific actions taken are a function of the particular situation. Thus Wolman and Peterson (1981) concluded that the unique features of each limit produce distinctive responses and that the strategies employed to cope with a limit depend on the type of limit. Bowen and Lee (1979) argued that the existing state context, existing state–local fiscal arrangements (which are varied and complex) and the content of the particular limit all affect the impact of a limit. An additional factor that contributes to the uniqueness of each limit and its impact is that limits tend to be omnibus packages with many provisions, some that may have little connection with the primary purpose of the limit but were included for political reasons or convenience.

THE FUTURE

How will TELs affect school finance in the next decade? That depends to a great extent on the likelihood of the adoption of additional limits and on the nature of such limits. Was the spate of limit adoptions in the late 1970s an omen of what is to come or is it a phenomenon that has already passed its peak? If further limits are adopted, where is that most likely to occur and what type of limit will be involved – a "meat ax" such as Proposition 13 or a more modest limit on growth in revenues or expenditures? In order to answer these questions, it is necessary to look at the pattern of adoptions across states and over time.

Limits placed on the ballot for voter approval have had, at best, modest success even in the late 1970s, and other attempts to place additional measures on the ballot through an initiative have failed to gain sufficient signatures. Furthermore, the tendency in both 1978 and 1980, when most of these measures were on the ballot, was for the more extreme or radical proposals, the ones that would have made the greatest changes in the current state–local finance structure, to be defeated. Generally, those that were approved were the more moderate proposals. Lucier (1979) argued that even Proposition 13 should not be considered a vote for cutbacks rather than restrained growth because of the existence of the state surplus. In 1978 Nevada approved a Proposition 13 copy, but since constitutional amendments must be approved twice, that was not a binding decision. When it came up again in 1980, after the legislature had adopted a statutory limit in 1979, it was defeated. Including Nevada, twelve measures were voted upon in ten states in the November 1978 elections; seven were approved. In 1980 ten measures involving limits were on the ballot; three passed. Six states defeated variants of Proposition 13. In addition to Proposition 2½ the other two successful proposals were in Arkansas, which adopted a millage rollback provision following reassessment, and Missouri, which adopted a limit on the growth of state and local taxes tied to increases in personal income. In Michigan a version of the Tisch proposal was on the ballot again, as were two measures that would have involved considerable tax shifts, one backed by the MEA and the other referred by the legislature; all three failed. The campaign for the Tisch proposal was very similar to that in 1978, with a narrowly based, poorly financed support group and unanimous opposition by the "Establishment." The results of the 1980 elections led commentators to conclude that "tax fever" had subsided (Ranney 1981; National Conference of State Legislatures 1980; Coalition of American Public Employees 1981). Since 1980 there have been no new adoptions of TELs.

Efforts to explain which states have adopted some type of limitation have not been particularly successful. Ladd (1978) found that states with high expenditure growth and high property tax burdens were more likely to impose limits on local governments between 1970 and 1976, as were those that already had some type of limit. Rand researchers used a similar methodology and found for the 1970 to 1978 period that a high property tax burden and a history of limitations were again associated with a tendency to adopt limits but not high local expenditure growth (Pascal et al. 1979). Mikesell (1979) suggested that referenda on limits tended to appear on the ballot in 1978 in states where residential property tax rates were above the national median or the recent (1966 to 1976) growth in state spending was above the national average. He also noted a regional pattern, with referenda most frequent in western and central states and infrequent in the East. (This reflects the fact that the initiative process is generally not available for state statutes or constitutional amendments in the East.) MacManus (1981) found that adoption of fiscal controls prior to Proposition 13 was more likely in states that were high on various measures of fiscal stress but that such measures did not explain which states approved or defeated ballot measures in 1978. Kuttner (1980) also argued that high residential property tax burdens and, in particular, a shift from business to residential property tax owners contributed to the adoption of limits in several states. However, other researchers (National Governors' Association 1978; Sigelman, Lowery, and Smith 1981; Hansen 1981; Ellickson 1979) have not found consistent relationships between state spending and taxing policies and adoption of limits. Results have also been inconsistent as to the importance of the initiative process (Craig 1979; Sigelman, Lowery, and Smith 1981).

Several factors may contribute to the differences in results from these studies. Part of the explanation may be varying definitions of the universe of limits or fiscal controls; measures included in one study are not necessarily counted in others. Another may be different time periods. Several authors (Pascal et al. 1979; Sigelman, Lowery, and Smith 1981; MacManus 1981) suggested that once the tax revolt became a "national phenomenon," the characteristics of individual states were no longer as important in determining whether a particular state would consider or adopt a limit, and that political rather than fiscal factors became more important.

Perhaps most important, the methodologies that have been used to examine this issue may have been poorly suited to tap the complexity of the phenomenon. Gold (1981b) criticized the multistate statistical studies that have tried to examine the impact of limits because they generally have used a single dummy variable (limit or no limit) to represent the impact of limits. Given the complexity and diversity of limits and the extent to which the impact of a limit is a function of its provisions, it is not surprising that the studies have not shown consistent or significant impacts. A similar criticism appears appropriate for the statistical studies of limit adoptions. The measures studied are complex and the likelihood of a measure being approved by the voters does appear to be a function of the nature of the proposal (statutory versus constitutional, advisory or nonbinding versus binding, and the restrictiveness of the measure).

Furthermore, political factors appear to be significant in explaining the outcome of referenda campaigns, and some of these are not captured in the statistical models. Lack of responsiveness by the legislature to perceived grievances about property taxes contributed to the passage of severe property tax limitations in California, Idaho, and Michigan. Kuttner (1980) argued that the reason that referenda failed in several states was because the state had already taken action to address such problems. Poorly organized and financed campaigns contributed to the defeat of other referenda. Several of the statistical studies found that adoption of limits or voting behavior on limits are best explained by political factors, such as ideology, past voting records, and political culture (Hansen 1981; Sigelman, Lowery, and Smith 1981; Williams 1976; Morgan 1981).

Thus, state-specific configurations of political and fiscal phenomena seem to provide the explanations for the adoption of limits. This suggests that there was not a national "tax revolt" that was manifested in the adoption of limits in the late 1970s. Concern about government efficiency and the feeling that taxes are too high did not suddenly appear in the late 1970s, although the salience of those issues may have increased due to economic conditions in that period, with double-digit inflation contributing to higher taxes when real incomes were growing very little. However, the size of the state–local sector was not growing and in fact had begun to decline as a proportion of the GNP. Thus there was a reservoir of discontent about taxes, but whether it was mobilized and resulted in a TEL measure being adopted depended on conditions within individual states.

The late 1970s were marked by a variety of measures that resulted in reductions in the size of the state–local sector or in slower growth in that sector. Some states adopted limits, while most enacted various types of tax reductions. Beginning in 1980 the times have changed; the rate of adoption of TELs has slowed considerably and most states, with the exceptions of those that have energy resources, have been faced with the necessity to raise taxes (and/or cut expenditures) in order to balance their budgets. These developments reflect both the stagnation in the economy and the fact that some states overreacted when they cut taxes a few years earlier. Furthermore, the policies of the current administration are accelerating the decline in federal aid to state and local governments that had begun at the end of the Carter administration. All these factors suggest that in the next few years:

- Many state and local governments will be faced with the problem of maintaining service levels in the face of slowly growing (or declining) real revenues;

- There will not be another surge of adoptions of limits; and

- Where limits are adopted, they will tend to be moderate ones, limiting growth, rather than ones calling for actual declines in revenues or expenditures.

Have tax and expenditure limitations had a significant impact on school finance? At a general level, the answer is not much, although there are noticeable exceptions, such as California with the large increase in the state share of funding. The reasons for the lack of impact are several. Many of the state limits are not particularly constraining. The effect of other limits has not yet really been felt (e.g., due to the state surplus in California or the depressed economic conditions in Michigan). Some local limits have been accompanied by increased state aid, which has contributed to a different mix in revenues and a greater state share, even if it has not facilitated expenditure equalization. Finally, some of the limits are simply too recent, and there is too little information available to be able to evaluate their impact. In addition the initial responses of governments to newly imposed limits may be a poor indicator of the long term effects and responses.

It would be an overstatement to say that TELs, at least with regard to school finance, are "full of sound and fury but signify nothing" or "paper tigers" as Wilken and Callahan (1978) suggested. However, as a general rule their effects are marginal and subtle and are a function of both the nature of the measure and how it is implemented. Many of the initiated measures left a number of the details about implementation unspecified, which is one reason there is often much confusion during the campaign about the possible effects of the proposal. Thus the politics of the implementation of a limit, about which very little has been written, can contribute significantly to the ultimate impact of the measure. California and Massachusetts appear to have made quite different decisions in constructing new state aid packages in the wake of severe property tax limitations, while the legislature rewrote the statutory limit in Idaho. There was a surge of adoptions of local limits in the 1930s, which were later found to be rather ineffective (ACIR 1962). In the long run, similar conclusions may be reached about the limits adopted in the late 1970s, especially as they are modified over time and officials learn how to get around them. The adoption of additional severe limits does not appear very likely.

California and Massachusetts appear to represent exceptions, rather than the rule, in terms of adoption and impact of limits. It does not appear likely that many states will follow their example in the near future. California has had two additional limitation measures on the ballot since June 1978. One passed, Proposition 4, which placed mild limits on the growth of state revenues, and the other, Proposition 9, which would have dramatically reduced state income taxes, was defeated. Thus even in California, once the problems of rising residential property taxes and the large state surplus had been addressed by Proposition 13, the voters were unwilling to adopt a radical measure such as Proposition 9. To the extent that further limitations are adopted, they will probably represent legislative adoption (or referral to the voters) of moderate limits on expenditure and revenue growth, which has been the trend since 1979.

In retrospect it may appear that the great interest in TELs was simply one manifestation of a larger and longer-term development, the reduction in the relative, if not the absolute, size of the public sector, which both preceded and outlived the brief flurry of TEL activity between 1978 and 1980. Slower growth had begun for state and local governments before both Proposition 13 and the declines in federal grants-in-aid. Similarly, the adoption of moderate, statutory spending limits also preceded Proposition 13 in New Jersey, Colorado, and Tennessee. The major impact of property tax limitations has been to shift the mix of state–local revenues away from the property tax and to further centralize revenue raising at the state level, which has been the trend for more than twenty years (ACIR 1981).

The available evidence on the politics of TELs suggests that there was not a "national tax revolt" in the late 1970s. What occurred could not be explained in national terms nor be characterized as a tax "revolt." While voters were concerned about the level of taxes and efficiency, they generally were not seeking reductions in services, and measures that would have produced such cutbacks were usually rejected. In the cases where more severe limits were approved, the explanation appeared to be a combination of a very specific and visible grievance about property taxes (as opposed to a more general, unfocused discontent about taxes) and an equally apparent lack of responsiveness from the state government. By the early 1980s the message of a smaller, more efficient public sector (but not necessarily one that does less) has permeated all levels of government. The acceptance of that message by public officials and a stagnant economy are having far more impact on state and local governments than are formal limitations. They also are likely to obviate the interest in or perceived need for limits. Thus TELs may have been more a symptom of a change in attitudes and direction rather than a significant factor contributing to that change, except in a few instances where public officials were out-of-step with the changing times. Additional factors that may decrease interest in TELs are uncertainty about the future federal role, the possibility that state and local governments may assume some responsibilities previously handled or financed by the federal government, and reductions in state revenues due to the changes in the federal income tax.

REFERENCES

Advisory Commission on Intergovernmental Relations (ACIR). 1962. *State Constitutional and Statutory Restrictions on Local Taxing Powers.* Washington, D.C.

_____. 1980. *Significant Features of Fiscal Federalism, 1979-80 Edition.* Washington, D.C.

_____. 1981. *Significant Features of Fiscal Federalism, 1980-81 Edition.* Washington, D.C.

Attiyeh, Richard, and Robert Engle. 1979. "Testing Some Propositions about Proposition 13." *National Tax Journal* 32, no. 2 (June): 131–46.

Austermann, Winifred, and Dan Pilcher. 1980. "The Tax Revolt Transformed." *State Legislatures* (July/August): 25–33.

Baratz, Joan, and Jay Moskowitz. 1978. "Proposition 13: How and Why It Happened." *Phi Delta Kappan* 60, no. 1 (September): 9–11.

Bishop, Reid. 1982. Assistant Superintendent, Idaho State Department of Education. Personal communication (March 12).

Bloom, Howard. 1979. "Public Choice and Private Interest: Explaining the Vote for Property Tax Classification in Massachusetts." *National Tax Journal* 32, no. 4 (December): 527-34.

Bowen, Frank, and Eugene Lee. 1979. *Limiting State Spending: The Legislature or the Electorate.* Berkeley, Calif.: Institute of Governmental Studies, University of California, Berkeley.

Bradbury, Katharine, and Helen Ladd, with Claire Christopherson. 1982. "Proposition 2½: Initial Impacts (pt. I)." *New England Economic Review* (January/February): 13-24.

Brown, L.; A. Ginsburg; J. Killalea; R. Rosthal; and E. Tron. 1978. "School Finance Reform in the Seventies: Achievements and Failures." *Journal of Education Finance* 4, no. 2 (Fall): 195-212.

Bureau of Government Research. 1980. *School Budget Caps in New Jersey, 1976-1980: Four Years of Experience with Expenditure Limitations.* New Brunswick, N.J.: Rutgers University.

Cattanach, D.; R. Lang; and L. Hooper. 1976. "Tax and Expenditure Controls: The Price of School Finance Reform." In *School Finance Reform: A Legislators' Handbook*, edited by J. Callahan and W. Wilken, pp. 60-72. Washington, D.C.: National Conference of State Legislatures.

Citrin, Jack. 1979. "Do People Want Something for Nothing: Public Opinion on Taxes and Government Spending." *National Tax Journal* 32, no. 2 (June): 113-30.

Coalition of American Public Employees. 1981, *Cape Update* (May/April).

Courant, P.; E. Gramlich; and D. Rubinfeld. 1980. "Why Voters Support Tax Limitation Amendments: The Michigan Case." *National Tax Journal* 33, no. 1 (March): 1-20.

_____. 1981. "Why Voters Support Tax Limitation Amendments: The Michigan Case." In *Tax and Expenditure Limitations*, edited by H. Ladd and T. N. Tideman. Washington, D.C.: The Urban Institute Press.

Craig, Eleanor. 1979. "Are Tax and Spending Lids Predictable?" *Proceedings of the Seventy-Second Annual Conference of the National Tax Association-Tax Institute of America.* Oklahoma City, Oklahoma, October 28-November 1.

Education Finance Center, Education Commission of the States. 1979. "Public Opinion and Proposition 13: Attitudes of Californians toward Education and the Implementation of Proposition 13." *Finance Facts* Special Issue (February).

Ellickson, Phyllis. 1979. "The Fiscal Limitation Movement: Present Context and Outlooks." Rand Note: N-1160-FF. Santa Monica, Calif.: The Rand Corporation.

Elmore, Richard, and Milbrey McLaughlin. 1982. *Reform and Retrenchment: The Politics of California School Finance Reform.* Cambridge, Mass.: Ballinger Publishing Company.

Fox, Mark. 1982. Idaho State Department of Education. Personal communication (March 8).

Freiman, Marc. 1980. "Why Voters Support Tax Limitation Amendments: A Comment." *National Tax Journal* 33, no. 4 (December): 493–96.

Freiman, Marc, and Patrick Grasso. 1982. "Budget Impact and Voter Response to Tax Limitation Referenda." *Public Finance Quarterly* 10, no. 1 (January): 49–66.

Goertz, Margaret, and Jay Moskowitz. 1979. "Caps and Kids: The Impact of New Jersey's Education Budget Caps." Paper presented at Annual Meeting of the American Education Finance Association, Washington, D.C., January 15.

Gold, Steven. 1981a. "Homeowner Property Taxes, Inflation and Property Tax Relief." *National Tax Journal* 34, no. 2 (June): 167–84.

_____. 1981b. "Results of Local Spending and Revenue Limitations: A Survey." Legislative Finance Paper #5. Denver, Colo.: National Conference of State Legislatures.

_____. 1982. "How Restrictive Have Limitations on State Spending and Taxing Been?" Legislative Finance Paper #15. Denver, Colo.: National Conference of State Legislatures.

Hansen, Susan. 1981. "The Tax Revolt and the Politics of Redistribution." Paper presented at the Annual Meeting of the American Political Science Association, New York City, September 3–6.

Hansen, W. Lee, and F. Howard Nelson. 1978. "Impact of the 1973 Wisconsin School Finance Reform." In *Selected Papers in School Finance, 1978*, edited by Esther Tron, pp. 111–24. Washington, D.C.: U.S. Department of Health, Education, and Welfare.

Katz, David. 1979. "Proposition 13 and the Public Schools: The First Year." Program Report No. B–18. Stanford, Calif.: Institute for Research on Educational Finance and Governance, Stanford University.

Kuttner, Robert. 1980. *Revolt of the Haves: Tax Rebellions and Hard Times.* New York: Simon and Schuster.

Ladd, Helen. 1978. "An Economic Evaluation of State Limitations on Local Taxing and Spending Powers." *National Tax Journal* 31, no. 1 (March): 1–18.

Ladd, Helen, and Julie Boatright Wilson. 1982a. "Education and Tax Limitations: Evidence from Massachusetts' Proposition 2½." Boston; John F. Kennedy School of Government, Harvard University.

_____. 1982b. "Proposition 2½: Explaining the Vote." Boston: John F. Kennedy School of Government, Harvard University.

_____. 1982c. "Proposition 2½: Variations in Individual Preferences and Expectations across Communities." Boston: John F. Kennedy School of Government, Harvard University.

_____. 1982d. "Who Supports Tax Limitations: Evidence from Massachusetts' Proposition 2½." Boston: John F. Kennedy School of Government, Harvard University.

_____. 1982e. "Why Voters Support Tax Limitations: Evidence from Massachusetts' Proposition 2½." Boston: John F. Kennedy School of Government, Harvard University.

Levy, Mickey. 1975. "Voting on California's Tax and Expenditure Limitation Initiative." *National Tax Journal* 28, no. 2 (December): 426–35.

Lipset, Seymour Martin, and William Schneider. 1980. "Is the Tax Revolt Over?" *Taxing and Spending* (Summer): 73–81.

Lipson, Albert, with Marvin Lavin. 1979. "Political and Legal Responses to Proposition 13 in California." Rand Report: R-2483-DOJ. Santa Monica, Calif.: The Rand Corporation.

Lowery, David, and Lee Sigelman. 1981. "Understanding the Tax Revolt: Eight Explanations." *American Political Science Review* 75, no. 4 (December): 963–74.

Lucier, Richard. 1971. "The Oregon Tax Substitution Referendum: The Prediction of Voting Behavior." *National Tax Journal* 24, no. 1 (March): 87–90.

_____. 1973. "The Prediction of Public Choice Behavior in the Washington Tax Substitution Referendum." *National Tax Journal* 26, no. 4 (December): 625–30.

_____. 1979. "Gauging the Strength and Meaning of the 1978 Tax Revolt." *Public Administration Review* 39, no. 4 (July/August): 371–79.

MacManus, Susan. 1981. "State Tax Revolts in the Seventies: Economic Necessities or Political Opportunities?" In *Perspectives on Taxing and Spending Limitations in the United States*, edited by Charlie B. Tyer and Marcia W. Taylor. Columbia, S.C.: Bureau of Governmental Research and Service, University of South Carolina.

Magaddino, J.P.; E. Toma; and M. Toma. 1980. "Proposition 13: A Public Choice Appraisal." *Public Finance Quarterly* 8, no. 2 (April): 223–35.

Massachusetts Municipal Association. 1982. "Report on the Impact of Proposition 2½." Boston.

May, Peter, and Arnold Meltsner. 1981. "Limited Actions, Distressing Consequences: A Selected View of the California Experience." *Public Administration Review* 41, Special Issue (January): 172–79.

Menchik, M.; J. Fernandez; and M. Caggiano. 1981. "How Fiscal Containment Affects Spending and Services in Cities." Working draft for Conference on Prospects for Local Government, sponsored by The Rand Corporation, Santa Monica, California, April 27–28.

Mikesell, John. 1979. "The Season of Tax Revolt." In *Fiscal Retrenchment and Urban Policy*, edited by John Blair and David Nachmias. Urban Affairs Annual Reviews, Vol. 17, Beverly Hills, Calif.: Sage Publications.

Morgan, Edward. 1981. "Public Preferences and Policy Realities: Proposition 2½ in Massachusetts." Paper presented at the Annual Meeting of the Northeastern Political Science Association, Newark, New Jersey, November.

_____. 1982. "Public Education and the Taxpayers' Revolt: Interpreting Proposition 2½ in Massachusetts." Summary Report presented at the Annual

Meeting of the American Education Finance Association, Philadelphia, March 19.

National Conference of State Legislatures. 1980. "Results of Ballot Proposals Show Tax Cut Fever Cooling." *News Release* (November 7). Washington, D.C.

National Governors' Association. 1978. *Tax and Expenditure Limitations, 1978.* Washington, D.C.: Center for Policy Research.

Odden, Allen. 1978. "School Finance in Colorado: An Update." Papers in Education Finance, Paper No. 8. Denver, Colo.: Education Commission of the States.

Osman, Jack, and John Gemello. "Revenue/Expenditure Limits and Override Elections: The Experience of California School Districts." Project Report No. 81-A9. Stanford, Calif.: Institute for Research on Educational Finance and Governance, Stanford University.

Palaich, Robert. 1980. "Statewide Tax and Expenditure Limitation Referenda: What Are the Implications for Schools?" Paper presented at the Annual Meeting of the American Education Finance Association, San Diego, California, March 16-18.

Palaich, R.; J. Kloss; and M. Williams. 1980. "The Politics of Tax and Expenditure Limitations: An Analysis of Public Opinion, Voting Behavior and the Campaigns in Four States." Report No. F80-2. Denver, Colo.: Education Finance Center, Education Commission of the States.

Pascal, A.; M. Menchik; J. Chaiken; P. Ellickson; W. Walker; D. Tray; and A. Wise. 1979. "Fiscal Containment of Local and State Government." Rand Report: R-2494-FF/RC. Santa Monica, Calif.: The Rand Corporation.

Ranney, Austin. 1981. "Opinion Roundup." *Public Opinion* 4, no. 1 (February/March): 40-41.

Ruhf, Marilyn. 1981. "A School Sampling: 'Enrichment,' Athletics, and Class Sizes under 2½." *Impact: 2½* no. 15-16 (December 1): 1-4.

Shalala, D.; M. Williams; and A. Fishel. 1973. "The Property Tax and the Voters: An Analysis of State Constitutional Referenda to Revise School Finance Systems in California, Colorado, Michigan and Oregon in 1972 and 1973." Occasional Paper Number 2. New York, N.Y.: The Institute of Philosophy and Politics of Education, Teachers College, Columbia University.

Sigelman, L.; D. Lowery; and R. Smith. 1981. "The Tax Revolt: A Comparative State Study." Paper presented at the Annual Meeting of the Southwestern Political Science Association, Dallas, Texas, March.

Speich, Don, and Stephen Weiner. 1980. *In the Eye of the Storm: Proposition 13 and Public Education in California.* Washington, D.C.: Institute for Educational Leadership, George Washington University.

Tompkins, Susanne. 1981. "Proposition 2½—Massachusetts and the Tax Revolt." *The Journal of the Institute for Socioeconomic Studies* 6, no. 1 (Spring): 21-32.

Tvedt, Sherry. 1981. "Enough is Enough: Proposition 2½ in Massachusetts." *National Civic Review* 70, no. 10 (November): 527–33.

Wilken, William, and John Callahan. 1978. "State Limitations on Local Taxing and Spending Power: A Paper Tiger." Unpublished paper, National Conference of State Legislatures, Washington, D.C.

Williams, Mary Frase. 1976. "Politics and Voting Behavior in Statewide Tax Referenda." Paper presented at the Annual Meeting of the American Political Science Association, Chicago, September.

_____. 1979a. "Colorado: A Dozen Years of Fiscal Referenda and School Finance Reform." Unpublished materials prepared for the National Conference of State Legislatures, Washington, D.C.

_____. 1979b. "Michigan Politics." Unpublished materials prepared for the National Conference of State Legislatures, Washington, D.C.

Winkler, Donald. 1979. "Fiscal Limitations in the Provision of Local Public Services: The Case of Education." *National Tax Journal* 32, no. 2 (June): 329–42.

Wolman, Harold, and George Peterson. 1981. "State and Local Government Strategies for Responding to Fiscal Pressure." *Tulane Law Review* 55, no. 3 (April): 773–819.

Wright, J. Ward. 1981. *Tax and Expenditure Limitation: A Policy Perspective.* Lexington, Ky.: The Council of State Governments.

7 THE POLITICS OF PUBLIC AID TO PRIVATE SCHOOLS

Chester E. Finn, Jr.*

INTRODUCTION

If this essay were being written 150 years ago, it would be called simply "the politics of school aid." From the founding of the earliest American colonies almost until the Civil War, there was no distinction between "public" and "private" education. Schools were generally regarded as community institutions but were customarily operated under church or other nongovernmental auspices and funded with a mixture of tuition monies, charitable support, and miscellaneous subsidies given them by the town fathers (or state assemblies) out of resources belonging to the "public" sector.

Politics, to be sure, played a part in schools, and these were often spirited, sometimes rancorous and divisive. Schools had to justify their support by satisfying the diverse needs, demands, and expectations of multiple constituencies: their students' families, their own trustees or governing boards, the elders of their churches or other organizational sponsors, the selectmen or councils of the towns in which they were located, and frequently the legislators of their colonies or states. But the schools were not creatures of government. Since there were no compulsory attendance laws—Massachusetts enacted the first such law in 1852—and no expectation that educa-

*Chester E. Finn, Jr., Professor, Education and Public Policy, Vanderbilt University.

183

tion would be universal, let alone free, state and local jurisdictions could and did devise varied, even idiosyncratic, patterns of financial support for and regulation of schools.

The middle third of the nineteenth century witnessed the "invention" of public schools as they are known today: educational institutions operated by agencies of government (usually a complex blend of state and local), wholly financed from compulsory taxation, free to all who attend them, and ultimately accountable to elected officials (hence to the electorate) for their policies and activities.

The pre-Civil War pioneers of public education—Horace Mann, Henry Barnard, John Pierce, and Samuel Lewis—had many hopes and were motivated by several strong impulses. Lawrence A. Cremin (1961: 9–10), one of the most distinguished historians of American education, characterized Mann's ideas thusly:

> [H]e had poured into his vision of universal education a boundless faith in the perfectability of human life and institutions. Once public schools were established, no evil could resist their salutary influence. Universal education could be the "great equalizer" of human conditions, the "balance wheel of the social machinery," and the "creator of wealth undreamed of." . . . The theory supporting Mann's faith represented a fascinating potpourri of early American progressivism, combining elements of Jeffersonian republicanism, Christian moralism, and Emersonian idealism. Mann understood well the relationship between freedom, self-government, and universal education. . . . Mann's school would be common, not as a school for the common people . . . but rather as a school common to all people. It would be open to all, provided by the state and the local community as part of the birthright of every child. . . . The genius of Mann's design . . . was the vesting of political control in the people. . . . For by the artful device of lay control the public was entrusted with the continuing definition of the public philosophy taught its children. . . .[1]

Public schooling gradually spread across the United States and by the end of the nineteenth century was accessible to virtually every child. Not surprisingly, the emergence of explicitly "public" schools transformed the relationship between government and the older kinds of schools that now began to be seen as "private." This was a gradual change that followed no uniform pattern. Direct and indirect governmental aid to privately controlled schools dwindled, and a number of once-private institutions evolved into governmental schools. But many organizational hybrids endured, and some still do today. These can be seen in a few towns in northern New England that continue to pay the tuitions of students to attend local "academies," especially at the secondary level, rather than operating complete sets of "public" schools. It is also evident in the arrangements that many states make for severely handicapped children to be educated in private—often residential—schools that specialize in such instruction.

The spread of universal and compulsory education had two other major impacts on private schooling. It tended to encourage the establishment of private schools to serve those who for one reason or another did not like what they found in the public schools and who discovered that they could not alter those schools to suit them. This was true to some extent of social elites, and it is not coincidental that many of today's better-known preparatory schools were founded in the late nineteenth century. But the largest movement came from ethnic and religious groups that found the public schools apathetic or hostile to their own views of faith and morality or just plain unfriendly to them as people. Not everyone welcomed Horace Mann's educational values or the Protestantism that dominated American public schools in the nineteenth century. Thus the largest set of private educational institutions in the United States—the parochial schools of the Roman Catholic church—was formally established in the late 1800s in reaction to that dominant Protestantism and to the nativism that made many Catholic immigrant families feel unwelcome in the public schools of the period. Essentially the same development can be seen today in the spread of fundamentalist Protestant schools, which is primarily motivated by dismay over the secularism, immorality, and indiscipline of public education.

The other significant impact of compulsory schooling laws is also still being felt by private education. When the state requires children to attend school, it must have some means of enforcing that requirement, that is, some way of determining what constitutes an acceptable school. The public schools present no definitional problems, but how is the state to know whether a nongovernmental entity that calls itself a "school"—be it Andover or a tutorial conducted by parents in their own living room—is a satisfactory source of compliance with the compulsory attendance law? This is no easy question, and efforts to answer it have plunged practically every state into complex—and highly-charged—issues of regulating private education.

These issues, it should be noted, would arise even in the absence of any public financial support for private education. So long as the state has the power to require children to attend school but lacks the authority (as the Supreme Court held in 1925) to oblige them to attend government schools, it must somehow define the terms by which its own requirements can be satisfied.

But the definitional task grows manifestly harder when government also supplies financial assistance to private schools or their students. Short of scattering money in the streets or handing it out to everyone who wants some, the funding agency must define eligible recipients and take some steps to ensure that the aid is used for the purposes intended. This means, in a word, regulation—the inevitable concomitant of public financial support. It need not necessarily be complex or burdensome, but there is no getting around the fact that aid is always associated with some regulation, if only through the determination of eligibility.

The linked issues of aid-and-regulation also invoke related passages in the federal Constitution, namely the first amendment stipulations that "Congress shall make no law respecting an establishment of religion, or prohibiting the free exercise thereof." Inasmuch as 80 percent of private schools are church-affiliated, it is impossible to have any public policies affecting them, beneficially or otherwise, without reckoning with those two pillars of the republic (and with kindred provisions in most state constitutions).

The constitutionality of proposals for public support of nonpublic education is usually tested against the "establishment" clause while government regulations affecting private schools are ordinarily debated in relation to the "free exercise" clause. But that has also been something of an oversimpliciation, and it becomes more of one with every passing month. For the fastest-growing and politically most active sector of private education—the schools run by fundamentalist Protestant churches—is especially sensitive to real and perceived infringements by government on the free exercise of religion. This gets carried to what many observers regard as needless extremes, such as the unwillingness of some fundamentalist schools even to be counted in government-sponsored tallies of education statistics. But for purposes of this discussion it is sufficient to point out that, whereas for most of the past three decades the protection of the first amendment was generally invoked by persons who did not want government to help private education, today it is at least as frequently invoked by persons within private education who do not want government to do anything to harm their schools.

THE DEEPENING SCHISM

The relationships between government and private education in the early 1980s are characterized by confused policy, schismatic philosophy, and stalemated politics. There are two large divisions. The first is the split within private education between those whose foremost objective is to obtain public financial support for their schools and those whose premier concern is to vouchsafe the autonomy of their schools.

The second is the split between those outside private education who value it and believe public policies should strengthen it, and those, also outside private education, who believe that its welfare is not a fit concern of government. This, too, is oversimplified. Some persons in the latter category wish private schools no ill and may contribute (privately) to their support, perhaps even enroll their children in them, but have philosophical objections to governmental encouragement of nongovernmental education. Others regard private schools as destructive of important social and educational values and would have government take vigorous action to discourage, harass, or regulate them such that they will lose their distinctive appeal. At the same time, "friends" of private education may have radically different ideas about what constitutes favorable public policy, some viewing it chiefly in terms of financial support, others in terms of maximum institutional freedom, with some incurable optimists believing the two to be compatible.

In the main—but again oversimplifying—the older, better-established private school groups and their allies in the political world tend to be found among the aid-seekers.[2] This is partly because they regard their schools as quasi-public institutions, have long since worked out fairly satisfactory relationships with state and local educational agencies, and do not see additional financial support as likely to result in much more or much different regulation than they are already accommodating. They are not especially mistrustful of government; indeed, many are linked through their sponsoring denominations to health and social service agencies that cooperate closely with government and depend heavily upon it for financial support. They have lived through earlier school aid battles, are not above compromising, and feel deprived, even cheated, of what they regard as the portions of previous aid schemes that were meant for their schools. Furthermore, they suffered from the sharp downturn in private school enrollments that occurred in the late 1960s and early 1970s, the era in which the current campaign for private school aid began, and tend still to think that such aid is essential to their long-term institutional security.

By contrast, the newer private education groups, primarily the fundamentalist sects and their schools, see a greater threat from proximity to government than from fiscal neglect by it. Although many such schools operate on financial shoestrings, they do not presently lack for students and most are too new to have experienced the hard times of a decade ago. Moreover, they are riding the national wave of religious fundamentalism *cum* moral revivalism *cum* political conservatism and are accustomed of late to succeeding in their efforts. Because their leaders, their teachers, their benefactors and their students (or at least the parents of their students) tend to view all issues through the lenses of religious faith and scripture, and because they also tend to regard the secular state as hostile and immoral, they approach absolutism in their construction of the proper relationship between government and private education: Government should in no way seek to influence the activities of the school, of those who work in the school, or of those who study in the school, and if that means abjuring all forms of financial assistance from public sources, so be it.[3] (There is one significant exception. Even the most fundamentalist of schools insist on being exempt from taxation and on the deductibility of contributions to them. But in their eyes—and the eyes of many others—that does not constitute aid from government, merely exemption from another form of governmental harassment and red tape. Of course it is an exemption that brings palpable economic benefits to their schools as well. This issue is further discussed below.)

THE POLITICAL CONTEXT: FIVE REALITIES

The schism within private education is the *first* of five elemental realities that form the context within which any contemporary examination of these issues must take place. Private education is not a single community of interest within the world of public policy. Other than the fact that all three are educational institutions operating under private auspices in the Washington metropolitan area, the

Sidwell Friends School, the Our Lady of Perpetual Help School, and the Clinton Christian School have practically nothing in common. Besides obvious differences in religious affiliation, they have dissimilar educational philosophies; they embody somewhat different moral and ethical values; they generally enroll youngsters from separate social, economic, and geographic communities; they belong to different national associations; and it is unlikely that a teacher or administrator from any one of them would take—or could get—a position at either of the others. To be sure, all charge tuition to their students (though in very different amounts) and all receive (deductible) contributions. That means from time to time a public policy issue may arise around which they—or their national spokesmen—can make common cause. But their shared interests are less consequential than their differences, and any alliances are apt to be temporary and fragile.

The *second* basic reality is that the governmental pie from which education aid is sliced is no longer growing. The sharp reductions that the Reagan administration proposed in 1981 and 1982, and that Congress has partially accepted, are evidence of the erosion of federal financial support for education—as well as for many other domains of domestic social policy. Ascendant conservatism and various tax limitation referenda are having much the same effect on many state and local budgets, which also must compensate as best they can for Washington's cutbacks. The continuing decline in school enrollments in most communities leads many people to assume that education should be able to make do with less money. And although widespread public dissatisfaction with the quality of schooling might seem, to an educator, like a solid reason for devoting additional resources to it, voters often seem disposed to draw the opposite conclusion.

While dissatisfaction with public schools is one reason for increasing interest in private schools and in government support for them, the old maxim of political economy that "you can't get blood from a turnip" also continues to be true. It is far easier to obtain government aid for new recipients when the totality of such aid is increasing and correspondingly more difficult when the total is level or declining. Even elected officials who are disposed to help private education are apt to be more reluctant to do so when such help is, or seems to be, at the expense of the public schools attended by approximately 90 percent of all students.

This reluctance is intensified by the anxiety-verging-on-panic that presently afflicts much of *public* education, and the near-paranoia manifested by many spokesmen for public education vis-à-vis private education. This is the *third* political reality: Rightly or wrongly, private schools are today viewed by many in the public education establishment as threats to public schools, as competitors for students, and as rivals in the already difficult campaign for popular approbation and resources. That establishment retains many political allies. It can tap a considerable reservoir of popular support for the *idea* of free public education, even from many who are displeased with the *performance* of particular public schools. Moreover, it has an awesome arsenal of ideological, rhetorical, and cultural weapons—as well as ready access to major shapers of public opinion and a relatively newfound willingness to roll up its sleeves and plunge into practical politics, unabashedly making sizable campaign contributions to and rounding up votes for candidates who are attentive to its interests.[4]

The *fourth* reality is that private elementary and secondary education has never—not in a century, anyway—enjoyed full legitimacy in the eyes of the predominantly liberal elites that continue to shape many of the nation's ideological, cultural, and social views, even if those views do not presently dominate the policy agenda of the federal government. The major private foundations, the elite universities, the editorial pages of many metropolitan newspapers, the most prestigious think tanks and research institutes, and the writers for many illustrious journals of opinion do not generally hold private schools in the same high regard as private universities, private hospitals, or private libraries—not to mention private newspapers, magazines, and foundations! Paradoxically, more than a few members of the selfsame elites send their own children to private schools even as they say, write, and do things that call into question the present legitimacy and future viability of such institutions. Such questions, it may be noted, are more apt to be oblique, linked to such concerns as racial integration (and the alleged role of private schools in impeding it, both by inadequately integrating themselves and by providing a haven for those fleeing public school desegregation), than frontal assaults on the desirability or quality of nongovernmental schooling per se.[5]

This is not to suggest that opinion-shapers are engaged in some sort of anti-private school vendetta even as they garner the benefits of such education for their own privileged youngsters. Many bear no animus against private schools but simply believe, sincerely and consistently, that these schools offer social benefits comparable to private swimming pools or golf clubs—mildly snooty and vaguely exclusive luxuries that a free society cannot deny to those who want (and can afford) them but that government has no business encouraging, aiding, or abetting. Some lament that private schools give the most ardently education-minded families too easy an alternative, thus deflecting their political, organizational, and economic energies away from the improvement of public education. And for some, the common school ideal of a free public institution attended equally by all the children of a community looms so large as a social and political value as to cast shadows across anything that might appear to undermine it.

Such sentiments occasionally have an ugly underside that is not rendered any more attractive by the fact that it may be unconscious. Bigotry may be too strong a term for it, but distaste may be too mild. It is simply the fact that the two largest segments of private education today—the Roman Catholic and Protestant fundamentalist schools—are affiliated with religions whose orthodoxies and dogmas are frequently unpalatable to the members of liberal elites, whose adherents are often not the kinds of people with whom members of those elites tend to associate, and whose motives in forming and supporting separate schools often seem questionable when judged by the political and social values of those elites. Such questions are, if anything, intensified by the entanglement of private schooling with some of the ideas of the new right and the Moral Majority and by its overlap with such volatile issues in public education policy as busing, school prayer, creationism, and sex education.

Although the ideological hegemony of the liberal elites is weaker than before—the consequence of recent election returns, the more conservative mood of the nation, and the proliferation of conservative research institutes and journals of opinion—education policy remains among its more vigorous outposts, and no issue in education policy galvanizes it to greater effort than public support for private schooling. Hence the fourth reality, much the oldest of them all, endures today.

The *fifth* reality, by contrast, is so new that even many persons within private education have not yet grasped its import. Private schools, overall, are in reasonably sound institutional health at the present time. Though practically none has any surplus income, and some—especially Catholic schools in declining northeastern industrial cities—are short of students, most are fully enrolled and a number have waiting lists. (The several hundred traditionally selective independent schools have simply become more selective.) While several sectors of private education—especially, again, the Catholic schools—have continued shrinking both in total enrollments and in the number of institutions, the rate of that shrinkage has slowed dramatically in the past five years, and recent data indicate that even Catholic enrollments have stabilized in the last year or two. Meanwhile, other sectors are growing in numbers of students and schools, and for the fundamentalist Protestant denominations that growth may be near-explosive. (Their reluctance to cooperate with statistical surveys means that government data about fundamentalist schools are incomplete and unreliable, but one of the companies that publishes their textbooks boasts that such schools are opening at an average rate of three per day.) Although aggregate private school enrollments have by no means returned to the 13 percent of total elementary/secondary students that they commanded in the mid-1960s, available evidence indicates that they have edged above 10 percent and are heading for 11 percent. It should, of course, be borne in mind that this percentage depends both on actual private school enrollments and on the total number of youngsters in school. The latter figure continues to fall, but the public schools now absorb more than their share of the total decline, whereas ten years ago private schools did.

There is no reason to suppose that the currently healthy condition of private education will last, any more than the sickly condition of 1970 did. What is significant for contemporary analyses, however, is that most of the impetus behind the present quest for public aid to private education—especially at the federal level but also in many states—is "left over" from the time when it looked to many as if without such aid private schools would all but disappear. Thus the quest continues to have the political, rhetorical, and programmatic trappings of a campaign to channel public resources into nonpublic education in order to "preserve" it. Yet it is difficult to persuade any objective observer of the present situation that private education as a whole is in any immediate peril. It is rather as if the campaign to save the Chrysler corporation were being waged several years after the automaker had turned the corner and was showing a modest profit.

It is not surprising that today's chief aid-seekers are the spokesmen for Catholic schools and other sectors of private education that genuinely believed their existence to be in jeopardy a few years ago and that are not sanguine about their institutional future, no mátter what the most recent statistics may suggest about the present.[6] Neither is it surprising that their staunchest allies in government have been officials who cherish Catholic and other mainstream private schools, who formed their ideas about the condition of those schools and about the proper relationship between private schools and government during the time of crisis and decline, whose districts or states include frostbelt communities most apt to have private schools that are still in peril, and who espouse the kinds of programs—tuition tax credits being the best known—designed to channel a substantial amount of additional resources into the ordinary operating budgets of practically every private school.

Nor is it surprising that the sectors of private education that now tend to be most concerned about the *terms* by which public aid may be provided and about other regulatory issues are those with no history of shrinkage or decline but with recent experience with what they regard as governmental harassment. It follows that *their* staunchest allies in government are officials who assign great value to the independence of private organizations, who are more apt to see governmental action of any kind as a threat than as a boon, and whose constituencies are sunbelt jurisdictions with relatively few Catholic (and other traditional private) schools but with large numbers of new fundamentalist churches and born-again voters.

The five realities that shape the politics of public support for private education, then, are a schismatic private school community with internally divergent policy priorities, a leveling-off or decline in aggregate government support for education, deepening insecurity combined with intensifying activism on the part of public school leaders, enduring doubts in much of the American political culture as to the legitimacy of private education, and an at least temporarily obsolete formulation of the key problem that public support is intended to solve.

CURRENT EFFORTS TO OBTAIN AID:
FOUR THEMES

Against this backdrop, one can more easily disentangle four distinct themes in recent efforts to secure public support for private education. In practical political terms, of course, they are rarely separated, but for analytical purposes it is useful to understand them separately.

The *first* theme, noted above, is to save private schools from vanishing and to assure their institutional vitality by subsidizing them with something resembling unrestricted revenues. The underlying assumption is that they are socially and educationally valuable institutions in their present form and that as such they have a claim on public financial resources. Because Supreme Court interpretations of the establishment clause raise vexing questions about the constitutionality of unrestricted government payments directly to church-affiliated schools, actual schemes crafted to attain this objective generally take the form of financial assistance to families that pay private school tuitions. The best known proposal is a partial credit against the parents' federal income tax for tuitions paid to private schools. Although taxpayers would reap the initial economic benefit, the expectation is that this would lead to increased revenue for the schools. Revenue gains could be realized through facilitating higher tuition charges or by enabling parents to pay tuitions who would not otherwise be able to, thereby expanding enrollments, or by reducing the need for schools to give tuition reductions and other kinds of financial aid to students. No such proposal has yet been enacted by the federal government, and a number of similar schemes enacted at the state level have been struck down by the courts, though a modified (and small) one endures in Minnesota.

The *second* theme is to preserve economic benefits that private schools already receive from government without levying additional requirements or regulations on them. Like the first, this is an essentially conservative notion: avoiding the loss of something that already exists. But that is not an easy task in a period when many programs and benefits are being cut back and there is keen competition for the remaining funds.

Private schools and their students already benefit directly and indirectly from a number of federal and state programs, although in virtually every case they receive those benefits not because they are private schools (or the students enrolled therein) but because they fit into other, larger classes of beneficiaries.

Exemption from taxation has already been noted. This is generally available to all nonprofit organizations and institutions with charitable, religious, social welfare, or educational purposes, and if one defines it as a benefit, it is the largest one currently available to private schools. Not surprisingly, the most intense federal political controversies involving private schools in the past three years have stemmed from attempts by the Internal Revenue Service (under considerable pressure from court decisions) to impose much more stringent standards of racial nondiscrimination on private schools seeking such exemptions and from the Reagan administration's attempt to reverse that policy. That episode will be discussed below. For the moment it is sufficient to note that private schools and their allies have thus far succeeded in retaining the tax exemption benefit and in fending off additional regulations.

They have fared less well in preserving several smaller benefits, partly because these were of so little importance that they did not try very hard, partly because the pressures were intense to achieve savings in the larger programs in which these benefits are embedded. An example was the decision by Congress in the summer of 1981 to phase out Social Security payments to eighteen- to twenty-one-year-old students who are the dependents or survivors of Social Security beneficiaries. The vast majority of such students are of course enrolled in colleges and universities. The handful who attend private secondary schools while receiving such payments are not much more than a symbol of one way private education has been aided without much fuss or controversy when it is incorporated into larger classes of beneficiaries. But that particular symbol is now being erased.

Other reductions in federal school aid enacted in 1981 generally affect private schools only to the extent that they participated in programs aimed primarily at public schools. In most instances private schools did not experience a unique loss except in the school lunch program. Institutions charging very high tuitions were excluded from future participation in that program presumably on the theory that these must be wealthy schools (or schools patronized by wealthy persons), hence they have no proper claim to such assistance.[7]

The fifty states have extraordinarily varied patterns of assisting private schools with certain activities and expenses for which they also assist public schools. These range from practically nothing in some jurisdictions to quite elaborate arrangements whereby the private sector receives direct or indirect state help with pupil transportation, health care, books and supplies, the costs of administering tests, and sundry social services. These programs are run in various ways, but in essentially every case the benefits to private schools and their students are incidental to benefits for public education. It seems in every case that the aid is categorically restricted to specific activities and may not be used for ordinary instructional costs (though to the extent that the private schools would otherwise divert funds for these specific activities it can be said that the state is indirectly supporting their instructional budgets).

The *third* theme is less conservative. It consists of efforts to obtain for private schools (or their students or parents) benefits and assistance that they believe they have been wrongly denied. The essential argument here is for distributive justice. Its specific manifestations range from the highly specific to the vaguely general. Under the former heading come efforts to secure for private school students who are eligible for various kinds of government categorical assistance (e.g., the economically disadvantaged, the handicapped, the non-English speaking) their full portion of such assistance. Under the latter heading comes economic relief for families aggrieved because they pay their full share of the taxes that support public education but receive none of the benefits since they send their children to private schools and who, because they also pay tuitions, feel doubly burdened.

Many such efforts have valid bases in current law. The legislation authorizing most federal school aid programs, for example, stipulates that categorically eligible private school students must receive benefits comparable to those received by similarly situated public school students. But few if any of the programs have been administered in ways that cause this to happen.

Where there is a state or federal program of assistance to public school students that does not include similar private school students, the effort to obtain justice is obviously based on more general rationales, such as the constitutional mandate for equal protection. Where there is no extant program at all but simply an ardent plea to relieve the tuition-paying parents of private school students from what they deem to be unfair burdens, the basis for the effort is essentially political: Are there enough such parents to cause state or federal officials to respond to their demands?

The *fourth* theme is much more radical—and correspondingly further from realization. It is to bring about social and educational *reform* via financial support of various kinds for private schools or their students.

Although the reformers' schemes are many and varied, virtually all of them rest on one or more of the following propositions:

- Parents bear the principal responsibility for the upbringing and education of their children and are therefore the proper (and most qualified) persons to select the specific kind(s) of formal schooling that are best for their children. Public policy should encourage this.

- Well-to-do families in most communities already have the ability to choose the schools they want for their children, either by moving to neighborhoods or towns with public schools that suit them or by paying the tuition at private schools of their choice. Public policy should bring similar choices within reach of low and moderate income families that wish to exercise them.

- The United States is a heterogeneous society in which people—individually, and in groups and communities—hold varied and sometimes quite divergent ideas about the desirable character and content of formal education. These differ along such dimensions as curriculum, pedagogical style, discipline, morality, values, religious content, and academic standards. Public policy should foster educational pluralism and diversity that are responsive to those differences within the society rather than seeking to impose a uniform or homogeneous definition of schooling.

- Government monopoly of schooling leads to mediocre and inefficient education while the forces of marketplace competition for students and resources would result in schooling of higher quality, greater effectiveness, and lower cost (or, at least, more efficient resource use).

The best-known proposal to carry out the reform theme embraces all these propositions. The idea of education vouchers, in its pure form, would terminate government support of public schools as institutions and would instead supply parents with chits that they could use to pay for their children's education at any schools of their choice. All schools would be private, no matter what auspices they operated under, inasmuch as all would compete for students and would receive income only to the extent that they succeeded in that competition. (There are, to be sure, voucher variants in which some schools would continue to operate under direct governmental auspices. And the one voucher experiment that has been conducted in the United States to date was actually confined to the *public* schools of Alum Rock, California.) This would, it is claimed, enhance parental control of their children's education, equalize educational opportunities for the poor, encourage the operation of distinctively different and varied schools, and improve educational quality through competition.

Less sweeping reform schemes tend to emphasize just one or two of these ideas. The proposal to provide federal scholarships to needy private school students on essentially the same basis as such aid is now provided to college students—dubbed "baby–BEOGs" when the U.S. Senate considered it in the summer of 1980—is aimed at equalizing opportunities and providing parental choices for the poor. The idea of voucherizing the federal Title I program—enabling the families of disadvantaged children to obtain compensatory education wherever they wish—is partly aimed at equality of opportunity but is more solidly grounded in the belief that the educational services obtained thereby will be more effective—of higher "quality"—than those provided exclusively by the public schools. Even the tuition tax credit idea has been justified on grounds of equality of opportunity and improved school quality, though that proposal (at least in its most familiar manifestations) is not especially well-designed to achieve those objectives.

Those who would reform education via private schooling include both liberals and conservatives. The intellectual ancestry of the voucher idea, for example, numbers both Milton Friedman and Christopher Jencks among its prominent members. Unaccustomed to working together, persons of such divergent ideologies have difficulty uniting their efforts behind particular proposals, a problem that is exacerbated by large differences over such crucial details as the extent to which the behavior of participating schools (and parents) should be regulated by government. But the reform schemes encounter several additional political obstacles. The private schools themselves are chiefly—and understandably—interested in continuing to do what they now do, not in altering their activities on behalf of somebody else's notions about whom they should serve or how they should conduct themselves. Much of their enduring support in Washington and in state capitols comes from officials who like what private schools now do but—if conservative—are wary of government-sponsored social reform schemes of all kinds or—if liberal—are reluctant to espouse proposals that appear to imply the end of public schooling in its present form. Only if private school leaders were ardent in their enthusiasm for such reform schemes would there be any real chance of rallying these officials to vigorous advocacy. But the leaders of private education are a fairly cautious lot—focused on existing institutions, missions, and students, infrequently disposed to enlist in "other people's battles," and reluctant to rile the public school establishment unnecessarily.

The closer a reform proposal gets to the disestablishment of public schooling, of course, the more vigorously it is opposed by leaders of that establishment. Vouchers, in that sense, are the ultimate threat. But the national teacher unions and their many organizational allies have been adept—and, from their standpoint, sincere—in depicting less sweeping proposals as a "foot in the door" or way station on the path to destruction. Indeed, it could fairly be said that the reform theme is the one that troubles them most, implying as it does that public schools in their current form are deficient or even harmful. They have been notably less vigorous in opposing proposals and programs that provide modest amounts of aid to private schools on essentially the same terms as public schools. (The most spirited opposition to *those* programs has come not from public education spokesmen but from single-issue church–state separation groups.)

The final obstacle faced by reformers is uncertainty or confusion as to which *level* of government would take responsibility for particular policy proposals. Social reformers generally paint their ideas on a national canvas, but as long as more than 90 percent of all primary/ secondary school funding comes from state and local governments it is unrealistic to think that the federal government could single-handedly mount anything so sweeping as a full-fledged voucher scheme, at least not without enormously increasing its education outlays. While Washington could change the ways its own education aid is disbursed (e.g., by "vouchering" Title I), could underwrite experimental or demonstration programs, or could mount limited new programs of categorical aid (e.g., "baby–BEOGs"), any thoroughgoing change in the organization or financing of schooling necessarily entails state and local collaboration. But the reformers have had little success at the state level. Those few jurisdictions that have seriously considered vouchers (such as the referendum on the Michigan ballot in 1980) have defeated them. The voucher proposal that has attracted the most national notice—the attempt by John Coons, Stephen Sugarman, and others to introduce their "education by choice" scheme into California—has not yet garnered enough signatures to get onto the ballot.

THE LIMITED APPEAL OF THE MOST
APPEALING IDEA

The major contemporary efforts to provide public aid to private education, as noted, have been based primarily on the theme of saving private schools from oblivion. But this, as has been shown, is not a very persuasive policy argument at the present time.

It might appear that well-formulated proposals based on the theme of educational *reform* would stand the greatest chance of winning widespread support and approval at the present time, if only because popular discontent with the educational status quo is so widespread. As recent research by James Coleman and others (1981) has shown, private schools offer more than an *a la carte* alternative to fussy educational consumers dissatisfied with the *table d'hote* menu of public education: They offer at least reasonable likelihood of greater nourishment as well. It is not that public schools lack the ability to offer comparable (or greater) educational nutrition but simply that private schools appear to be somewhat more likely to have the kind of educational environments most conducive to better student achievement.

This suggests that proposals designed to bring that environment within reach of more students would have considerable appeal, particularly if coupled with the progressive social policy goal of equalizing opportunity for low income and minority group students and with the hypothesis that public schools, facing heightened competition for students and resources, would take steps to improve their own educational performance as well.

Certainly that set of ideas has the greatest appeal to the author and could possibly be converted into the most powerful rationale for new forms of public support to private education: more persuasive, in any event, than preserving private education in its current form at a time when preservation does not appear to require public support; more compelling than retention of existing modes of support, most of which are small anyway and have little to do with distinctive characteristics of private education; and surely more invigorating than attempts to win for private education a more reasonable approximation of "its share" of existing school aid monies at a time when these are generally dwindling.

But the intellectual power of this case for public support is not apt to be translated into effective political power in the near future. For only a scattering of intellectuals, analysts, and reformers is likely to find it compelling. To understand why, it is necessary to recall the contextual realities with which this chapter began. Because private education is in reasonably sound institutional health at a time when public education is deeply anxious about its own well-being, any proposal to improve education as a whole by channeling public resources into private education will evoke mixed feelings from the friends of private education and intense opposition from every element of public education. Because the overall shrinkage of government aid to education implies that added support for private schooling would mean further cuts in the assistance available to public schooling (a perception that statements by Reagan administration spokesmen reinforce), the likelihood of building an alliance that would join all educators and their political supporters around such a reform plan is more remote than ever. Because private education still enjoys dubious legitimacy in much of the media, in the dominant intellectual-cultural elites, and in the other usual bastions of support for major social reform initiatives, schemes that rely heavily on new public support for private education are sure to evoke more criticism than acclaim.

There is a special irony here, for the greatest beneficiaries of such proposals (assuming they were properly designed) would be the low income and minority groups that are objects of great concern on the part of liberal social critics, editorial writers, civil rights and labor groups, and others. But so tangled are the webs of education politics and ideology that even the idea of equalizing opportunities for high quality schooling evokes the hostility of most such interests when it is linked to support for nonpublic education.[8]

At least as important as organized opposition, however, is the continuing ambivalence of private education itself to any schemes that would bind it more closely to public policy. Even the mainstream schools are reluctant to become instrumentalities for the attainment of other people's public policy objectives, and the fundamentalist schools are actively opposed to all such interventions by government.

Although these anxieties have multiple sources, they can be understood in relation to a single idea, perhaps the most powerful one to have entered this policy arena in the past several years: the idea that public support for private schools may be *harmful* to them. This is not, to be sure, so very different from the concern that dogged federal aid to schools generally in the 1950s and early 1960s: the fear that aid would bring control and with it a lessening of freedom, diversity, and institutional sovereignty. But it has taken on added strength and significance for private schools in recent years.

Private school leaders have seen their public education counterparts become tangled more and more tightly in regulatory and accountability snarls associated (sometimes only remotely) with new forms of categorical assistance from the federal and state governments. They have witnessed private colleges and universities—their closest institutional relatives—coming under the sway of more regulations and court decisions that are tied to the receipt of federal aid, even aid that is confined to their students. They have watched as church-affiliated colleges in states such as New York were obliged to loosen or renounce their sectarian links in order to qualify for public funding. They have read the results of studies suggesting that the special educational effectiveness of private schools—hence much of their distinctive appeal to students—is associated at least in part with their freedom from the external controls and constraints borne by public schools. They have noted the preliminary findings of scholars monitoring the effects of a new, voucher-like program of public aid to private schools in Canada's British Columbia—namely, that the assistance may create unhealthy institutional dependency and erode the qualities that previously made private schools special. They have, perhaps, also grown a bit weary of the political gyrations and programmatic contortions that have been necessary to get even the most limited forms of public support for private schools over the hurdles of state and federal constitutional provisions as interpreted in a string of ever more quixotic court decisions.[9] Most vividly of all, for several years now they have been bloodied in battles with the Internal Revenue Service, the White House, the Congress, and the courts over retention of the most indirect (if also the most valuable) government benefit they now enjoy, their exemption from taxation.

THE TAX EXEMPTION ISSUE

The tax exemption issue has a long and extraordinarily intricate saga that can only be outlined here.[10] Although Congress has never explicitly stated in law that a precondition for tax exemption for a private school is racial nondiscrimination, a series of court decisions and Internal Revenue Service rulings that began in 1970 established with reasonable certainty that this should indeed be one of the conditions. It could be satisfied, at least in the early 1970s, by a school that formally adopted a policy of nondiscrimination and published that policy in its literature.

By the mid-1970s, however, civil rights groups, some federal judges and others had concluded that *professing* nondiscrimination was insufficient and that the Internal Revenue Service (IRS) should require private schools to submit additional evidence that they did not discriminate in practice.

To this were added two highly charged political controversies of the period. First, it was said that private schools were providing a refuge for families seeking to avoid public school desegregation generally and compulsory busing particularly, indeed that some private schools were being established (and others expanded) specifically for this purpose. Second, the vigorous campaign mounted by Senators Packwood and Moynihan and others to enact a federal tuition tax credit program brought to the fore the issue of whether such tax credits would aid "segregation academies" and, if not, how the government could ensure that this did not happen.

The Carter administration responded in August 1978 by publishing proposed new IRS regulations governing nondiscrimination by private schools seeking (or holding) tax exemptions. These produced the largest outpouring of comment—some 150,000 letters in all—of any IRS regulation in memory, and the vast majority of it was highly critical. The essential problem, in the eyes of private school leaders, was that certain schools were to be presumed to be discriminatory unless they could prove otherwise and that the principal means of proving otherwise was to be enrollment of a quota of minority group students.

The mainstream private schools were outraged because many of them had made vigorous efforts to enhance educational opportunities for poor and minority youngsters, because their statements of

nondiscrimination were sincere and genuine, and because the new
IRS procedures could cause complications for some institutions, such
as Orthodox Jewish day schools that, under religious law, could only
accept students of a particular faith and therefore could not reasonably fulfill racial quotas.

Fundamentalist school leaders were even more alarmed. For many,
this was the first direct confrontation with any kind of intrusive or
threatening government regulation and they did not welcome the
prospect. Others had already been effected adversely by various state
requirements and were wary of entangling themselves with the federal government as well. The fact that many fundamentalist schools
are integral parts of individual—and usually quite homogeneous—
church congregations means that diversity of students is not a highly
prized educational or social value, and the essentially religious character of these schools meant that any supervision at all by secular
authorities was seen as a threat to their religious freedom. In a few
cases, the doctrines of the guiding religious faith themselves were said
to forbid racial integration. In other cases, the schools were simply
not much interested in enrolling black youngsters (and still others
were not much interested in enrolling *white* youngsters) and did not
want to be compelled to do so. Practically all of them disputed the
contention that exemption from taxation was a government benefit
anyway; they saw it, instead, as being spared a form of governmental
harassment.

The private schools effectively mobilized congressional support for
their position, and after extensive hearings Congress prohibited the
Internal Revenue Service from implementing its new regulations. But
Congress also failed to offer any constructive policy guidance or to
clarify the law, so the practical effect of its ban (embodied in several
consecutive Treasury Department appropriations and still in effect
today) was to reinstate the standards and procedures that the IRS
had followed until August 1978—namely, that a private school was
ordinarily to be believed when it stated that it did not discriminate.

That did not put an end to the matter, however, for it left several
issues unresolved. A group of Mississippi private schools had been
held to a stricter standard by a federal court that had, in effect, applied to them the procedures that the IRS had proposed for the
entire country in 1978. These schools, and their congressional allies,
naturally wanted relief. Moreover, two lawsuits were working their
way through the appellate courts that concerned the extremely vexing

situation of schools (The Goldsboro Christian Schools and Bob Jones University) that claimed a religious basis for their practice of racial discrimination, thus posing a direct conflict between two sets of constitutionally protected rights. Finally, because the IRS never formally withdrew the procedures it had proposed in 1978, some private school spokesmen felt that they still had a sword hanging overhead.

President Reagan was elected on a platform that pledged to "halt the unconstitutional regulatory vendetta launched by Carter's IRS Commissioner against independent schools," and fundamentalist leaders in particular felt that Mr. Reagan was speaking to them when he promised not to use the tax code as an instrument of social reform or institutional regulation. Hence they expected the Reagan administration at the very least to withdraw the 1978 IRS procedures, and in the autumn of 1981 they pressed it to do so. The administration went much further, however, and in January 1982 announced that it found no legal basis for denying tax exemptions to racially discriminatory private schools and would, therefore, proceed to grant exemptions to such schools until and unless Congress changed the law.

Faced with protest from civil rights leaders and others outraged by this reappearance of the ghost of Jim Crow, the president a few days later urged Congress to pass legislation denying tax exemptions to discriminatory private schools and sent a draft bill to Capitol Hill. Within several weeks, however, it became clear that Congress had no intention of passing such legislation; the administration found itself in a most awkward situation and, after several more twists and turns, decided to ask the Supreme Court to resolve the issue, which is where matters stood in mid-summer.

This episode had several damaging results. It cast a pall of suspicion over all private schools, including the vast majority that do not discriminate. It dimmed the prospects for enacting tuition tax credit legislation and other aid (and reform) proposals. It gave momentary encouragement to persons harboring some of the least attractive impulses in American society. Ironically, it also ended up deepening the sense of suspicion and paranoia of fundamentalist school (and religious) leaders vis-à-vis the government and thus reduced the likelihood that they would willingly become involved with any subsequent aid or reform schemes that might give the hated regulators added leverage over them.

FOR THE FUTURE

Painful though it was, the issue of racial discrimination and tax exemptions was a revealing preview of the policy issues and political dynamics that are apt to characterize the relationship between government and private education through the remainder of this decade. Indeed, its implications are even wider. Well before the recent sequence of events involving the Reagan administration, a careful observer who is himself sympathetic to private schools in general and fundamentalist schools in particular had written that, "One of the great unreported stories of the last few years was the way the Carter Administration helped create a militant, politicized Christian right by trying to drive fundamentalist schools out of business via new IRS regulations" (Uzzell 1981: 7). The subsequent actions of the Reagan administration unintentionally but undeniably intensified the militancy, the politicization, and the wariness both of the Christian right and of mainstream private education leaders, as well as the anxiety of others who cherish the privateness of private institutions but who in many cases believe that certain elemental social norms and individual rights should also be respected.

These tensions are sure to remain, and the idea that governmental aid—indeed governmental entanglement of any kind—may be harmful to private education is certain to gain added force. Hence it seems likely that vouchsafing the limited benefits government now provides to private education while otherwise fending it off entirely will be the theme that dominates the politics of public policies toward private schooling in the years ahead. This is not only a different objective from obtaining additional public support; it evokes quite different political behavior and enlists different allies. It is defensive, conservative, and minimalist, rather than venturesome, expansive, and reformist. The elected officials it is most likely to fire with enthusiasm are those disposed to curb the powers of government, not to enlarge the domain of governmental assistance.

For even the most modest, roundabout, and nonintrusive forms of public support for private institutions entail some degree of public accountability. As noted at the outset, it is not possible to aid a school or a student in any way—even just sparing it from some otherwise universal burden or obligation—without beginning to define what is a school, what is a student, or what constitutes education.

Once across that threshold it is not a great distance to prescribing various forms of institutional conduct and educational practice and to policing compliance with them.

To one who regards schools as essentially public institutions regardless of the auspices under which they operate, who believes that society's obligation to educate its young carries with it at least limited powers to determine what constitutes an education, and who believes that any social institution, public or private, has the responsibility to comply with certain basic social norms and expectations, none of this is especially surprising or necessarily worrisome. But government is given to excesses, even in those (rare) instances when its motives are pure. It is known to engender dependency in those it aids, to have enormous difficulty dealing with institutions it does not control, and to prize uniform treatment and homogeneous behavior more highly than diversity and sensitivity.

Hence the politics of private education are changing. They are moving, without any reliable compass or clear landmarks, out of an era dominated by efforts to obtain financial support from government and into an era likely to be dominated by efforts to curb government and keep it from doing harm. But the older agenda will not be entirely supplanted by the new one, and both sets of issues will remain. This means the policy arena will be filled, but the participants (and spectators) will not always know who is on which team, for alliances will shift abruptly as issues are redefined, as priorities change, and as objectives become incompatible.

Even in the days when goals were clearer and alliances more stable, the arena of public policies affecting private education was not adequately described by the conventional political language of "who gets what." This has always been a field strewn with religious belief, ideology, confused constitutional doctrine, intricate individual motives, conflicting values, deepset historical patterns, a good deal of wishful thinking, a measure of narrow-mindedness, and perhaps a bit of prejudice. That may be why it has been so little analyzed.[11] But the volatile and knotty character of the policy issues now enveloping private education will serve only to render the topic more complex, as will the near-revolutionary changes that are convulsing the political economy of the entire nation and the upheavals in prevailing educational priorities as well.

Though the analyst's task grows more difficult, there is a good chance that private education will emerge from this period stronger than it entered. But this is not likely to be solely the result of substantial financial support garnered from a beneficent government through purposeful actions in the political sphere. It is at least as likely to result from restraint by government—and restraints imposed on government through actions in the political sphere. But it may also turn out that government—and politics—will have less to do with it than will the innate characteristics of private education in the 1980s: confidence, enthusiasm, a reasonably clear sense of mission, stubbornness, high standards, and more than three centuries of experience.

NOTES TO CHAPTER 7

1. See also Cremin's (1980) magisterial *American Education*. For an altogether different (and much more ideological) perspective, see Blumenfeld (1981).
2. These are generally the groups and organizations that belong to the Council for American Private Education, a Washington-based "umbrella" organization that represents the interests—particularly at the federal level—of the mainstream private schools.
3. An especially clear spokesman for this view is William Bentley Ball, an attorney who has represented fundamentalist schools in a number of key state and federal lawsuits. See, for example, his *Constitutional Protection of Christian Schools* (Ball 1981) and his testimony before the Senate Finance Committee (U.S. Congress 1981).
4. As is well known, the largest component of the public school establishment, the National Education Association, took a vigorous drubbing at the polls in 1980 when Jimmy Carter and many other Democrats whom it supported were defeated. But this seems to have heightened its resolve to work harder in the future. It happens that government aid to private schools is one of the three national issues—the other two being the overall level of federal education spending and the existence of the Department of Education—that most powerfully unite the establishment into a reasonable, cohesive political force numbering hundreds of organizations and millions of individual members.
5. Space does not permit a full discussion of the multiple issues of civil rights and private education, except to note that they are very complicated. Most private schools are not segregated (except sometimes by religion) and many are well-integrated. Hundreds of thousands of black, Hispanic, and other minority youngsters attend private schools, and recent research findings indicate that many are extraordinarily well-educated in them (see, for example, Greeley 1982). The "under-representation of minority youngsters in private education as a whole has much to do with the cost of such educa-

tion to families and with the *absence* of any systematic government aid to low-income students attending private schools. At the same time, there is no denying that some private schools exist primarily because parents did not want their children to be bused to newly desegregated public schools. Whether the dominant impulse was avoidance of desegregation or of busing is unknown and probably unknowable. The motivations that govern families' choices of schools are many and intricate — at least for those who have such choices. No one who has seen the all-white academies founded ten or fifteen years ago in some communities would deny that the motives behind them are not altogether admirable. But no one who has visited Catholic inner-city schools — or who has seen the Marva Collins story on television — would deny that private education is also very beneficial to a great many minority youngsters.

6. It is unclear to what extent Catholic church and lay leaders still feel strongly about government aid. Their staff organizations and lobbyists continue with efforts to organize support for tuition tax credits and other such programs, but this may have as much to do with organizational momentum as with genuine priorities. Certainly aid for private education was conspicuously missing from the otherwise lengthy list of well-publicized policies enunciated by the American hierarchy at its December 1981 meeting in Washington. On the other hand, some critics have long held that the hierarchy has lost interest in its schools or at least lost enthusiasm both for spending much money to maintain them and for expending much political capital to obtain money from other sources for that purpose.

7. The sweeping legislative changes embodied in the Education Consolidation and Improvement Act of 1981 also included some that may provide additional benefits to private schools and their students. The new Chapter 2 program in particular, which consolidated a number of categorical federal school aid programs in a "block grant," provides far more explicitly and precisely for full and equitable private school sharing in activities funded with the block grant than had been the case under much of the antecedent legislation.

8. Conservatives who basically favor private education may also oppose efforts by government to enlist it in social reforms that they do not favor. Judging from the comments that they voiced when the Senate resoundingly rejected the "baby–BEOGs" idea in 1980, anything that smacks of a "handout" program for the poor is not apt to win much support on the political right, even if one of its consequences is aid for private schooling.

9. There is no doubt that the tortured condition of constitutional law in this area confuses the politics and exhausts the participants (for a recent penetrating discussion see Cord 1982). Until the Supreme Court has the opportunity to rule directly on a major federal aid program, uncertainty will prevail. Until such an aid program is enacted, the Court will not have that opportunity. As long as there is reasonable likelihood that the Court would

overturn such a program, however, the chances of passing the legislation creating it are slender.

10. A good summary—and some very difference conclusions—can be found in Rabkin 1982.

11. The quantity and quality of the analyses are rapidly increasing, however. For two recent compilations containing a number of good essays, see Manley-Casimir 1982 and Everhart 1982.

Note: Two good recent bibliographies may be found in American Enterprise Institute for Public Policy Research 1981 and Monroe C. Gutman Library 1982.

REFERENCES

American Enterprise Institute for Public Policy Research. 1981. *Debating National Education Policy: The Question of Standards.* Washington.

Ball, William B. 1981. *Constitutional Protection of Christian Schools.* Grand Rapids, Mich.: Association of Christian Schools International.

Blumenfeld, Samuel L. 1981. *Is Public Education Necessary?* Old Greenwich, Conn.: Devin.

Coleman, James; Thomas Hoffer; and Sally Kilgore. 1981. *Public and Private Schools.* Washington, D.C.: National Center for Education Statistics.

Cord, Robert L. 1982. *Separation of Church and State: Historical Fact and Current Fiction.* New York: Lambeth Press.

Cremin, Lawrence A. 1964. *The Transformation of the School: Progressivism in American Education.* New York: Random House.

Cremin, Lawrence A. 1980. *American Education: The National Experience.* New York: Harper & Row.

Everhart, Robert B. 1982. *The Public School Monopoly.* San Francisco: Pacific Institute for Public Policy Research.

Greeley, Andrew M. 1982. *Catholic High Schools and Minority Students.* New Brunswick: Transaction Books.

Manley-Casimir, Michael E. 1982. *Family Choice in Schooling.* Lexington, Mass.: D.C. Heath, Lexington Books.

Monroe C. Gutman Library. 1982. *Current Issues in Education: Tuition Tax Credits & Educational Vouchers*, vol. 1, no. 1. Cambridge, Mass.: Harvard Graduate School of Education.

Rabkin, Jeremy. 1982. "Behind the Tax-Exempt Schools Debate." *The Public Interest* no. 68 (summer): 21–36.

Uzzell, Lawrence A. 1981. "Letter to the Editor." *Change Magazine* 13, no. 8 (November/December): 7–8.

U.S. Congress. Senate. 1981. *Hearings on Tuition Tax Credits* before the Subcommittee on Taxation and Debt Management, Commitee on Finance, 97th Cong., 1st sess. Washington, D.C.: Government Printing Office.

8 FINANCING URBAN SCHOOLS

*Joseph M. Cronin**

INTRODUCTION

Many urban schools in the 1970s lost their leadership position in American education. They appeared at times profligate in expenditure per pupil, defective in educational performance, and derelict in compliance with civil rights laws. More than a few were sluggish in achieving the retrenchment and reform needed to restore credibility and respect in the eyes of the general public. There were, of course, exceptions—school districts that desegregated more or less voluntarily, urban school boards that somehow achieved cutbacks or compliance at federal or state urgings, and city schools with successful school improvement programs. But the stereotype of waste, extravagance, and poor performance lingers. It fuels the voucher movement as well as Reagan economics—the repeal of federal education programs and the new constraints on state and local finance of education. This chapter explores the political punishments meted out to urban schools and the implications for financing those schools.

What should be the basis of urban school finance? What challenges and obstacles must be overcome? What political and demographic forces confront those who try to provide for adequate city school

*Joseph M. Cronin, President, Massachusetts Higher Education Assistance Corporation and Former State Superintendent of Education (Illinois).

finance? Does urban school finance differ appreciably from rural or suburban school finance? These are the larger questions that face policymakers as well as practitioners concerned about the finance of urban education in the 1980s.

THE GREAT CITIES: GOLDEN AGE
TO POVERTY (1930s-80s)

When examining education in the great cities of America, one must recognize (1) the great progress that was made from the 1880s to 1940s, in terms of educational improvements and accomplishments— especially in providing access to college and gainful employment for the children of immigrants and (2) the serious erosion in financial support from 1950 to 1980 in terms of local support for education and the importance of state and federal support in providing an adequate education for urban children.

In the 1930s and 1940s urban schools reigned supreme in American education. City schools represented the very best of American education. From 1930 to 1950 Boston Latin School sent more than 100 graduates each year to Harvard College—more than any other public high school or private preparatory school, including Groton, Exeter, St. Paul's, and Middlesex. The Bronx High School of Science in New York City was up front in the line of technical preparation. East High School in Denver was the best in the state.

Big city schools were well-funded in the years from 1940 to 1960 because of heavy reliance on property taxes. Business and industry, located mainly in the major cities of America, added great wealth to the property tax base and provided high revenues for city schools. Furthermore, major cities were inhabited by immigrant groups who cared passionately about education—the Chinese, Japanese, Jews, and Irish—each of which supported the use of the city's tax base and used the schools as an engine for economic and professional mobility.[1]

While education in general was progressing during the 1930s, 1940s, and 1950s, different hardships were faced in each decade:

- During the Great Depression of the 1930s there were years of depressed salary levels for school workers; during some months, teachers were paid in scrip;

- During the 1940s most male teachers fought in World War II, decimating the high school faculties; and

- During the 1950s qualified teachers in science, mathematics, and industrial arts were much too scarce, and there were difficulties facing the Sputnik challenge.

Politically, however, these were great years for urban decisionmakers. City school districts enjoyed tremendous state supported leeway in the governance of their school systems. Most states with large cities either issued a special charter or set aside a special section of the law authorizing unique governance, budgeting, bonding, teacher certification, and other provisions to suit the preferences of the city. School laws for cities of more than 200,000 (or a million) inhabitants grew out of the decades when only the cities had genuine bureaucracies, and most rural areas and suburbs housed their children in one- or two-room schools. Until the 1960s, moreover, state education agencies served mainly the needs of smaller, essentially rural schools. Cities presumably possessed the talent and wealth to solve their own problems. Urban school boards needed the leeway to construct a six-story schoolhouse, to run their own normal schools, and to finance their own city school employee retirement systems.

City school districts also were able to recruit the "best and the brightest" to staff their schools. Thousands of scholars and intellectuals, unable to find other work during the Depression, became school teachers. Ph.D.s, scientists, engineers, and accountants were not yet in great demand and were grateful to find jobs as teachers, if only to have employment indoors. Class size was large, but the general public looked up to the teachers, however shabby their pay and conditions of employment.

The schools also enjoyed strong community support. City students were composed mostly of white ethnic majorities. Their families were poor but intact. Parents supervised homework assignments and generally sternly disciplined a child who misbehaved in school. Truant officers behaved as "hooky cops" to enforce compulsory attendance laws. Students had no legal rights. They were paddled, bullied, or expelled if they resisted the discipline of learning or the rules of the school.

The business community also helped maintain the excellence of urban schools. Businessmen decided how much city schools should cost and paid the taxes. Industry was the mainstay of the property tax base. Graduates of high schools qualified for good entry-level jobs; others could find employment as stockboys, runners, yard hands, or otherwise unskilled laborers for which there existed a substantial demand. This was the precomputer, precontainer era. Youth exploitation still had to be prohibited; youth employment was not yet an issue.

It was an honor and privilege for the city dwellers to serve on city school boards, especially the appointed school boards of Chicago, Philadelphia, Pittsburgh, Buffalo, and New York City. The most talented American educators plotted their careers—from small city, to medium city, and if they were really excellent to the top job in the largest cities. Thus did Harold C. Hunt move from Kalamazoo, Michigan, to New Rochelle, New York, then to Kansas City, and finally to Chicago in 1947. Along the way he became president of the American Association of School Administrators, the Charles William Eliot Professor of Education at Harvard, and in the 1950s Undersecretary of Health, Education, and Welfare. Hundreds of younger educators tried to follow in his footsteps and emulate his success as a practitioner.

But during the 1960s the cities became more difficult to administer and govern. Minorities migrated from the South, Mexico, and Puerto Rico. Labor unions formed in the public sector and employed the strike as an economic weapon. Good highways and the availability of home mortgage money lured middle-class whites to the green suburbs. City schools shrank in size and importance—Boston, from 135,000 pupils in 1935 to fewer than 90,000 in 1965—even before racial desegregation was an issue or family size began to decline.

Industry in the 1960s and 1970s began to relocate in suburbs or to move south or west. The new technological firms developed around university communities or around the outer metropolitan rim of major cities. Young families left the cities to older families and the older, less demanding industries and teachers.

THE NEW 3 Rs FOR THE CITIES

By the 1970s and 1980s demographic changes made the financing of urban schools more complicated because of three factors: race, retrenchment, and receivership. As middle-income whites moved to the suburbs and minorities moved into cities, city school districts were left with an increasing minority population and the issue of school desegregation, which caused community unrest and increased budgets. Complicating this issue was an overall enrollment decline that could have reduced budgets, but that met community resistance to school closings, augmented by union demands to retain staff, lower class size, and provide more services. Although helped some- what by increased state and federal aid, many city school districts nevertheless faced eroding budget conditions and ended the decade in the hands of state receivership boards.

Race

Race became an issue as the growing numbers of minority popula- tions attended city schools and raised controversy over issues such as discrimination, desegregation, and decentralization. Beginning in about 1966 these issues—racial separation, inadequate minority staff- ing, school boycotts, prolonged court cases, and contentious debates over community control—all served to complicate the issues of pay- ing for and governing city schools. The notion that schools simply transmitted the prevailing or dominant culture appeared to unravel. Minority advocates began to challenge the arguments that schools would serve as engines of stability and employability. New taxes and increased aid from the individual states became more difficult to obtain. The issues of reassigning students, recruiting teachers of dif- ferent color and language background, and empowering neglected racial groups became central in school finance and governance. When states could not handle these volatile issues, the U.S. Congress and the court system did—by enacting civil rights laws, economic oppor- tunity programs, and federal education statutes during the 1960s.[2] The dollars were modest but symbolic of a new interventionist spir- it; the message was clearly conveyed to cities that those who main- tained barriers against student integration or faculty affirmative action would be branded as outlaws.

Three of the key political questions of responsibility, money, and power were:

1. Does the city desegregate by itself or with the county or metro- politan area?
2. Who pays the costs of desegregation?
3. How long does the court retain jurisdiction over the case?

As minority enrollments increased in central cities, plaintiffs predicted that, beyond a point, desegregation could not work within urban school district boundaries. Richmond, Detroit, Baltimore, and Atlanta were examples of cities whose school enrollment by the early 1970s became mostly black. The United States Supreme Court in 1971 had approved the Charlotte–Mecklenburg County merger for desegregation purposes. Elsewhere housing segregation in suburbia denied minority families access to high quality schools, in itself an argument that state policy and suburban segregation contributed to racial concentration in cities. One remedy, a metropolitan desegregation plan, was mandated in the Detroit case but rejected by the Supreme Court by a five to four vote (*Milliken* v. *Bradley* (1977)). However, the Louisville–Jefferson County, Kentucky, and Wilmington–New Castle County, Delaware, school district mergers for desegregation purposes were allowed to take place.

It would appear that desegregation on a metropolitan basis is more likely to occur in southern cities (because of a long tradition of strong county government) than in northern cities. Miami, Tampa, Orlando, Clearwater, Jacksonville, and Fort Lauderdale in Florida provide the most obvious examples, in addition to Nashville, Louisville, and Charlotte. Except for Wilmington, Delaware, the larger northern cities that have desegregated on a metropolitan basis—Boston, Hartford, Rochester, and Milwaukee—relied upon voluntary suburban school district and student participation.

Courts have ordered states to provide financial assistance for desegregation. In Atlanta the judge mandated an increase in black school administrators. The judge in Detroit mandated a greatly expanded compensatory education program for disadvantaged minorities. Judges in Cincinnati, Milwaukee, and St. Louis agreed to student choice and transportation to magnet or specialized theme schools, all of which cost more money than regular schools. State legislatures in Massachusetts and Wisconsin voted to provide funds to make desegregation work, especially to provide financial assistance for magnet schools and special programs. In all instances the desegregation mandates increased costs—for transportation, new education services, or staff training. While the education benefits may be desirable, the fact is that court ordered or voluntary desegregation efforts generally increase education costs for city schools.

In terms of governance, desegregation plans have forced large city and state education agencies into close working relationships that would have been unthinkable in the autonomous 1930s. States actually review and approve proposals for educational innovations at specific school sites within many city school district boundaries. Cities once enjoyed substantial local control and near-total authority over enrollment and educational decisions for each school. Court decisions and legislative policies sharply constrain the local city school board and often require the city and the state to share costs and responsibility for a desegregation plan's success.

Federal courts also may choose to retain jurisdiction over city school desegregation indefinitely, further changing the historic autonomous governance patterns. Judge Hoffman in Illinois requires that the South Holland school officials submit for approval any change in school assignment patterns. Judge Arthur Garrity in Boston monitors very closely the decisions of the Boston School Committee and placed the South Boston High School under special court supervision when the board did not comply with directives. Courts appoint as their desegregation "eyes and ears" masters or expert panels to advise them of progress, problems, and the need to summon the parties to the bench and admonish them or issue supplementary orders. Since the media always report any conflicts over desegregation, the public as well as the board is repeatedly reminded of the limits on the scope of local school decisionmaking.

Generally courts act as a force for stability and continuity. However, when lower court decisions are rewritten or overturned by higher courts, city school policies change radically on short notice. The *Milliken* case forced Detroit and the state of Michigan to increase substantially compensatory education for minority children. In 1980 the Los Angeles desegregation remedies that were in place and working were reviewed and invalidated during the same school year. Chicago endured a series of stop-and-go court cases over a period of fifteen years amid an abundance of confusion and controversy. Both federal and state decisionmakers often enter the conflict to enforce or cajole city officials to file more adequate desegregation plans. The quality of dialogue is interrupted by the changing demography, the volatility of the issue, and the unpredictability of federal policy and judicial rulings. Race is one issue that will continue to plague the cities and that will increase the financial burdens of school districts hard pressed to maintain adequacy of funding.

Retrenchment

Retrenchment—that is, the decline of city populations and of city school populations in the older, more mature cities (especially of the North and Midwest)—poses problems of reconciling enrollment declines with expanding school costs. Cities have become less densely populated—a boon in terms of public health but a challenge to urban school planners. Families became smaller in the 1970s in both suburbs and cities. Fewer children attended school; fewer teachers and schools were needed. But it is difficult to close a school; political opposition exists at all corners, and community resistance is intense.

A good measure of the financial problems of American cities during the 1970s can be traced to the sluggish response to enrollment decline, the reluctance to reduce the school employment rolls, and the refusal by various officials—not always school boards—to close down half-empty buildings and consolidate schools. As always, there were exceptions. Some cities and their schools grew as most of the others declined in size and student enrollment, especially cities of the South and West such as Houston, Dallas, Phoenix, and San Diego.

One troubling aspect of the financing of city schools in the 1960s and 1970s was that the total staff increased even as the student population declined. From 1965 to 1970 this phenomenon can be explained partially by the implementation of new federal programs that encouraged the hiring of additional staff and teacher aides in many classrooms. A drop in student enrollment allowed the use of empty rooms for specialized services—for disadvantaged, handicapped, or bilingual populations or whatever special need a funded program might address. In addition, teacher unions encouraged the lowering of class size and the hiring of auxiliary personnel.[3] Combined, these factors meant that the cost of education per pupil rose much more rapidly than the rate of inflation.

Thus, the understandable community resistance to close a neighborhood school as enrollments dropped was augmented by union pressure to add special programs and reduce class size as the alternatives to reducing staff or consolidating programs, and the influx of federal money provided the funds to support many of these services. As a result, staff-per-pupil ratios increased; schools remained in operation much longer than would have been possible before 1965; and urban school costs rose dramatically.

Changes in state school aid formulas between 1965 and 1980 also contributed to this chain of events, in part as a response to city school pleas of poverty and discrimination (Goertz 1981). Even as enrollments continued to drop, more money was added which postponed retrenchment.

States intervened in retrenchment decisions only indirectly, usually by decreasing the state aid dollars paid to school districts on the basis of the actual number of students. But even here, adjustments were made to cushion or postpone the loss of aid, which helped to postpone the budgetary decisions that retrenchment inevitably requires. Illinois school districts in the 1970s won some temporary relief from the state legislature when it agreed to allow the calculation of state aid to be based on the last three years of attendance. Legislatures in nearly fifteen other states followed suit. "Save harmless" clauses, which mandated no decrease in state aid, were developed in even more states. In addition, city school districts annually sought the use of an average student *enrollment* statistic as the student count for state aid in order to cushion city schools even further against the negative effects of higher truancy and dropout rates in disadvantaged neighborhoods. This argument was given legal support in the *Levittown* v. *Nyquist* (1978) school finance court case in New York. While cities find suburban-dominated legislatures reluctant to enact urban adjustments in state school aid formulas, they nevertheless feel obligated to press for fiscal relief and more often than not are successful.

In general, however, states stood by as city school boards wrestled with unions, neighborhood school champions, special interest groups, and others who opposed cutbacks in budgets or services as enrollments dropped and retrenchment became necessary. As will become evident in the next section, cities were allowed substantial freedom to close or not to close buildings and to reduce or not to reduce employment, provided they did not overspend.

Receivership

Another complication in financing urban schools that recurred in the 1970s was *receivership*, the point at which expenses so exceed revenues and cash needs so exceed the willingness to pay taxes that bankers and political officials impose fiscal control systems on schools to stave off bankruptcy and restore the fiscal health of the budget. This was necessary on occasion during the 1930s when a few school systems teetered on the edge of insolvency. It recurred in 1975 in New York City when its fiscally dependent schools hovered on the brink of bankruptcy,[4] and it has occurred in a number of other large city districts since that time.

On April 7, 1975, New York City mayor Abraham Beame informed Governor Hugh Carey that the city could not pay $40 million in short-term debt due eight days later. The mayor asked for help in the form of early payment of state aid, since the city could not market additional tax anticipation notes. Since city schools relied on city officials and the city budget for operating funds, the school system was dramatically effected by this event. As part of the resolution of the problem, a Municipal Assistance Corporation was created to help raise funds for New York City, and an Emergency Financial Control Board was empaneled to serve as a watchdog over city service expenditures, including those of the school system. Thousands of teachers were laid off in the ensuing attempts to balance the city's budget.

In Ohio during the late 1970s a number of city school districts, unable to pass tax referenda, ran out of funds and closed schools for several weeks to save money in order not to incur an illegal budget deficit. Cleveland, the largest city, beset by the unrest accompanied by teacher strikes and court-ordered desegregation, faced the biggest problem, and also closed its schools early to balance its budget. In 1980 the state superintendent of public instruction argued that such prolonged closings were detrimental to the education of students and proposed the creation of a State Emergency Advance Bank to provide "advance" state aid to districts to help them avoid closings while also prohibiting such closings. As a condition for receiving such funds, however, local school districts had to submit plans showing how they would curtail costs and balance the school budget within a fixed period of time. Several urban school systems in Ohio, including Cleveland, are now under the scrutiny of this state entity.

In November 1979 Chicago schools lost the municipal investment grade rating needed to market bonds when Moody's and the banks discovered that debt service sinking fund money had been borrowed to meet payrolls. By early 1980 the governor and legislature, working closely with city bankers and the mayor of Chicago, imposed a

School Finance Authority on the city to review budgets and to raise money through bond sales.

Other large cities moved close to the brink of bankruptcy but were saved either through state action or timely retrenchment decisions or both. What New York, Cleveland, and Chicago endured was a change in both governance and finance—a loss of school board control over financial decisionmaking and new limits on budgets, expenditures, staffing levels, and contracts. In addition, the pace of staff retrenchment and school closings accelerated in each case. New York city lost 50,000 students between 1971 and 1975; the schools lost 14,000 positions. Cleveland lost 60,000 students between 1968 and 1979; the schools lost 2,000 positions. Chicago lost 96,000 students between 1971 and 1979; the schools lost 3,000 positions.

Race, retrenchment, and receivership actually became intertwined in these cities. Cleveland's student assignment practices and desegregation remedy were closely monitored by a federal judge who directed state officials to find both educational and financial solutions. The Chicago schools were under desegregation review by the U.S. Department of Health, Education, and Welfare and the Illinois State Board of Education, both of which from 1976 to 1979 had threatened to cut off or withhold state and federal funds that amounted to more than half of the city school budget; the issue was the failure to desegregate student assignment patterns. The more bank officials heard about fund cut-off threats, the more nervous they became about the credit worthiness of the Chicago schools and their tax-exempt notes. New York was beset by desegregation issues that included professional staff testing and selection and student assignment, both of which became complicated as the city on which it depended for funds nearly went bankrupt; simultaneously the service needs of its students increased as the concentration of handicapped, bilingual, and low achieving students grew astronomically.

In each case, difficult decisions to close down half-empty schoolhouses and lay off staff had been deferred or delayed during the 1970s. Employee unions—not only teachers but also custodians and school engineers—fought to protect their assignments and preserve staffing levels. In the end, race issues and retrenchment postponement led to budget overruns and state controlled receivership, a far cry from the golden age of the 1940s and 1950s when city schools were the best, finances were healthy, and community opinion strong.

COURT MANDATES AND FEDERAL AID

In addition to the demographic changes that toppled many urban school districts from a golden era of excellence in the 1940s and 1950s to the status of receivership in the 1980s, two other factors constrain the prognosis of financial health for urban schools in the 1980s—court mandates and the changing role of the federal government.

Court Mandates

As discussed above, court actions related to desegregation constrained many urban school districts in the 1960s and 1970s, requiring changes in both pupil and staff assignment procedures, mandating changes in the educational program ranging from remedial instruction to staff development, and altering the governance structures, all of which placed new strains on eroding budgets. But desegregation was not the only arena in which city school districts experienced court intervention and court-imposed cost mandates. One unanticipated outcome of the civil rights movement, which included court intervention on race discrimination issues, was the involvement of the courts in nearly *all* aspects of education, especially for urban schools.

Handicapped children won rights to improved service, and their parents won the right to participate in class assignments and program-planning decisions through court decisions in the early 1970s and finally through the enactment of the Education of All Handicapped Children Act. A major class action lawsuit brought by the Pennsylvania Association for Retarded Children gave legal impetus to make provision for adequate education services in the public schools for all handicapped students. Several other suits followed. By the end of the 1970s all states had comprehensive laws mandating services for the handicapped. The costs to urban schools, with high percentages of handicapped children, were enormous while the mandate to provide full services, which could include placement in expensive private schools, was unequivocally enforced.

Bilingual children also won efforts to extend and expand special services, especially after the 1974 *Lau* v. *Nichol* decision requiring bilingual education for students with limited English proficiency. With state-mandated transitional bilingual education and with most students needing bilingual instruction living in the larger cities, more costs had to be absorbed.

General education programs also came under court review in some states. In 1976 New Jersey enacted a major school finance law that carried with it measures to enforce a "thorough and efficient" education clause in the state constitution (Wise 1979). The law gave the state authority to review all local district education programs. Several years later the New Jersey commissioner of education appointed a special administrator to take charge of the Trenton city schools after state review found the local education program inadequate.

Thus, cities found themselves in the 1970s awaiting court decisions or constantly spending money to appeal court decisions, most of which they lost. Even when they won, as in the Los Angeles school desegregation case, great sums were spent on compliance with the lower court decision, on the appeal itself, and then more on putting a somewhat shrunken school system together again.

Of course, some cities managed to avoid or postpone the court decisions. It may have helped New York City, Chicago, and Philadelphia to be so very huge—although Chicago faced great pressure from state and federal officials to desegregate anyway. A few cities found judges or legislators willing—as in New York state for a while, Wisconsin, and Ohio—to make available additional state funds, making desegregation and other court mandated solutions profitable and educationally attractive.

Changes in Federal Policy

The alteration of the financing and governance of urban school districts brought on by changing demographic conditions and the mandates of the courts prior to the 1980s is now exacerbated by a radical and fast-paced change in the federal role in education. Federal aid, while never the largest source of city school district dollars, has provided large sums of money for three major services required in urban school systems—programs for educationally disadvantaged students from low income and poverty backgrounds (which sometimes constitutes 50 percent of a city's school enrollment), subsidies for free or reduced cost meals, and desegregation.

From 1965 to 1980 Congress vigorously encouraged city school boards to spend funds for programs for the most disadvantaged students and also suggested how these billions should be spent. The federal funds carried with them certain stipulations and strings:

- Money for the disadvantaged could only be spent on targeted schools and could not supplant local funds.

- A mandatory parent advisory council would review the program and spending plan.

- Children would need to be pulled out of class for extra help so that a clear "audit trail" could be established for the expenditure of federal funds.

During 1981 the president and Congress considered plans to consolidate many of the federal programs, of which Title I was simply the largest for city schools. After little discussion, the Education Consolidation and Improvement Act of 1981, Chapter I, changed the federal program structure by stating that:

- City schools with scarce dollars or tax limits could substitute as much as 10 percent of the federal dollars for the past local or state funds if the latter had shrunk;

- Parents still should be consulted but the advisory council no longer would be required; and

- "Pull out" programs, often thought to be counterproductive, would no longer be required.

Another section of the law, Chapter II, combined thirty-one categorical and separate programs into one block grant that included many smaller basic skill and curriculum grants but also the Emergency School Assistance Funds, which produced millions of dollars for the larger cities undergoing desegregation.

The price of federal program consolidation and deregulation, however, is a reduction in the level of federal funds in 1982 and the likelihood of further reductions in the future. The cutbacks come at a time when these extra services have become established as expected programs, when city budgets already are stretched beyond reasonable limits, when the politics of urban aid are unstable, and when the likelihood of increased state aid is generally low. The new federal law also provides for "equal expenditure" of funds on students attending nonpublic schools, further diluting federal aid to urban public schools. Furthermore, the U.S. Secretary of Education no longer will allocate the emergency funds to desegregate city schools; these funds—much reduced in size—will be blended with all the other programs and allocated by state officials to all public and interested nonpublic schools.

While from one perspective, the federal dollars never were that great (10 or 15 percent of a city school budget), for fifteen years federal dollars nevertheless helped fund certain categories of cost and encouraged expenditures on other populations judged to have special needs—the poor, the minorities, the handicapped. Federal funds provided seed money for sex equity workshops, for ethnic heritage curriculum projects, for gifted and talented classes, and for other discretionary programs not always affordable in city school budgets.

Federal cuts come, however, at the same time as energy costs (transporting children, heating buildings) soar and as state revenues, often dependent in part on automotive sales and domestic construction, taper off and sag. State funds for city schools in the 1980s will be more difficult to obtain. As city populations shrink and suburban populations expand, cities become more dependent on the good will of a majority of nonurban legislators whose constituents generally reject city school financial rescue operations and bailouts. States, in short, are unlikely to make up for any loss in federal revenues.

THE CURRENT SITUATION IN BRIEF

As the 1970s end and the 1980s begin, it is not difficult to notice the erosion of city school boards' decisionmaking authority:

• Courts have ordered student and staff reassignments and other remedies designed to eradicate any trace of racial injustice. Often, judges retain jurisdiction over even administrative decisions, such as personnel appointments to administrative posts and the closing of old school buildings. School board decisions to achieve certain economies therefore are subject to challenge, court debate, and judicial decision, but only after the passage of several months of time during which the judge assesses all the facts necessary to rule.

• Legislatures, while continuing to establish general policies and standards for schools, now do so more often, with more expertise, and in greater detail. The new laws—for handicapped and bilingual education, for example—are much more explicit about the rights of children and parents. Frequently, a parent who is upset about a decision employs an advocate or counsel and seeks to appeal a professional decision, an act almost unheard of a decade ago and expensive for all schools, especially urban schools, which are subject to more appeals.

• The federal government, which for fifteen years helped fund new programs for disadvantaged students concentrated in urban school districts, is now trying to regress from such a commitment. These programs have existed for so long that most parents and students expect them. Urban districts are left to cope with "giving the bad news" and cutting programs to balance budgets.

• Finally, for financial reasons control boards insist on reviewing budgets, contracts, and proposed expenditure and personnel plans as a price for arranging for bonds, tax anticipation notes, and other emergency funds. Bankers and private financiers exercise considerably more direct control over city school boards than ever possible in earlier years. What is more, the likelihood of additional school finance authorities and control boards grows with inflation and the difficulty of urban school boards to live within expenditure limits and revenue caps.

During the 1960s and 1970s the fashionable debate was over whether cities should be fiscally dependent or independent and whether city school boards should be elected or appointed. Slowly it became clear that if a federal judge decided how many schools to close and how the children would be assigned and if financial control boards monitored the budgets, the old questions faded in importance. Even an elected, fiscally independent board can make few important decisions if a judge is mandating what to do and if bankers refuse to arrange financing without the assurance of a control board approving the budget.

PROSPECTS FOR AN URBAN RENAISSANCE

Too often social scientists and critics tend to detail the dismal trends and structural inadequacies of urban institutions. The success stories of big city schools often remain untold and the triumphs of individual educators and urban school boards go unchronicled. Despite the bleak events described in the prior sections of this chapter, many urban districts are rebounding to positions of excellence.

During 1980 a study group of distinguished educators visited Atlanta public schools as the guests of Alonzo Crim, Superintendent of Schools. Derek Bok, President of Harvard University, reported his satisfaction at seeing orderly, productive schools throughout the entire district.

In 1981 the Board of the San Francisco Unified School District offered a new five-year contract to Superintendent of Schools Robert Alioto. His record of accomplishment was impressive. Early in his tenure, Proposition 13 was enacted in California; Alioto simply accelerated the closing of several dozen old schools rather than complain about the new budget constraints. He inherited a school system with test scores at the bottom for most big cities. But he confronted the principals and told them they were accountable for learning and that if ineffective, they would be replaced. A thorough curriculum revision and staff retraining brought San Francisco test scores to the top of those for big cities.

Other cities have made urban school improvement a priority, and the Ford Foundation recently committed $30 million to this effort. Detroit city schools, under Superintendent Arthur Jefferson, raised the average reading scores in grades one to seven (Maeroff 1982). New Orleans schools raised both reading and mathematics scores in all twelve grades. Philadelphia, New York City, and Newark schools report improvement in student performance—especially in response to programs of expanding parent involvement in the schools and in placing greater responsibility for instructional leadership upon the principal.

During the 1980s many young families will decide whether to live in the new and distant suburbs or to remodel some of the grand old homes in the central city, paying for renovations with the savings from transportation. Urban "gentrification"—the wholesale and largely private renewal of once-decaying neighborhoods—occurs for the most part after school desegregation and after city housing prices reach a rock-bottom low. Young, well-educated couples buy in this market, and their success at rebuilding one or more houses attracts others like themselves to the neighborhood. (The South End of Boston and now Dorchester are two examples; each city has others.)

But this trend will not suffice to save big city schools. Any school system needs a cadre of concerned constituents and clients willing to speak out for adequate financing of the schools. Cities have served the poor and the children of the poor in the past and will continue to do so in the future. Cities need leadership and advocacy in the form of voices raised not only for reading and writing but for art, music, school libraries, and computer studies. City children later in life must compete with suburban children in the marketplace of ideas, jobs, and services. The city schools need enough funds to provide exemplary school programs to encourage families to stay with the school system and to supply colleges, companies, and government with students and graduates.

During the 1980s:

- Retrenchment will continue, largely because of the shortage of federal and state funds.

- Race also will continue as an issue. Minority enrollment will increase mainly because of Asian and Hispanic immigration, while black enrollments will stabilize and even decline somewhat in total numbers.

- States will continue to prescribe expected standards for sound budgetary practices, pupil achievement, and teacher literacy.

- The federal government's role will recede in providing funds and promulgating regulations through 1985, but national manpower policy in the long run will be unable to ignore the schools of central cities or the potential of urban education.

At any given time, some great city school system is in trouble—schools on the brink of bankruptcy, the state on the verge of cutting off funds, or trying to raise another $100 million. Even so, the rebirth of many urban centers during the 1980s will counteract the drying up of federal support. Later in the 1980s the federal equation may well be redesigned so that American cities and their education systems get the financial nourishment they need.

NOTES TO CHAPTER 8

1. The politics of urban education begins with the issue of how to cope with immigrants (see Handlin 1982). See also Tyack (1974) for a summary of the history of urban schools. For a review of school governance in large cities, see Cronin (1973). See also Novak (1971) and Levine and Havighurst (1971) for further discussion of the immigrant issue.

2. Orfield (1978) provides a comprehensive background of the extension of the civil rights and desegregation issues to major city schools.
3. Contrary to popular belief, the teacher-per-pupil ratio in virtually all U.S. school systems dropped sharply in the 1960s and 1970s. The 1979 Statistical Report of the National Center for Educational Statistics shows that ratio falling from 28.7 in 1960 to 20.9 in 1978 (elementary level) and from 21.7 in 1960 to 18.1 in 1978 (secondary level) (U.S. Department of Health, Education, and Welfare 1979: 80).
4. Cronin (1980) provides a more detailed description and analysis of New York City, Chicago, and Cleveland school crises and the federal-political solutions chosen.

REFERENCES

Cronin, Joseph M. 1973. *The Control of Urban Schools.* New York: The Free Press.

_____. 1980. "Big City School Bankruptcy." Policy Paper No. 80-C3. Stanford, Calif.: Institute for Research on Educational Finance and Governance, Stanford University.

Goertz, Margaret E. 1981. "School Finance Reform and Cities." In *Perspectives in State School Support Programs*, edited by K. Forbis Jordan and Nelda Cambron–McCabe, pp. 113-42. Cambridge, Mass.: Ballinger Publishing Co.

Handlin, Oscar. 1982. *The Uprooted.* Boston: Little, Brown and Company.

Lau v. Nichols, 414 U.S. 563 (1974).

Levine, Daniel, and Robert J. Havighurst, eds. 1977. *The Future of Big City Schools: Desegregation Policies and Magnet Alternatives.* Berkeley, Calif.: McCutchan Publishing Corporation.

Levittown v. Nyquist, 408 N.Y.S. 2d 606 (Sup. Ct., Nassau County, 1978).

Maeroff, G. I. 1982. *Don't Blame the Kids: The Trouble with America's Public Schools.* New York: McGraw-Hill, Inc.

Milliken v. Bradley, 433 U.S. 267 (1977).

Novak, Michael. 1971. *The Rise of the Unmeltable Ethnics.* Toronto: MacMillan, Inc.

Orfield, G. 1978. *Must We Bus? Segregated Schools and National Policy.* Washington, D.C.: Brookings Institution.

Tyack, David B. 1974. *The One Best System.* Cambridge, Mass.: Harvard University Press.

U.S. Department of Health, Education, and Welfare. 1979. *The Condition of Education.* Washington, D.C.

Wise, Arthur. 1979. *Legislated Learning: The Bureaucratization of the American Classroom.* Berkeley, Calif.: University of California Press.

9 THE POLITICS OF DECLINING ENROLLMENTS AND SCHOOL CLOSINGS

William Lowe Boyd*

In 1965 *Fortune* magazine featured a cover story about education as America's great new growth industry. This was something less than one of *Fortune*'s most distinguished predictions. By the late 1960s many public school districts were experiencing declining enrollments at their primary grade levels; by the early 1970s it was becoming fashionable to speak of education as a declining industry.

It may provide some solace for educators, who were caught by surprise and ill-prepared for decline, to note that business and financial analysts also failed to anticipate the changeover from growth to decline. Unlike business leaders who invested too late in this growth field and had to sell out at a loss, however, educators cannot abandon the field. They must hold their ground and learn to manage a declining industry. This has not proven to be an easy task, for educators are facing a variety of new kinds of social, economic, and political problems.

This chapter focuses on the political problems of decline, particularly the central question of how to manage the conflict that accompanies the hard choices and cutbacks necessitated by a decreasing demand for educational services. The combination of declining en-

*William Lowe Boyd, Professor of Education, Pennsylvania State University.

Part of the research for this chapter was supported by the National Institute of Education (Grant No. NIE–G–78–0086). Views expressed are solely those of the author.

231

rollments, an aging population, adverse economic developments, and disappointment with the performance of public schools has eroded public support and reduced willingness to invest in education (Kirst and Garms 1980). In turn, tight resources and anxiety about potential cutbacks have intensified competition, factionalism, and conflict in school politics. These problems have been exacerbated by the addition of "mandates without money" (Levine 1979).[1] In other words, the combination of increasing demands (often mandated but with little or no funding) for specialized educational services (e.g., special, gifted, and bilingual education) with the need to maintain regular programs in a time of stable or decreasing enrollments and revenues is forcing painful and controversial reassessments of educational programs and priorities (Mosher, Hastings, and Wagoner 1981).[2] These realities have intensified special interest group activity and contributed to further politicization of education. In this context the universal complaint of school officials is that, although there is a reluctant acceptance of the need to cut back, no one wants his ox to be gored. As a result school authorities have learned anew that the political function of government is "the management of conflict in matters of public importance" (Banfield and Wilson 1963: 18).

A large literature, mainly prescriptive but partly empirical, has grown up recently on the management of declining enrollments. Much of this literature deals with the technical aspects of retrenchment—for example, how to close schools, cut costs, and consolidate programs. All of the literature is concerned, at least in passing, with the perplexities of the political aspects of the problem. The recent appearance of an excellent, comprehensive review and annotated bibliography of the literature on declining enrollments (Zerchykov 1981) makes it unnecessary to attempt to summarize this literature here. Instead, this chapter concentrates on some central issues in the politics of decline: (1) What are the distinctive features and problems of policymaking and conflict management in decline? (2) How are retrenchment decisions, and especially school closing decisions, made? (3) What are the political and organizational consequences of decline? Answers to these questions are drawn from the literature in general and from the author's own research in fifteen suburban school districts (Boyd 1979, forthcoming; Boyd and Wheaton 1982).

POLICYMAKING AND CONFLICT
MANAGEMENT IN DECLINE

There is wide agreement among analysts that policymaking and conflict management in decline differ significantly from their characteristics under growth conditions (Behn 1978a, 1980b, 1980c; Berman
and McLaughlin 1978; Cyert 1978; Freeman and Hannan 1975,
1981; Levine 1978, 1979). First, resource allocation decisions become far more difficult in decline. The contest, as Behn (1980d:
603) noted, is no longer "over who should get how much of the expansion of the [budgetary] pie, but over who should be forced to
absorb what share of the cuts." Stated another way, there is a fundamental shift from *distributive* to *redistributive* politics: A shrinking
budget creates clear winners and losers, and no slack resources remain with which to buy off the losers with side payments on secondary issues.

Second, participation is intensified. Consistent with research on
decisionmaking showing that humans weigh losses more heavily
than gains (Tversky and Kanneman 1974), retrenchment activates
wide and intense participation as all organization members, and beneficiaries feel a personal stake in the decisions to be made (Behn
1980c: 618).

Third, retrenchment decisions are complicated by considerations
of equity and entitlement. The problem here goes beyond the well-
known fact that staff layoffs according to seniority tend to conflict
with affirmative action objectives. Bardach (1976) argued that a distinguishing feature of the politics of policy termination, particularly
where government is involved, lies in the ability of vested interests to
advance a powerful moral claim regarding the inequity of changes
that would deprive them of arrangements they have learned to rely
upon. Thus, what Behn (1978a) called the "entitlement ethic" supports the view that government has a responsibility to maintain the
facilities and jobs that people have come to count on. Indeed, civil
servants with tenure may rightly feel that they are being deprived of
a property right when their jobs are abolished.

Fourth, morale plummets in declining organizations. Incentives for
performance and promotion and career opportunities all tend to dry
up. Talented people, who by definition are mobile, tend to abandon
the organization for greener pastures (Levine 1978).

Fifth, organizations cannot be cut back simply by reversing the sequence of developments by which they grew (Berman and Mc-Laughlin 1978). Levine (1979) called this problem the "paradox of irreducible wholes."

Finally, while growth can be managed on an ad hoc basis without grave peril, retrenchment cannot. Systematic planning and analysis become essential (Behn 1980c). Yet the ability to do this frequently is challenged by the view that the administrative component in organizations should be cut to the bone before the service delivery component is weakened (see Levine 1979).

In point of fact, research reveals that declining school districts reduce their teaching staff much more rapidly than their administrative staff (Freeman and Hannan 1975, 1981). Freeman and Hannan rejected the argument concerning the greater need in decline for planning and analysis and interpret their data as indicative of the self-serving political power of school administrators. The truth of the matter probably lies somewhere between the extreme positions. On the one hand, the management literature makes it quite clear that decline requires more centralized management and planning. On the other hand, the bulk of the administrative staff in school systems is employed in system maintenance activities and is not engaged in planning and analysis (Boyd and Crowson 1981). Still, administrative staff services may be required on a transitional basis for an orderly winding down of the school system. In sum there appear to be rational as well as political reasons for the lag in the reduction of the administrative component in declining school systems.

Discussions of cutback management in the public services show that such management and associated politics share many commonalities across functional service areas. For instance, whether one is closing a mental hospital, a juvenile delinquent home, an army base, or a public school, many of the problems in the process are similar (Bardach 1976; Behn 1976, 1978a, 1978b, 1979, 1980b). The difficulties facing educators in retrenchment, however, actually are less severe than those facing managers in many other public services.

Behn (1980a) pointed out that the reasons for retrenchment in public school systems are unambiguous, unalterable, and no one's fault. There is a clear drop in the demand for schooling due to declining enrollments. Unlike public services that must be cut back mainly because of inadequate funding (due to shifting priorities, tax cuts, or constant funding combined with inflation), retrenchment in public schools is primarily necessitated by an unavoidable decrease in demand. This fact helps to convince people of the real need for retrenchment, which is the first step in cutback management. Moreover, the need for retrenchment in public schools does not reflect failure. People simply are not having as many children as they used to, and this obviously is not the fault of school officials. Consequently, in announcing the need for retrenchment, school officials do not have to face the recriminations that discourage many public officials from undertaking the arduous tasks of cutback management.

Variation in Contexts and Constraints

It is important to recognize the extent to which retrenchment policy-making is affected by the wide variation in circumstances among school districts faced with declining enrollments. Research over the past decade has led to a new appreciation of the significance for educational reform of the variety of settings and constraints found in school districts (Mann 1978). In many ways this variety is an even more important consideration for districts facing decline than it was for districts experiencing growth. Entrenched interests and bricks and mortar constraints loom larger in the absence of the opportunities created by an expanding budget and physical plant. Moreover, although declining enrollments are a national problem (with the exception of areas in the sunbelt states and other pockets of growth), their impact on individual school districts varies. As Florio (1976: 2) noted, "Enrollment is a local phenomenon, in each district a unique configuration of birth rate, population migration, age of community, economic growth in a community, and other factors."

The literature in general indicates that an understanding of the unique situation confronting each school district requires that categories of constraints such as the following be taken into account:

- *Enrollment constraints* — the rate and distribution (by grade level and location) of growth or decline within the district;

- *Fiscal constraints* — including such factors as amount of state and other aid, local tax rates, assessed valuation per pupil, and so on;

- *Fiscal management attitudes* — extent to which conservative or liberal fiscal attitudes prevail on the school board and in the community;

- *Conflict management resources and attitudes*—availability of managerial skills in the populace; extent to which school board and populace favor a political bargaining or rational-consensual mode of decisionmaking;

- *Educational program preferences*—including degree of complexity and specialization of educational program, grade organization, and so on;

- *Facility constraints*—including size, age, condition, flexibility for use, and location of buildings, plus alternative building utilization possibilities;

- *Teacher contract/union constraints*—provisions affecting reduction in teaching force and such;

- *Faculty/professional staff constraints*—age of staff, distribution in salary schedule, rate of attrition through retirement and mobility, and so on; and

- *Environmental and subcommunity constraints*—considerations related to the socioeconomic, racial, ethnic, and religious population distribution and mixture within the district; geographic features affecting school attendance area boundaries; extent of existence of areas with special claims to the maintenance of their neighborhood schools that school boards *wish* to respect or believe they *must* respect (Boyd 1979; see also Crespo and Haché 1982).

As important as these various factors seem to be, it is possible to assert that what really counts are fiscal constraints. Such constraints obviously are quite important in shaping the response to decline since, as Zerchykov (1981) observed, ability and willingness to pay in large part determine whether declining enrollments are viewed as a problem. If some declining districts are much harder pressed financially than others, it is reasonable to expect that they will be forced to institute more cutbacks sooner than will more affluent districts. To the extent that this assumption is correct, a simple economic explanation may, by itself, account for most of the observed variance in school district behavior.

Two data sets provide some support, but also some qualifications, for this argument. Table 9–1 shows that, in the case of the fifteen suburban school districts studied by Boyd and Wheaton (1982), fiscal strain (as measured by slow budget growth) does not neces-

Table 9-1. Rankings on Enrollment Decline and Fiscal Strain.

School District	Locale[a]	Percentage Decline (as of 9/79)	Since Peak Enrollment Year	Ranking on Fiscal Strain	Percentage Change in Budget, 1976–77 to 1979–80[c]	Fiscal Strain Category
1. Oakton	C	47.5	1968	4	+ 8.8	High
2. Camden	C	47.4	1969	7	+13.4	Medium
3. Weston	C	42.6	1970	2	+ 6.6	High
4. Alton	C	39.8	1970	1	− 2.4	High
5. Northview	C	38.1	1968	8	+15.3	Medium
6. Leland	M	31.8	1968	6	+13.2	Medium
7. Greenwood	C	31.4	1969	12	+21.7	Low
8. Trenton[b]	C	29.9	1968	5	+10.3	High
9. Buckley	M	25.9	1971	11	+20.3	Low
10. Arbutus	M	20.9	1971	9	+18.2	Medium
11. Empire	M	19.3	1972	10	+18.9	Medium
12. Smithville[b]	C	15.5	1971	3	+ 8.7	High
13. Mesick[b]	M	7.5	1976	13	+32.1	Low
14. Karlin	M	6.9	1971	14	+32.9	Low
15. Arcadia	C	4.8	1977	15	+44.7	Low

a. Locale: C = Chicago; M = Marasmus.

b. Denotes districts that still had not closed a school as of June 1981.

c. Based on actual dollars, unadjusted for inflation.

Source: Boyd and Wheaton (1982).

sarily predict one of the most important responses to declining enrollments—school closings.[3] Even though the Trenton and Smithville districts were high on fiscal strain and had substantial enrollment decline, neither had closed a school as of June 1981. At the same time, the two districts *lowest* on *both* enrollment decline and fiscal strain (Karlin and Arcadia) nevertheless had closed schools.

Table 9-2 presents data on ten large city school systems studied by Cibulka (1982a). Although there is a rough correspondence among the rankings of the cities on enrollment decline, service reductions, and expenditure changes, there are some anomalous relationships, such as in Dallas and Los Angeles. However, in another paper dealing with the same cities, Cibulka (1982b: 15) showed that, "In most cities the first school closing effort, or the first effort to close a large number of schools at one time was closely linked to a budget problem." On balance, the two data sets suggest that there may be a closer linkage between fiscal strain and school closings in cities than in suburbs. This is likely because the bulk of the evidence, discussed later, indicates that large school districts (i.e., cities) tend to experience more conflict in responding to decline and are more inclined to delay action on retrenchment (allowing fiscal strain to increase) than smaller districts do.

Like individuals and organizations, communities and the school districts serving them age and go through developmental stages that have far-reaching implications (Kimberly et al. 1980; Iannaccone and Lutz 1970). While the social changes producing the demographic trends associated with declining enrollments surprised most people in our society, these trends can be viewed as somewhat predictable developments in the life cycle of communities (Zikmund 1975). For instance, aging central cities and older suburban communities generally have experienced substantial enrollment decline. In "bedroom" suburbs, rapid growth in population and school enrollments often has been followed by abrupt and precipitous decline in enrollments. Indeed, many suburban communities have gone from adolescence directly to old age and also find themselves facing an unexpected and unwelcome variety of *urban* problems (Masotti and Hadden 1973). In the case of rural school districts, however, enrollment decline and school consolidation are not new developments but longstanding problems (Burlingame 1979).

Table 9-2. Comparative Data on Enrollment Loss, Selected Service Reductions, and Expenditure Changes, 1974–75 to 1980–81.

School Systems	Enrollment Decline		Selected Service Reductions			Expenditure Changes[d]		
	Degree (percentage)	Rank	School Plants Closed[a] (percentage)	Net Staff Changed[b] (percentage)	Rank[c]	Aggregate (percentage)	Per Pupil (percentage)	Rank[e]
Atlanta	21.1[f]	4	16.0	– 5.0	4	–23.3	– 0.7	2
Baltimore	30.1	2	7.5–10[g]	– 1.1[h]	5	–23.2	+10.0	4
Boston	20.1	5	26.0	29.0[i]	1	– 2.4	+23.6	6
Chicago	14.6	7	13.0[j]	–11.2	2	–28.9	–11.7	1
Dallas	14.5	8	0.0	+46.0	8	+ 7.5	+24.3	7
Los Angeles	10.0	10	0.0	+40.1	7	– 9.2	+ 1.0	4
Milwaukee	25.9	3	15.3	– 9.3	2	–11.7	+19.1	5
New Orleans	13.2	9	5.0	+20.7	6	– 1.1	+14.0	6
New York	15.5	6	8.1	–28.1	3	–26.2	–12.6	1
Seattle	30.5	1	22.0	–33.0	1	–24.2	+ 8.8	3

a. Note that while most closings occurred since 1974–75 and they share a common base period for comparison with net staff changes, these figures do not include school closings made in a few cities in the early 1970s. (Since the exact year of these early closings was not always available, it was thought best to calculate all systems on a uniform base.) Percentage calculated on basis of 1980 school facilities.

b. Includes operations fund (or its equivalent) positions only. Hence, excludes some federally funded positions and in some cities state-funded categorical positions. Despite local differences in the base measurement, percentage shifts should be valid, assuming positions were not shifted out of operations fund to external funds between 1974–75 and 1980–81.

(notes continued overleaf)

Notes to Table 9–2. *continued*

c. Computed by using the ranking of school systems on each of the two measures. The points were added to obtain a composite rank. The lower the score, the greater the service reductions, relative to each other.

d. Adjusted for 1967 dollars using the consumer price index (CPI) for each city. The all-city average was used for New Orleans because a city average is not available.

e. Computed same as service reductions. See note *b* above.

f. Computed between 1974 and 1980 because 1981 figure was not available.

g. Exact number unavailable. Hence the range between the lowest estimate and the highest is provided.

h. Adjusted with Budget and Financial Management data to April 30, 1981. Includes all sources of funds.

i. Reflects adjustments to 1981 based on court reports and annual (October) report to state. Excludes state and federal positions. Update to 1981 is included here because staffing cuts were made late in Fiscal 1981 and early in Fiscal 1982 but were not clearly separated by fiscal year. Moreover, 1981 budget is largely the same as 1980, less CPI adjustments.

j. This figure is approximate because it includes schools that were closed but replaced. It was possible to identify and subtract only one of those cases from the list. On the upside, the figure omits the closing of 1,120 mobile and other units, estimated to be the equivalent of fifty-six school buildings (at twenty classrooms per school). If these are included, the percent of schools closed could be estimated at 20 percent.

Source: Cibulka (1982).

A New Politics of Education?

The bulk of the evidence on the politics of declining enrollments suggests that there are systematic differences between the experience of urban, suburban, and rural school districts. There is some debate, however, concerning the explanation for these differences. Iannaccone (1979) has argued that variations in political patterns in declining districts can be explained best in terms of the traditional politics found in various kinds of school districts. While Iannaccone's interpretation is persuasive regarding urban school districts, it is less convincing when applied to suburban districts and still less so when viewed in relation to the overall social and fiscal context of public education.

Iannaccone (1979) contended that declining enrollments have not created a new politics of education but rather have simply produced pressures exposing existing cleavages and activating the traditional patterns of politics found in different kinds of school districts. Quite to the contrary, however, there is strong evidence that declining enrollments have produced a distinctively new politics of education. First, decline has dramatically increased the frequency of *redistributive* politics. In the past, middle-class suburban school districts usually were able to confine their politics to *distributive* issues, whereas urban districts, due to their greater social heterogeneity, were prone to generate conflict-producing *redistributive* issues (Weeres 1971). These differences in patterns of political issues affected how middle class management resources were used in urban and suburban settings (Boyd 1976a, 1976b; Weeres 1971). Now, however, suburban districts, as well as urban districts, are confronting frequent redistributive decisions. The plentiful management skills of middle-class suburban populations, which used to be employed mainly to minimize conflict, now are being used, in substantial part, to mobilize conflict—that is, to resist cutbacks (Boyd 1979). Moreover, redistributive politics have been significantly escalated in large urban districts due to the frequently acute combination of declining enrollments and severe fiscal strain arising from municipal overburden, the high cost of educating disadvantaged urban populations, and a trend toward disinvestment in urban education (Cibulka 1982a).

Second, declining enrollments and fiscal resources have forced school officials, and other active participants in the policymaking contest, to learn the dynamics of the new game of cutback management. Adaptation to this new game, the distinctive features of which were outlined at the opening of this chapter, has been complicated by its interaction with collective bargaining, which in many school districts was another new process that had to be learned at the same time as cutback management (Murnane 1981).

Third, the redistributive, zero-sum game produced by declining enrollments and retrenchment has not merely activated old cleavages; it also has created new cleavages, such as the one alluded to earlier between advocates of special and regular educational services. But the most imposing new cleavage is associated with the dramatic changes in the social and fiscal context of public education in the 1970s (Kirst and Garms 1980). Demographic and economic trends have conspired to substantially reduce the priority that public education can claim on the public fisc. Families with children in the public schools are now a minority group in many school districts. The newest cleavage thus is between the shrinking group of supporters of public education and the expanding group of taxpayers and senior citizens who feel that spending for education should be reduced. From the point of view of school governance, this further complicates the already thorny issue of to whom public school systems should be responsive and accountable.

Rationality and Retrenchment

How have educators typically sought to circumvent the rancorous conflict that usually attends retrenchment policymaking? Consistent with the influential heritage of the municipal reform movement, the extensive literature of professional advice on the management of declining enrollments emphasizes the need to follow a strategy of broad citizen involvement in policymaking through a rational planning, problem-solving, and consensus-building process (Zerchykov 1981). Such an approach is supposed to produce both agreement and high-quality decisions. As it turns out, the emerging evidence makes it increasingly clear that the professional advice strategy is misguided. Both Zerchykov's (1981) review of the literature and

Berger's (1982c) secondary analysis of seventy case studies, via the case survey method, show, contrary to the conventional wisdom, that the more comprehensive and extended the planning process, the greater is the opposition to school closing decisions.[4] Berger (1982c: 21) concluded, therefore, that school officials "may want to consider swifter, less technical planning techniques to avoid [or reduce] community protest."

On the other hand, as Berger (1982c) noted, minimizing opposition is only one of several goals in retrenchment policymaking. School officials consequently must seek a delicate balance between not entirely compatible objectives: (1) discovering the "best" or at least a desirable and defensible educational solution or adjustment to declining enrollments that, at the same time, is politically viable; (2) securing community and staff understanding and consent; (3) maintaining legitimacy for the policymaking process; and (4) moving rapidly enough toward closure on retrenchment decisions to avoid the apparent tendency for conflict and opposition to increase over time. In view of the tension among these objectives, it is not surprising that school officials actually tend to depart from the professional advice strategy. But there are signs of variation among the inclination of different types of school districts. Upper-middle-class suburban school districts seem most prone to try to follow the strategy, while working-class and large urban school districts are much less inclined to pursue the "rational" model.

Of course, much of the recent literature on policymaking in organizations debunks the rational planning model. Particularly for public sector organizations, but also increasingly for private sector organizations (Pfeffer 1981), the policymaking process is described as incremental, chaotic, and political (see Lindblom 1959; March and Olsen 1976) rather than comprehensive, systematic, and rational. At the same time, however, there is evidence that organizations under the pressures of decline ultimately tend to be forced to abandon ad hoc, incremental policymaking in favor of calculated risks that provide more comprehensive responses to the problems they face (Behn 1980c; Glassberg 1978; Rubin 1980; but see also Hirschman 1970).

It nevertheless is true that policy frequently evolves in a none too tidy way out of a process that is partially deliberate and partially accidental. A good example of accidental policy development is provided by two of the suburban working class school districts in the

Boyd and Wheaton (1982) study. As a by-product of reluctance to close schools and ad hoc decisions made (or avoided) with reference to the problem of declining enrollments, the Alton and Weston districts, without desiring to, moved toward small, combined-grade classes in a number of their elementary schools.[5]

Of course, the business of calling attention to what is claimed to be the unusually loosely coupled, anarchic character of public schools as organizations and policymaking systems has by now become something of a growth industry (see Cuban 1975; March and Olsen 1976; Meyer and Rowan 1977; Rowan 1981; Weick 1976). As a consequence the mounting chorus of voices chanting this refrain may obscure the fact that school districts actually vary in the degree to which they pursue (and in a few cases, in some ways approach) the ideal of rational policymaking.[6] In the high socioeconomic status suburban districts in the Boyd and Wheaton (1982) study, plentiful management resources and associated attitudes inclined them to assiduously pursue the rational planning model. Their policy development process for decline thus was characterized by:

- Extensive data collection and analysis;

- Considerable use of expertise;

- Formation of numerous committees and task forces involving citizens and educators;

- Numerous attempts to clarify and set educational goals; to establish policies and models for systematic and consistent responses to decline-related problems; and to develop and apply criteria for school closing decisions; and

- Extensive public discussion of the problems of decline and of alternative solutions for these problems.[7]

By contrast, in the working-class districts in the study, where management resources were scarce, policy development was more inclined toward political bargaining than rational planning. As a result, the process usually was characterized by:

- Much less data collection and analysis;

- Little use of expertise;

- Fewer committees and less citizen involvement;

- Fewer attempts to clarify or set goals and criteria;

- Less public discussion, more inclination toward secrecy and suspicion;
- More inclination toward ad hoc and accidental policy development; and
- More overt politics and bargaining.

Some of the differences between the upper-middle- and working-class districts in the study can be illustrated by briefly contrasting Northview and Weston. In both districts the superintendents argued that declining enrollments necessitated a reorganization of schools and grades in order to maintain needed flexibility for the proper grouping of children. In high status Northview, child psychologists and university professors were brought in to board meetings to explain the importance of proper grouping. Extensive discussion of this subject, and analysis of enrollment projections under the existing arrangement of schools, convinced the Northview board, and most of the community, that a sweeping reorganization plan was necessary to maintain educational quality, even though it meant giving up the remainder of their neighborhood school system. (One elementary school already had been closed.)

In working-class Weston, the case for proper grouping was presented much more briefly, with less expertise invoked, and the substantive merits of the idea received far less discussion and scrutiny. Instead, the discussion quickly shifted to the importance of somehow maintaining the existing neighborhood school system. When the Weston superintendent continued to try to frame choices in response to decline in terms of grade reorganization or regrouping, the bulk of the interested public, and some board members, viewed this as a cover-up for what really was at stake—the demise of highly valued neighborhood schools.

While the reaction in Weston reflects a legitimate difference in values, it also reflects a difference in the importance placed on expertise and substantive analysis of educational policy questions. Thus, when school closings no longer could be postponed in Weston, the grouping issue still received little attention and the school board chose, from the alternatives before them, the plan that least altered their neighborhood school system.

Another example from the same study of the contrast in policy development approaches is the Alton School District. In the working class district of Alton, the only planning committee on declining enrollments was a small subcommittee of the school board itself, which met privately, apparently analyzed little data, and generally conducted itself with an air of secrecy and disdain toward curious citizens. While confidential discussions went on in all districts, citizens in the upper-middle-class districts would not have tolerated a planning approach relying almost entirely on a secretive elite.

Although Wheaton and Boyd found more overt politics and bargaining in working class districts, politics certainly was not absent in the high socioeconomic status districts. Rather, it often took place, with more subtlety than in the working-class districts, within the context of the "rational" approach. For instance, because of the complexity and ambiguity of the data and alternatives relevant to school closing decisions, these matters often were subject to debate and sophisticated "partisan analysis" (Lindblom 1968) by the citizen and employee groups potentially affected. Moreover, conflict often broke out, particularly over the initial school closings in a district (as was the case, for example, in Northview's first school closing), when it became clear who the losers were likely to be. In this regard, it was found that after the first one or two elementary school closings occur in a district citizens usually become more accepting of the idea that additional elementary school closings must take place and may not be as harmful as originally feared.

Particularly in high status districts, the use by school officials of at least the trappings of the rational planning approach helps to maintain the legitimacy of the decisionmaking process for most people, even though prospective and actual losers tend to be suspicious of the process. Sometimes their suspicions are well founded: As in many public facility closure situations the data on alternative school closing possibilities often fail to indicate one clearly superior solution. In these situations hints of political considerations and arbitrariness in the determination of decisions frequently make acceptance of the outcome especially difficult for the losers.

Although central office administrators in urban school districts typically attempt to follow a rational-technical model of decisionmaking for school closings, the process—and especially the public participation phase of it—tends to be overwhelmed or circumvented by the fundamental organizational and political dynamics common in large urban bureaucracies.[8] All too often the actual school closure decisionmaking in large urban districts seems to be characterized by incomplete information and analysis, blatant politics, and spectacular footdragging followed by precipitous and sometimes arbitrary decisions (see Cibulka 1982b; Colton and Frelich 1979; Cronin 1980). The flavor of this process in large urban districts is vividly conveyed by Metz (1981) in her account of the closing of the Andrew Jackson Magnet School, where the decision for closure took place a half hour after the first public mention of the idea. In a graphic illustration of the garbage-can theory of decisionmaking (March and Olsen 1976), Metz (1981: 147) showed how this decision "could not in any sense be described as a rational solution to a single problem." She also demonstrated the vulnerability of special schools, such as magnet schools, which tend to be used as movable pieces or pawns to ameliorate system-level problems through symbolic actions.

Above all, school closing and retrenchment decisionmaking in large urban school districts is characterized by problem avoidance and delay. Cronin (1980, and Chapter 8 of this book) reported that the bankruptcies in New York City, Cleveland, and Chicago were caused in part by the gross failure of all three school systems to make needed cutbacks. Enrollment in the New York City schools declined by 50,000 pupils from 1971 to 1975, but few schools were closed and the staff was not cut back. Cleveland lost 63,000 students from 1968 to 1979 but postponed closing any schools and actually increased its teaching staff. Chicago's enrollment declined by 96,000 students from 1971 to 1979, but very few schools were closed although hundreds of mobile classrooms were removed from schoolyards (Cronin 1980).

Similarly, in 1981 the Little Hoover Commission in California criticized the Los Angeles school district for not closing a single school despite having lost over 100,000 students in the previous eight years. And in what *Education Week* (1982a: 3) characterized as "a belated attempt . . . to bring five years of stability to the system," the Minneapolis school board voted in March 1982 to close eighteen schools, a quarter of the city's total schools. This action, taken in an attempt to reduce an anticipated $97 million deficit over the next five years, will require more than half of the district's students to attend different schools in the next school year.

Why should large urban school districts be so prone to delay on retrenchment? If anything, the massive and dramatic nature of their enrollment declines and fiscal problems would seem to demand *prompter* attention and action than the more modest problems faced by smaller districts. The answer, in part, as documented by Berger's (1982c) case survey, is that urban districts are prone to face more opposition to school closings than nonurban districts. But why should this be the case? A complete answer requires an examination of the implications of a fundamental dilemma of cutback management.

The fact that there tend to be clear winners and losers in retrenchment policymaking is, of course, the reason why conflict management is so difficult in decline. A way out of this difficulty might appear to be across-the-board or dispersed, rather than concentrated, cutbacks. But there is a debate and dilemma associated with this option: On the one hand, across-the-board cutbacks in time will weaken the entire enterprise (and possibly antagonize too many people), while on the other hand, concentrated cuts involve painful surgery and are sure to galvanize vociferous opposition from the affected parties.

In the short run, however, across-the-board cuts are quite attractive because they minimize conflict. As Behn (1980c: 615) has argued persuasively, however, referring to the ultimate danger of bankruptcy and receivership, there are two fundamental stages in retrenchment:

> During the first, the small declines in resources combine with the inability (or unwillingness) to recognize the long-run trends to produce short-run solutions: across-the-board cuts and deferred maintenance. Eventually, however, reality is forced upon the organization—either by its leaders who explain it, or by outsiders who place strict conditions upon their continued support. Only once the organization is in this second stage can the serious business of managing the decline begin. And it is in the interest of the manager (or, at least, in the interest of the manager who plans to stay with the organization over the long-term) to get past the first stage as quickly as possible.

To get past the first stage of decline, leaders must understand and explain to their constituents and organization members the opportunity cost of *not* cutting back (Behn 1980c). Otherwise, everyone will focus on the obvious, immediate costs of the cutbacks themselves.

As Zerchykov (1981) noted, one of the reasons the professional advice literature almost universally urges a planning and consensus-building process is to seek agreement enabling focused cuts rather than eventually debilitating across-the-board cuts. But the empirical literature shows that the rational planning approach rarely produces

such agreement. Thus, it initially appears that conflict can be minimized only by sacrificing the more rational course of action in favor
of dispersed cuts: "If school managers make focused cuts they will
. . . be faced with intense organized political opposition but no countervailing organized support" (Zerchykov 1981: 175).

How then can school authorities "do the rational while accommodating the emotional [i.e., political] ?" (Zerchykov 1981: 7). A major
conclusion of Boyd and Wheaton (1982) is that school officials need
not be deterred by the inability of the rational planning approach to
perform as advertised: *The politics of school closings really is far
more a divide-and-conquer than a plan-and-agree process.* The secret
of school closings, sensed by some school officials, is *concentrated
cuts judiciously targeted* to minimize the likelihood of the formation
of resistance coalitions. There always will be resistance to school
closings, but if it is isolated it will have little effect. Because citizens
in other neighborhoods may not mind seeing someone else's ox
gored, they will be unlikely to join forces with the losers unless they
believe their neighborhood school soon will be in jeopardy also.
Thus, the lack of active, organized support in *favor* of school closings
is not the obstacle to school closings that it might appear to be: A
countervailing force is not needed against weak and isolated opponents. Moreover, rather than being the artifact of Machiavellian tactics, the isolation of opponents to cutbacks will tend to occur spon-
taneously when participants truly understand the opportunity costs
of not cutting back.[9]

This analysis shows that small school systems, as most suburban
ones are, enjoy an important advantage over large systems in the
matter of school closings. Small districts usually need only to propose closing one or two schools at a time. In large city school systems plagued by decline, however, it is not uncommon for school
officials to propose closing a large number of schools simultaneously.
As Narver, Weatherley, and Elmore (1982) showed in the case of
Seattle, this creates the likelihood in cities of coalitions of affected
neighborhoods mounting significant opposition to school closing
proposals. This difference between large and small school systems
provides part of the explanation for the greater difficulties city
school districts are having in closing schools.[10]

The Seattle case actually is not entirely representative because
Seattle is atypical of large cities in America today in that it still has
a very large middle-class population. The high level of management

skills in Seattle's population doubtless contributed to the remarkable political mobilization by citizens reported by Narver, Weatherley, and Elmore (1982).[11] The more typical pattern in large cities, which does not require such a high order of sophisticated citizen involvement, can be inferred from Cronin's (1980) and Cibulka's (1982b) assessments of the politics of urban school closings.

Cronin (1980: 4) reported that "everytime the [Chicago School] Superintendent proposed closing a building, a delegation of parents, often led by an alderman or helped by school employees, would storm the Board of Education and cause such a furor that the proposed closing would be shelved." He concluded (1980: 15), from his appraisal of the New York City, Chicago, and Cleveland cases, that the principal reasons for urban school bankruptcies are:

- It is very difficult and unpopular to raise property taxes for city schools.

- It is very painful to close down individual school buildings, especially in cities where custodial unions have substantial strength and often assist city political leaders with election campaigns.[12]

- It is very tempting to try to "finesse" a deficit by engaging in short-term borrowing with tax exempt municipal bonds for just as long as the rating services and banks will allow.

Cibulka's (1982b) study of ten cities helps to flesh out the details of the political dynamics suggested by Cronin. Cibulka's data showed how and why urban school board members are less inclined to close schools than are their administrative staffs. This inclination springs from (1) the political orientation of urban school board members toward short-term pressures from constituents; (2) the fact that constituents emphasize claims of equity and program quality more than economy and efficiency; and (3) the difficulties retrenchment or decremental decisionmaking presents for the creation of winning coalitions in school board voting (Cibulka 1982b: 29). Since the second and third points relate to the first, the important thing to emphasize here is the evidence that Cibulka presented about the greater inclination in recent years for urban school board members to take a *delegate* orientation (i.e., "do what your constituents ask") rather than a *trustee* orientation (i.e., "do what *you* think is best for the whole school district") toward their representational role on the school board.

Cibulka notes that, as a result of a number of forces, many urban school board candidates in the 1970s were elected or appointed to represent a particular constituency or point of view. Some city districts, such as Atlanta and Milwaukee, even changed their laws to allow for the election of board members by areas within the school district rather than at-large. These developments, as they were intended to do, have made many urban school boards more representative of and responsive to segments of the public. As a result, large city school boards have increased the tendency they already had to be more politicized and to have more board members with political ambitions than is typically the case with school boards in smaller districts, where board members are more likely to serve mainly out of a sense of civic duty. When these conditions in urban districts are coupled with the political clout of unionized custodians and educators (and their ability to provide needed campaign support for the election of board members and other local politicians), a situation is created in which it is very difficult to get agreement to make the painful cutbacks essential for the long run financial stability of urban systems.[13]

As if these problems were not enough, because large and urban school districts usually are more socially heterogeneous than small and suburban districts, school closure decision-making is more likely to be complicated in the former by racial desegregation issues. As shown in articles on school closings in *Education Week* (1982a, 1982b, 1982c), thorny questions arise as to which schools to close in what neighborhoods, with what immediate and long-term effects on racial balance, and how to equalize the amount of busing that different racial groups will face. Because these issues are hard to resolve satisfactorily, they add to the conflict surrounding school closings and may prompt lawsuits that delay or block school closing decisions.

To summarize the discussion in this portion of the chapter, a tension exists between the professional advice literature on the management of decline and actual practice. Research shows that the professional advice literature is misguided, at least so far as conflict management is concerned, and that certain kinds of school districts are more likely than others to depart from the advice. Upper status districts are more inclined to follow the rational planning and consensus-building strategy, but it seldom enables them to avoid conflict. Significantly, however, it does provide a sense of legitimacy for the policymaking process and tends to produce results that appear more rational than the ad hoc, accidental, or dilatory policymaking that seems characteristic of working-class and urban districts. The political and organizational circumstances common to large urban school districts usually overwhelm efforts at a rational planning approach and make it very difficult to get agreement on the focused cuts necessary for real cutback management. The delay and temporizing about retrenchment that result exacerbate the already serious problems large urban school districts face. By contrast, because of differences in their political and organizational circumstances, small and suburban districts tend to be able to make focused cuts without excessive, harmful delays, though some, of course, fail to do so.

CONSEQUENCES AND IMPLICATIONS OF DECLINE

The most serious consequences of declining enrollments have been felt in large urban school districts, where delay in action on the problem has contributed to program deterioration, fiscal strain, and even in a few cases to bankruptcy and receivership. The latter cases have not only damaged the legitimacy and credibility of urban school boards in general but have led to an actual reduction in the scope of control and powers of the affected school boards (Cronin 1980). Declining enrollments are, of course, only one of the serious problems facing large urban districts, but Cronin (1980) argued that a lack of decisive action in this area was instrumental in pushing New York City, Chicago, and Cleveland into bankruptcy.

Considering the gravity of the problem and the fact that educators might be expected to have a somewhat easier time with cutback management than other public managers (due to the clear, unalterable, and blameless nature of the problem in their area (Behn 1980a)), one may still wonder why urban school officials would be so slow to act. The heart of the problem, as Rubin (1980) revealed, lies in the nature of the urban political process and the usual structure of incentives facing urban politicians, which discourages prudent fiscal management. Rubin emphasizes that politics works on a short-term, exchange system, with politicians allocating resources in return for political support. Cutbacks threaten the political exchange process by removing slack resources and new uncommitted funds. Since both cutbacks and new taxes are political liabilities, politicians, as Rubin (1980: 621) noted, may "satisfice" by:

> (1) encouraging new revenue sources such as federal grants or greater support from the state or other local jurisdictions; (2) denying there is a problem, and

delaying any cuts, except by attrition or deferred purchasing, maintenance, and equipment replacement; and (3) increasing borrowing to provide current services and capital projects for which they may take political credit. The administrative component of this strategy may involve [various methods of "creative financing" and] hiding deficits. . . . These responses may result in large, planned deficits in operating budgets. As long as these deficits are obscured, they may be politically preferable to the combination of cutbacks and new allocatable resources.

What seems needed, as Rubin contended, is a restructuring of the urban political incentive system (1) by making it hard to conceal deficits and (2) by providing new, inexpensive political resources to substitute for those now being allocated in the exchange process. Since urban school districts are susceptible to the same political problems found in urban municipal government, Rubin's recommendations are applicable to both arenas.

Although public schools still can be characterized as "domesticated organizations" assured, in the main, of clients and tax-supplied budgets (Carlson 1964), declining fiscal support and enrollments show clearly that they also are "open systems" dependent upon and vulnerable to their environments (see Crespo and Haché 1982), though not to the same degree as private sector organizations. One aspect of this dependency revealed by school closures is the need for cooperative relations with municipal government and community groups for the recycling or disposal of excess school buildings. In some settings, such as Seattle (Narver, Weatherley, and Elmore 1982), cooperation and flexibility in zoning adjustments have facilitated creative management of school property disposal, a new task area of major importance, especially for large declining school districts. In other locations, rigidity in zoning and resistance to alternative uses of school buildings have stymied property disposal and delayed realization of the associated economic benefits for school districts.

With the exception of large urban school districts, the organizational consequences of declining enrollments appear considerably more serious than the external political consequences, at least in the short run (see Cuban 1979). Over the long run, declining enrollments and an aging population are bound to reduce public political support for the finance of public schools, creating an increasing cleavage between direct and indirect beneficiaries of public schooling services. In the short term, it appears that when school officials close only one or two schools at a time they generally can ride out the period of angry opposition from citizens whose neighborhood schools are to be closed. Although opponents of closings sometimes can succeed in electing a representative to the school board, especially in the heat generated by the initial school closings in a district, they rarely can reverse the course of events. For example, in the Boyd and Wheaton study, very few school board members or school superintendents lost their positions, over the period from 1971 to 1981, because of actions associated with declining enrollments. Of the fifteen districts, three districts fired one superintendent each, and one district notorious for its volatility fired three superintendents. Of these six firings, only three can be even partially attributed to decline-related problems (Boyd and Wheaton 1982). Similar findings in the Washington, D.C., area are reported by Cuban (1979).

Even if the initial political, as opposed to organizational, consequences of declining enrollments are generally slight, it is still clear that neighborhoods that have lost schools have been hurt, at least in the short run. To the extent that school officials anticipate but wish to avoid intense controversies over closing neighborhood schools, they may want to consider Gately's (1979) proposal that neighborhoods that lose schools be given a temporary reduction in their school taxes as compensation for the costs imposed specifically on them in the interest of the welfare of the whole school district.

In most school districts, the response to declining enrollments has led to a period of tension and transformation in school–community relationships. Most importantly, with school mergers and consolidations, there has been a movement away from the once sacrosanct neighborhood school concept. This movement, however, usually has been accompanied by a complex symbolic politics regarding the meaning and maintenance (or redefinition) of neighborhood schools and neighborhoods (Wood and Boyd 1981). Whether one is explicit about it or not, the movement away from neighborhood schools to consolidated schools is likely to have highly significant and probably positive political consequences: Rather than identifying narrowly with the interests of neighborhood schools, parents will be more able to see the broader interests of the whole school system or at least their portion of the consolidated system. This redefinition of the schools' community should reduce factionalism and aid in the development of more unified parental support for the schools, a vital consideration in this time of adverse demographic and economic trends.

There is wide agreement among observers that declining enrollments are producing serious and far-reaching organizational and educational consequences for schools. Despite the consensus on the importance of these consequences, however, there still is much less systematic research in this area than on the financial, technical, and political aspects of managing the immediate problems caused by declining enrollments. Indeed, as Crespo and Haché (1982: 76) have observed, "Few attempts have been made to provide suitable conceptual frameworks for understanding the administrative and educational consequences or for dealing administratively or politically with the implications of declining enrollments in other than immediate, crisis-management terms."

The organizational consequences of decline have both objective and subjective or social psychological impacts (Crespo and Haché 1982), and they affect the full range of people, programs, and processes associated with schools. The specter and reality of forced layoffs of teachers and administrators and the much reduced opportunities for promotion and career advancement caused by declining enrollments have seriously damaged the morale of educators. Competition for resources and survival is rampant in rapidly declining districts and has produced an intense internal organizational politics. In New York City, for example, Duke, Cohen, and Herman (1981: 16) reported that:

> Schools contend with other schools, with the central administration, and with the private sector. Teachers compete among themselves or against administrators, and departments within a school may vie with one another. Even student groups are pitted against one another in a scramble to lay first claim to dwindling resources.

Similar illustrative findings can be cited in St. Louis, where school administrators misrepresented the enrollment and space utilization situation in their school buildings (Colton and Frelich 1979); in Arlington, Virginia, where tensions increased between the teachers union and the school board and administration (Cuban 1979); and in Chicago, where school principals interpreted school attendance area boundaries "creatively," undertook special programs and curricular adaptations as "a hook to get kids," and minimized implementation of school district initiatives encouraging student transfers if it appeared that "too much transfer" was likely to occur from their schools (Morris et al. 1981).

The combination of reduced resources and support, intensified competition and in-fighting, and increasing workloads has contributed to the mounting problem of teacher and administrator overload and "burnout." The interconnected and far-reaching ramifications of this problem can be illustrated by findings from Quebec and New York City.

In a study of fifteen school districts in Quebec, Crespo and Haché (1982) found that administrative roles and duties tended to be expanded as personnel were reduced, but tasks and functions still needed to be accomplished. As administrators accumulated more responsibilities, they tended to attend to the more urgent and expedient tasks and to neglect those associated with instruction and supervision of teaching. Moreover, the specialist roles that were eliminated, and the tasks that were redistributed, "were often those related to the pedagogical or curricular functions of the system [while] functions observed to be of more critical importance in the short-term management of decline, like personnel or finance, usually remained untouched" (Crespo and Haché 1982: 90).

These developments not only weakened administrative support of the educational functions of schools, but the overload on administrators "lowered the administrative responsiveness of the system." Furthermore, administrative overload compounded the problem of declining motivation, energy, and aspirations among tenured, aging administrators faced with shrinking opportunities for promotion. According to Crespo and Haché, the result was a tendency toward minimal job performance oriented toward routine organizational maintenance rather than innovation and development.

To the bleak picture sketched out above, one can add the observations of Duke, Cohen, and Herman (1981) in New York City. In a study of three high schools that were said to be only moderately affected by retrenchment, they found many signs of increased teacher burnout associated with cutbacks. Reductions in administrative and supervisory support have added to the problems of teachers:

> Because retrenchment has reduced the cadre of supervisors . . . [administrators lack] time to observe all classrooms by themselves . . . [and] have begun to require that teachers provide more documentation—e.g., detailed lesson plans and course objectives—to make "absentee supervision" easier. The extra paperwork is simply another burden for teachers already harried by larger classes and diminished resources. (Duke, Cohen, and Herman 1981: 16).

One of the most discussed dilemmas of decline has been the problem of how best to determine which teachers should be laid off. Should reduction-in-force (RIF) procedures be according to a person's seniority or performance or some mixture of these? In an important research project, Johnson (1980, 1982) has examined this question in six school districts located across the United States. Because of the difficulties of fairly assessing teachers' performance, tensions and problems in administering performance-based layoffs, and the likelihood that assessments will not stand up in arbitration, Johnson found that even school districts that wanted to use performance as the main criterion eventually shifted to seniority. Interestingly, while unions strongly back the seniority principle, Phelan (1982) found that a majority of the principals and teachers in his study wanted performance evaluations included as a RIF criterion. But he also found that performance evaluation procedures often were viewed as arbitrary and subjective, so seniority again emerged as the most acceptable approach.

The advantages of seniority are that all teachers are treated in an equitable and predictable manner, thus minimizing uncertainty and competition among teachers. The question can be raised, though, as to whom this approach is equitable and desirable for. If it serves most teachers' interests well (though not those of young teachers and minority persons hired recently under affirmative action) the same is not so clear for students' interests (but see Murnane 1981). Johnson (1982: 13) noted that as seniority is applied in some districts, "it provides no control over staff quality, it permits disruptions of ongoing classes, and it undermines the stability of school staffs." Also, depending on how it is applied, seniority can lead, as a result of "bumping" associated with RIF, to many teachers teaching outside their primary area of certification, where their expertise may be questionable. An encouraging note, however, is that both Johnson (1982) and Murnane (1981) observed that school district officials are beginning to learn how to bargain more effectively, formally or informally, to create better thought-out seniority-based layoff systems.

This discussion of the consequences of decline is far from exhaustive but points to the conclusion that the response to decline in many school districts probably is resulting in some serious deterioration of the educational program. Much more research is needed on this topic, but it appears that program deterioration is brought about by the combined effects of what may be the standard response to decline—a strong tendency toward organizational rigidity and delay in the initial stages (Berger 1982b) followed by ad hoc, expedient crisis-management later, producing a number of adverse short- and long-term effects on the educational climate and program (Berger 1982a; Crespo and Haché 1982; Whetten 1981). As Crespo and Haché (1982: 92) propose,

> The exclusion of long-term considerations in the formulation of strategies to deal with declining enrollments and the almost exclusive preoccupation with the short-term goals of solving the personnel, material, and financial problems associated with this phenomenon may be seen as a displacement of goals and resources from the primary area of student learning and achievement to that of maintaining system equilibrium under conditions of turbulence.

Similarly, commenting on the response by school districts in Massachusetts to the combined pressures of declining enrollments and fiscal cutbacks occasioned by the passage of Proposition 2½, Mulkeen (1982) has asserted that rather than choosing between programs school administrators maintained the same programs with less staff. As a consequence, "public employee doomsayers were made to look bad because school superintendents hid the agenda by weakening all programs" (Mulkeen 1982).

One does not have to look far to see that program cutbacks tend to come first in the "less essential" subjects and services such as art, music, counselors, and extracurricular activities (see Duke, Cohen, and Herman 1981). Such cutbacks are not to be taken lightly since these "extras," beyond their own value, often play a critical role in making schooling palatable for many students, and especially the more marginal students. Even if extracurricular activities are not decimated by cutbacks, there is the danger that school closings and consolidations will lead to the creation of still more large high schools, which provide settings unconducive to the social and scholastic benefits that have been shown to be associated with small schools (Garbarino 1981; Lindsay 1982).[14]

In drawing this discussion to a close, the point that educators should ponder, as Crespo and Haché (1982: 95) emphasized, is that "the quasi-absence of consideration for educational goals in the development of decline management strategies ultimately points to a decrease in the level of educational goal attainment."

CONCLUSION

In a cogent commentary on the contemporary educational scene, Tyack and Hansot (1982: 252) have succinctly summarized the dark side of the trends and dynamics discussed in this chapter:

> One could predict a dismal future for the public schools. Retrenchment could repeat the haphazard process of incrementalism [in policymaking that oc-curred during the growth period of the 1950s and 1960s], only in reverse: educators could set in motion a process of decrementalism, of peeling away parts of the system, with little sense of unified purpose. The economics of scarcity could stimulate factionalism and bitter competition among educational interest groups. As loyalty to public schooling as a common good erodes, parents who have the opportunity could choose exit to private schools rather than work to improve the public system. Public education could become a place of last resort.

Noting that "in an era of stagflation in the economy and conservative reaction against social services, those who are determined to preserve and improve public education must be able to state a coherent case," Tyack and Hansot (1982; 252, 255) called for creative leadership of the type described in Selznick's (1957) classic treatise on administration:

> In making budget cuts it will be tempting to find targets of least resistance rather than to make decisions based on collaborative reappraisal of what makes a coherent and effective system of instruction. But defined in another way, the need to decide what is essential—and to enlist colleagues and com-munity in that debate—can remedy the incoherence produced by easy money and rapid growth. . . . [C]utbacks need not signal decline of the public school as an institution (Tyack and Hansot 1982; 257–58).

One of the dilemmas revealed in this chapter is that it is precisely the "targets of least resistance" that facilitate the minimization of conflict in cutback management. While a focus on such targets may not necessarily preclude the development of a rational response to decline, in concluding it should be emphasized again that conflict management should not be an end in itself. It is true that excessive conflict or conflict that too long delays action can be injurious. But conflict and the debate that it sparks also can help to clarify issues and ultimately lead to better, more rational decisions, as Narver, Weatherley, and Elmore (1982) demonstrated in the case of Seattle.

Similarly, although pursuit of the rational planning model will not eliminate conflict, it ultimately may enable more rational policy choices (Boyd and Wheaton 1982). Educational leaders thus must recognize that conflict avoidance through sheer expediency in crisis-management can exact a very high cost in terms of long-run values.

Although the discussion earlier underscored the fact that leaders often must overcome opposition to cutbacks without the benefit of countervailing political support, leaders need not necessarily face the foes of retrenchment alone. In a seminal contribution to leadership in public management quite consistent in tone with Tyack and Hansot's recommendations, Behn (1980c) suggested how to create the support for cutbacks necessary to override the inevitable opposition: First, leaders can dramatize the opportunity costs of not cutting back by making clear the *specific* consequences for the organization and individuals and groups within it. Second, leaders can articulate a new "corporate strategy" or organizational mission that shows who will *benefit* by the transformation and contraction of the organization. By judicious use of these approaches leaders can both reduce opposition and increase support for necessary cutbacks.

In no-growth or contracting circumstances, public administrators must become adept at the leadership skills necessary for policy termination. With few or no new resources available to fund new services or innovations, change and reform are possible only through a redistribution of existing resources. For this to be done in the most thoughtful, desirable, and defensible way requires the highest order of public leadership.

NOTES TO CHAPTER 9

1. These mandates have led to an ironic rephrasing of an old refrain: "He who calls the tunes does not pay the piper."

2. Cronin (1980: 13) reported that during 1979, as a result of the federal mandate to serve handicapped children (Public Law 94–142), the New York City Board of Education "while still reducing other program costs had to hire 11,000 new staff, as teachers, counselors, and aides for handicapped students."

3. Pseudonyms are used for the fifteen districts in the study, which are located in two metropolitan areas. In 1978 the districts ranged in enrollment size from 1,000 to 17,000 students. On 1970 median family income

they ranged from $10,500 to $29,500. For further details of the study, see Boyd (forthcoming) and Boyd and Wheaton (1982).

4. Vivid case study examples of this proposition are provided by Morgan and Wofford (1977) and Poster and Gotti (1982).

5. Of course, small, combined-grade classes can be defended as desirable educational arrangements, if appropriate groupings of students can be made. In these cases, however, they were merely a means to the end of keeping neighborhood elementary schools open, and the grouping of students was increasingly a matter of chance rather than intention. To their credit the superintendents in both districts called attention to the educational implications of the choices their school boards were making.

6. The ideal of rational policy or decisionmaking, as March and Simon (1958) and others have shown, is of course entirely unattainable.

7. The range of alternative solutions considered, even in high status districts, tended to be quite narrow (see Boyd 1982).

8. Characterizing urban school politics as "closed system, privatized politics," Iannaccone (1979) noted that citizen participation often occurs *after* decisions to close schools and focuses on the implementation of the transfers of students.

9. For example, Boyd and Wheaton (1982) found in the Karlin school district that the opponents of a school closing were unable to garner support either from candidates running for the school board or for a proposed district-wide referendum on the closing of their school. The closing affected only a small segment of Karlin's population, and there were many voters who were more concerned about the district cutting back on expenses.

10. The long and impressive record of the Department of Defense in closing large numbers of military bases *at the same time* seems to contradict the proposition stated here (Behn and Lambert 1979). However, there are a number of factors specific to the Department of Defense case that may account for the lack of resistance coalitions in Congress to the multiple base closings. First, the multiple base closings are spread across many states, not confined to a single community area, so the multiple impact is not visible in one locality. Second, the affected citizens consequently are not able to directly form coalitions themselves but must rely on congressmen, the most influential of whom, Behn and Lambert reported, the Department of Defense studiously avoids offending. Third, military bases do not provide any direct local services. Fourth, most personnel on military bases that are closed do not lose their jobs but are transferred. Fifth, the Department of Defense will back down on proposed closings if local congressmen ask the right questions (Behn and Lambert 1979: 17). Sixth, and finally, the Department of Defense has a long-range planning approach

that leads to planned obsolescence, deterioration, and phasing down of activity at bases to be closed. Thus, when closing finally is announced these bases compare poorly to the other bases.

11. One example of the sophisticated citizen participation in Seattle is the ingenuity and legal expertise employed to block the closing of five schools in 1976 on the grounds that the school district had failed to file a required environmental impact statement (Narver, Weatherley, and Elmore 1982). Another example of enterprising citizen resistance to school closings is found in Portland, Oregon, where upset citizens in one area of the district are attempting to secede from the district, a legal possibility they discovered under the state's 1957 school reorganization act, which is primarily concerned with school district consolidation (*Education Week* 1982c: 11).

12. Cronin (1980: 19) noted that "In smaller cities the school custodian is viewed as a low status hired hand. In large cities the custodian-engineer is a feudal chieftain . . . an entrepreneur, a small businessman . . . who has a stake in keeping the schools not only clean but open.

13. In a very large sense, for school district as well as municipal government, "The crux of the retrenchment problem," as Levine, Rubin and Wolohojian (1981: 627) noted, "comes down to a fundamental trade-off . . . [between efficiency and democracy] : centralize [authority] and limit representative and responsive government [thereby facilitating decisive cutback management] , or leave authority more or less fragmented but open to interest group access, limiting the ability of government to prioritize and target cutbacks. Either way, something of value will be sacrificed." On this point, see also Boyd (1975).

14. Data are still scarce about the politics of closing high schools. The author's own research suggests that there is less resistance to closing junior highs than neighborhood elementary schools. Because of their distinct identity, visibility, and athletic teams, high schools are not likely to be closed easily.

REFERENCES

Banfield, Edward, and James Q. Wilson. 1963. *City Politics.* New York: Vintage.

Bardach, Eugene. 1976. "Policy Termination as a Political Process." *Policy Sciences* 7, no. 2 (June): 123–31.

Behn, Robert. 1976. "Closing the Massachusetts Public Training Schools." *Policy Sciences* 7, no. 2 (June): 151–71.

———. 1978a. "Closing a Government Facility." *Public Administration Review* 38, no. 4 (July/August): 332–38.

———. 1978b. "How to Terminate a Public Policy." *Policy Analysis* 4, no. 3 (Summer): 393–413.

_____. 1980a. "Declining Enrollment and Cut-Back Management: Making Retrenchment Look Easy." Paper presented at the Committee on Urban Public Economics Conference, New Orleans, Tulane University, October 31.

_____. 1980b. "The Fundamentals of Cutback Management." Paper presented at the Research Conference of the Association for Public Policy Analysis and Management, Boston, October 24.

_____. 1980c. "Leadership for Cut-Back Management: The Use of Corporate Strategy." _Public Administration Review_ 40, no. 6 (November/December): 613-20.

_____. 1980d. "Leadership in an Era of Retrenchment." _Public Administration Review_ 40, no. 6 (November/December): 603-04.

Behn, Robert, and D. P. Lambert. 1979. "Cut-Back Management at the Pentagon: The Closing of Military Bases." Paper presented at the Research Conference on Public Policy and Management, Chicago, October 19.

Berger, Michael A. 1982a. "Retrenchment Policies and Their Organizational Consequences." Paper presented at Conference on Managing Enrollment Decline, Vanderbilt University, Nashville, Tennessee, February 26.

_____. 1982b. "Stages in Decline: How an Educational Organization Scales Down." Paper presented at American Educational Research Association Annual Meeting, New York, March 23.

_____. 1982c. "Why Communities Protest School Closings." Paper presented at American Educational Research Association Annual Meeting, New York, March 20.

Berman, Paul, and Milbrey McLaughlin. 1978. "The Management of Decline." In _Declining Enrollment: The Challenge of the Coming Decade_, edited by S. Abramovitz and S. Rosenfeld, pp. 305-330. Washington, D.C.: National Institute of Education.

Boyd, William L. 1975. "School Board-Administrative Staff Relationships." In _Understanding School Boards_, edited by Peter Cistone, pp. 103-129. Boston: D. C. Heath.

_____. 1976a. "Community Status and Conflict in Suburban School Politics." _Sage Professional Papers in American Politics_, 3, 04-025. Beverly Hills, Calif.: Sage Publications.

_____. 1976b. "The Public, the Professionals and Educational Policy-Making: Who Governs?" _Teachers College Record_ 77, no. 4 (May): 539-77.

_____. 1979. "Educational Policy-Making in Declining Suburban School Distrists: Some Preliminary Findings." _Education and Urban Society_ 11, no. 3 (May): 333-66.

_____. 1982. "Retrenchment in American Education: The Politics of Efficiency." _California Journal of Teacher Education_ 9, no. 1 (winter): 67-78.

_____. Forthcoming. "School Governance in an Era of Retrenchment." Final Report to the National Institute of Education on Research Grant No. NIE-G-78-0086.

Boyd, William L., and Robert L. Crowson. 1981. "The Changing Conception and Practice of Public School Administration." In *Review of Research in Education*, edited by D. Berliner, pp. 311–373. Washington, D.C.: American Educational Research Association.

Boyd, William L., and Dennis R. Wheaton. 1982. "Policy Development in Declining Suburban School Districts." Paper presented at Conference on Managing Enrollment Decline, Vanderbilt University, Nashville, Tennessee, February 26.

Burlingame, Martin. 1979. "Declining Enrollments and Small Rural Cities and Districts." *Education and Urban Society* 11, no. 3 (May): 313–32.

Carlson, Richard O. 1964. "Environmental Constraints and Organizational Consequences." In *Behavioral Science and Educational Administration*, edited by Daniel E. Griffiths, pp. 262–76. Sixty-third Yearbook of the National Society for the Study of Education, Part 2. Chicago, Ill.: University of Chicago Press.

Cibulka, James G. 1982a. "Enrollment Loss and Financial Decline in Urban School Systems." Paper presented at Conference on Managing Enrollment Decline, Vanderbilt University, Nashville, Tennessee, February 26.

_____. 1982b. "The Politics of School Closings in Ten U.S. Cities." Paper presented at American Educational Research Association Annual Meeting, New York, March 20.

Colton, David, and Allan Frelich. 1979. "Enrollment Decline and School Closings in a Large City." *Education and Urban Society* 11, no. 3 (May): 396–417.

Crespo, Manuel, and Jean B. Haché. 1982. "The Management of Decline in Education: The Case of Quebec." *Educational Administration Quarterly* 18, no. 1 (Winter): 75–99.

Cronin, Joseph M. 1980. "Big City School Bankruptcy." Policy paper no. 80–C3, Institute for Research on Educational Finance and Governance, Stanford University, October.

Cuban, Larry. 1975. "*Hobson v. Hansen*: A Study in Organizational Response." *Educational Administration Quarterly* 11, no. 2: 15–37.

_____. 1979. "Shrinking Enrollment and Consolidation: Political and Organizational Impacts in Arlington, Virginia, 1973–1978." *Education and Urban Society* 11, no. 3 (May): 367–95.

Cyert, Richard M. 1978. "The Management of Universities of Constant or Decreasing Size." *Public Administration Review* 38, no. 4 (July/August): 334–49.

Duke, Daniel L.; J. S. Cohen; and R. Herman. 1981. "Running Faster to Stay in Place: Retrenchment in the New York City Schools." *Phi Delta Kappan* 62 (September): 13–17.

Education Week. 1982a. "Minneapolis Closes 25% of its Schools." 1, no. 25 (March 17): 3.

Education Week. 1982b. "Student Shift, Tight Budgets Heighten School-Closing Woes." 1, no. 26 (March 24): 1.

Education Week. 1982c. "To Save Local School, Parents Fight for New District." 1, no. 26 (March 24): 11.

Florio, David. 1976. *Declining Enrollment.* An NSBA Conference Report. Colorado Springs, Colo., August 4–6.

Freeman, John, and Michael T. Hannan. 1975. "Growth and Decline Processes in Organizations." *American Sociological Review* 40: 215–28.

Freeman, John, and Michael T. Hannan. 1981. "Effects of Resources and Enrollments on Growth and Decline in School Districts." Program Report No. 81–B1, Institute for Research on Educational Finance and Governance, Stanford University, April.

Garbarino, James. 1981. *Successful Schools and Competent Students.* Lexington, Mass.: D. C. Heath.

Gately, Dermot. 1979. "School Closure Decisions and the Cyclical Majority Problem." Unpublished paper, Department of Economics, New York University.

Glassberg, Andrew. 1978. "Organizational Responses to Municipal Budget Decreases." *Public Administration Review* 38, no. 4 (July/August): 325–32.

Hirschman, A.O. 1970. *Exit, Voice, and Loyalty.* Cambridge, Mass.: Harvard University Press.

Iannaccone, Laurence. 1979. "The Management of Decline." *Education and Urban Society* 11, no. 3 (May): 418–30.

Iannaccone, Laurence, and Frank W. Lutz. 1970. *Politics, Power and Policy: The Governing of Local School Districts.* Columbus, Ohio: Charles Merrill.

Johnson, Susan M. 1980. "Performance-Based Layoffs in the Public Schools." *Harvard Educational Review* 50, no. 2 (May): 214–33.

_____. 1982. "Seniority and Schools." Paper presented at American Educational Research Association Annual Meeting, New York, March 20.

Kimberly, J.R.; R.H. Miles; and associates. 1980. *The Organizational Life Cycle: Issues in the Creation, Transformation, and Decline of Organizations.* San Francisco: Jossey-Bass.

Kirst, Michael W., and Walter I. Garms. 1980. "The Political Environment of School Finance Policy in the 1980s." In *School Finance Policies and Practices—The 1980s: A Decade of Conflict,* edited by James Guthrie, pp. 47–75. Cambridge, Mass.: Ballinger Publishing Company.

Levine, Charles. 1978. "Organizational Decline and Cutback Management." *Public Administration Review* 38, no. 4 (July/August): 316–25.

_____. 1979. "More on Cutback Management: Hard Questions for Hard Times." *Public Administration Review* 39, no. 2 (March/April): 179–83.

Levine, C.; I. Rubin; and G. Wolohojian. 1981. "Resource Scarcity and the Reform Model: The Management of Retrenchment in Cincinnati and Oakland." *Public Administration Review* 41, no. 6 (November/December): 619–28.

Lindblom, Charles. 1959. "The Science of 'Muddling Through'." *Public Administration Review* 19 (Spring): 79–88.

_____. 1968. *The Policy Making Process.* Englewood Cliffs, N.J.: Prentice-Hall.

Lindsay, Paul. 1982. "The Effect of High School Size on Student Participation, Satisfaction, and Attendance." *Educational Evaluation and Policy Analysis* 4, no. 1 (Spring): 57–65.

Mann, Dale, ed. 1978. *Making Change Happen?* New York: Teachers College Press.

March, James G., and Johan P. Olsen. 1976. *Ambiguity and Choice in Organizations.* Bergen, Norway: Universitetsforlaget.

March, James G., and Herbert A. Simon. 1958. *Organizations.* New York: Wiley.

Masotti, Louis H., and Jeffrey K. Hadden, eds. 1973. *The Urbanization of the Suburbs.* Beverly Hills, Calif.: Sage.

Metz, Mary H. 1981. "The Closing of Andrew Jackson Elementary School: Magnets in School System Organization and Politics." In *Organizational Behavior in Schools and School Districts*, edited by S. B. Bacharach, pp. 127–59. New York: Praeger.

Meyer, John W., and Brian Rowan. 1977. "Institutionalized Organizations: Formal Structure as Myth and Ceremony." *American Journal of Sociology* 83: 340–63.

Morgan, H.M., and J.W. Wofford. 1977. *Declining Enrollment, Rising School Costs: One School's Response.* Lincoln–Sudbury, Mass.: Lincoln–Sudbury Regional School District.

Morris, V.; R. Crowson; E. Hurwitz, Jr.; and C. Porter–Gehrie. 1981. *The Urban Principal: Discretionary Decision-Making in a Large Educational Organization.* Research Report. University of Illinois at Chicago Circle, March.

Mosher, E.; A. Hastings; and J. Wagoner, Jr. 1981. "Beyond the Breaking Point? A Comparative Analysis of the New Activists for Educational Equality." *Educational Evaluation and Policy Analysis* 3 (January–February): 41–53.

Mulkeen, Thomas. 1982. "Comments on School Retrenchment in Massachusetts." Presented at American Educational Research Association Annual Meeting, New York, March 22.

Murnane, Richard J. 1981. "Seniority Rules and Educational Productivity: Understanding the Consequences of a Mandate for Equality." *American Journal of Education* 90, no. 1 (November): 14–38.

Narver, B.; R. Weatherley; and R. Elmore. 1982. "School Closures in Seattle: The Politics and Management of Decline." Paper presented at American Educational Research Association Annual Meeting, New York, March 20.

Pfeffer, Jeffrey. 1981. *Power in Organizations.* Marshfield, Mass.: Pitman Publishing Inc.

Phelan, William T. 1982. "Staffing Policies in Times of Retrenchment: Teacher Opinions." Paper presented at Conference on Managing Enrollment Decline, Vanderbilt University, Nashville, Tennessee, February 26.

Poster, John B., and Margaret R. Gotti. 1982. "The Limits of Consensus: Case Studies of School Closings." Paper presented at American Educational Research Association Annual Meeting, New York, March 22.

Rowan, Brian. 1981. "The Effects of Institutionalized Rules on Administrators." In *Organizational Behavior in Schools and School Districts*, edited by S. B. Bacharach, pp. 47-75. New York: Praeger.

Rubin, Irene. 1980. "Preventing or Eliminating Planned Deficits: Restructuring Political Incentives." *Public Administration Review* 40, no. 6 (November/December): 621-26.

Selznick, Phillip. 1957. *Leadership in Administration: A Sociological Perspective.* New York: Harper & Row.

Tversky, A., and D. Kanneman. 1974. "Judgement under Uncertainty." *Science* 185: 1124-30.

Tyack, David, and E. Hansot. 1982. *Managers of Virtue: Public School Leadership in America, 1820-1980.* New York: Basic Books.

Weeres, Joseph B. 1971. "School-Community Conflict in a Large Urban School System." *Administrator's Notebook* 19, no. 9: 1-4.

Weick, Karl E. 1976. "Educational Organizations as Loosely Coupled Systems." *Administrative Science Quarterly* 21: 1-19.

Whetten, David A. 1981. "Organizational Responses to Scarcity: Exploring the Obstacles to Innovative Approaches to Retrenchment in Education." *Educational Administration Quarterly* 17, no. 3 (Summer): 80-97.

Wood, Peter W., and William L. Boyd. 1981. "Declining Enrollments and Suburban School Closings: The Problem of Neighborhoods and Neighborhood Schools." *Educational Administration Quarterly* 17, no. 4 (Fall): 98-119.

Zerchykov, Ross. 1981. *A Review of the Literature and an Annotated Bibliography on Managing Decline in School Systems.* Boston, Mass.: Institute for Responsive Education, Boston University, September.

Zukmund, Joseph. 1975. "A Theoretical Structure for the Study of Suburban Politics." *The Annals* 422 (November): 45-60.

INDEX

ABOUT THE EDITORS

Nelda H. Cambron-McCabe is associate professor of educational leadership at Miami University, Oxford, Ohio. A former public school teacher, she has been a research associate with the Institute for Educational Finance and assistant professor at the University of Florida. She has participated in a number of state and national school finance projects and consultant studies. Currently she is the 1982–83 president-elect of the American Education Finance Association. In addition to her teaching and research interests in school finance and school law, she is also an executive editor of the *Journal of Education Finance*, coauthor of *Public School Law: Teachers' and Students' Rights*, and coeditor of the 1981 AEFA yearbook, *Perspectives in State School Support Programs* (Ballinger, 1981).

Allan Odden is the director of the Education Programs Division at the Education Commission of the States, which administers the Education Finance, Law, Governance and Improvement Centers. Previously director of the Finance Center, he directed school finance studies in several states. A former high school teacher in New York City's East Harlem, his school finance research has focused on the property tax, alternative measures of fiscal capacity, and equity. His current research efforts include the linkages between education finance, education improvement, and program implementation. He has been the lead author of the annual *School Finance Reform in the States* and the 1979–80 president of AEFA.

ABOUT THE CONTRIBUTORS

William L. Boyd is professor of education at Pennsylvania State University. Previously, he was a faculty member at University of Rochester. He specializes in educational policy and politics and has written on curriculum policymaking, the political economy of schools, and the changing conception and practice of school administration. He is a contributor to the *Encyclopedia of Educational Research* (5th ed.) and is coeditor of *Problem Finding in Educational Administration.*

Patricia Brown is assistant professor of political science at the University of California, Berkeley. She has recently completed a multistate study of school finance reform policies. Her teaching and research focus on policymaking and intergovernmental relations.

Joseph M. Cronin is president of the Massachusetts Higher Education Assistance Corporation and chairman of the New England Educational Loan Marketing Corporation. Previously, he was secretary of educational affairs in Massachusetts and state superintendent of education in Illinois. His experience includes the administration of education programs and budgets at all levels. He has taught at Stanford and Harvard and has written numerous articles, reviews, and books.

Richard Elmore is associate professor of public affairs and associate director of the Institute for Public Policy and Management, University of Washington. His current research includes work on the implementation of public policy and he has coauthored, with Milbrey McLaughlin, a study of school finance reform in California entitled *Reform and Retrenchment: The Politics of California School Finance Reform* (Ballinger, 1982).

Chester E. Finn, Jr. is professor of education and public policy at Vanderbilt University, where he is also lecturer in political science and co-director of the Center for Education Policy within the Vanderbilt Institute for Public Policy Studies. Formerly research associate at the Brookings Institution, legislative director for Senator Patrick Moynihan, and staff assistant to the president of the United States, he has written three books and numerous articles and is currently at work on a study of public policies affecting nonpublic schools.

Susan Fuhrman is research associate at the Eagleton Institute of Politics, Rutgers University. Following her graduate work at Teachers College, Columbia University, she taught state politics and education at that institution. Her research interests include the politics of school finance and state legislatures and education policy. She is coauthor of two recent monographs—*Legislative Education Leadership in the States* and *Shaping Education Policy in the States.*

Laurence Iannaccone is professor of education in the graduate school of education at the University of California, Santa Barbara. He has served on the faculties of the University of Toronto, Harvard University, Claremont Graduate, Washington University, and New York University. His writings include *Politics in Education* (1967), *The Politics of Education* (1974) coauthored with Peter Cistone, and *Public Participation in Local School Districts: The Dissatisfaction Theory of Democracy* (1978) coauthored with Frank Lutz.

John F. (Jack) Jennings is associate general counsel, Committee on Education and Labor, and also counsel and staff director, Subcommittee on Elementary, Secondary, and Vocational Education of that committee in the U.S. House of Representatives. He has been with the committee since 1967. His responsibilities include working broadly on federal education and social welfare legislation.

Tyll van Geel is professor at the University of Rochester in the Graduate School of Education and Human Development. After receiving his Juris Doctor from Northwestern School of Law and practicing law in Washington, D.C., he obtained a Doctor of Education from the Harvard Graduate School of Education. His research interests include educational law, the politics of education, and social philosophy with specific emphasis upon the relationship of government to education.

Mary Frase Williams is a social scientist currently on the staff of the School Finance Project of the U.S. Department of Education. Her interests are state and local finance and public policy. She has written extensively on the politics of education and on school finance. Previously she was a faculty member and chaired the Politics and Education Program at Teachers College, Columbia University.

AMERICAN EDUCATION FINANCE ASSOCIATION OFFICERS 1982-83

President   Walter I. Garms
President Elect   Nelda H. Cambron-McCabe
Secretary Treasurer   George Babigian
Past President   Edwin Steinbrecher

Directors

Kern Alexander   Joyce E. Krupey
Jay G. Chambers   Mary P. McKeown
Susan Fuhrman   Jay Moskowitz
Deborah Gallay   Sara L. Peterson
Terry Geske   James L. Phelps
Alan Ginsburg   Richard G. Salmon
Richard H. Goodman   William E. Sparkman
William A. Harrison   Stephen B. Thomas
Florence Henderson

Sustaining Members

American Association of School Administrators
American Federation of Teachers
National Education Association